William Palmer has published si
and four books of poetry. His
(Jonathan Cape, 2013) and his
Steps, came out from Rack Press in 2017. His stories and poems have appeared in many journals, including the *London Magazine, Poetry Review,* the *Spectator,* and *The Times Literary Supplement,* and have been broadcast on BBC Radio 3 and 4. He has reviewed regularly for the *Independent, Literary Review* and others. He was awarded the Travelling Scholarship of the Society of Authors in 1997.

Praise for *In Love with Hell*

'An enjoyable exploration of an enduringly fascinating subject . . . [Palmer] is above all a dispassionate critic, and is always attentive to, and unwaveringly perceptive about the art of his subjects as well as their relationship with alcohol . . . [his] treatment is even-handed and largely without judgement. He tries to understand, without either condoning or censuring, the impulses behind often reprehensible behaviour'

Soumya Bhattacharya, *New Statesman*

'A vastly absorbing and entertaining study of this ever-interesting subject'

Andrew Davies

'It is an achievement to take on this subject and succumb to neither puritanism nor romanticising. *In Love with Hell* will send you not to the drinks cabinet but back to your bookshelves to rediscover the brilliance that Palmer's writers couldn't quite drown'

Sarah Ditum, *The Times*

'Sympathetic and wonderfully perceptive biographies of eleven novelists and poets . . . Palmer is too wise a writer to pretend that novelists are a race apart . . . a heartbreaking read if you have learned to love the writers Palmer covers . . . By the end of this humane book, you are not falling into the sentimentality of the maudlin drunk if you wish the writers whom Palmer so tenderly examines had seen through alcohol's false promises before it was too late'

Nick Cohen, *The Critic*

Also by William Palmer

Fiction

The Good Republic
Leporello
The Contract
The Pardon of St Anne
Four Last Things
The India House
The Devil is White

Poetry

The Island Rescue
An Instruction from Madame S.
The Paradise Commissionaire
The Water Steps

In Love With Hell

Drink in the
Lives and Work
of Eleven Writers

William Palmer

ROBINSON

ROBINSON

First published in Great Britain in 2021 by Robinson
This paperback edition published in 2022 by Robinson

1 3 5 7 9 10 8 6 4 2

A CIP catalogue record for this book
is available from the British Library.

ISBN: 978-1-47214-499-7

Typeset in Adobe Garamond by SX Composing DTP, Rayleigh, Essex
Printed and bound in Great Britain by Clays Ltd, Elcograf S.p.A.

Papers used by Robinson are from well-managed forests
and other responsible sources.

Robinson
An imprint of
Little, Brown Book Group
Carmelite House
50 Victoria Embankment
London EC4Y 0DZ

An Hachette UK Company
www.hachette.co.uk

www.littlebrown.co.uk

To Lynda

'I like it,' he called to them, through the open window, from outside. Cervantes stood behind the bar, with scared eyes, holding the cockerel. 'I love hell. I can't wait to get back there. In fact I'm running. I'm almost back there already.'

Under the Volcano by Malcolm Lowry

Contents

Contents

Introduction

IN 2013, Olivia Laing published *The Trip to Echo Spring*, an excellent and penetrating study of six American writers who also happened to be alcoholics. The book's subtitle was *Why Writers Drink*. She was not asking the question, 'Why do writers drink?', rather, her subtitle carried the promise of an explanation. That this was not fully delivered is probably inevitable: the task, of dealing with a mysterious condition affecting writers, that most psychologically slippery cast of characters, resists any single answer.

Perhaps the question should be put as 'Why do some writers destroy themselves by drinking alcohol?' Before our health-conscious days it would be true to say that most writers, at least those with enough leisure and money, drank what we now regard as excessive amounts. Graham Greene drank on a daily basis quantities of spirits and wine and beer most doctors would consider as being dangerous to his health. But he was rarely out of control and lived with his considerable wits intact to the age of eighty-six. W.H. Auden drank the most of a bottle of spirits a day, but also worked hard and steadily every day until his death. Even T.S. Eliot in middle-age, for all his pontifical demeanour, was once observed completely drunk at a London Tube station by a startled friend. These are not writers who were generally regarded as alcoholics. It is a slippery word, as exemplified by Dylan Thomas's definition of an alcoholic as 'someone you dislike who drinks as much as you do'.

But it can be said that all of Laing's choices – F. Scott Fitzgerald, Ernest Hemingway, Tennessee Williams, John Berryman, John Cheever and Raymond Carver – were men who took the drinking of alcohol to more or less self-destructive excess. And men only? Laing did not include any women writers, although there are many, American and English, from Dorothy Parker onwards. The sad fact is that any work on this subject could fill several large volumes and contain the sodden lives, amongst those already mentioned, of Jack London, Eugene O'Neill, Sinclair Lewis, William Faulkner, Charles Jackson, Raymond Chandler, Jack Kerouac, and Richard Yates for the Americans, and a team including Patrick Hamilton, Jean Rhys, Henry Green, Evelyn Waugh, Dylan Thomas, William Sansom, Malcolm Lowry, Anthony Burgess, and Kingsley Amis for the British. Heavy drinkers all and some possibly alcoholics. The word is still controversial and often misunderstood and misapplied. What this book is interested in is the effect that heavy drinking had on writers, how they lived with it and were sometimes destroyed by it, and how they described the private and social world of the drinker in their work.

II

There is a continuing debate about the nature of alcoholism, but it is obvious that the long-term effects of heavy and continuous drinking are physically and mentally deleterious and in some cases catastrophic. In the past few years I have lost three close friends to drink: one died from cirrhosis of the liver, one collapsed into alcoholic dementia and died within a couple of weeks, and the third suffered a massive and fatal stroke after many bouts of illness. Two were in their late fifties when they died; the oldest was sixty-three. All three drank daily and heavily. None of them, I think, would have denied, in the end, that they were alcoholics. But then none of them was a writer. And, as we shall see, writers have many ways of denying, defining, or justifying their drinking. They can also describe its horrors.

Here is Fitzgerald enumerating some of his problems in a notebook:

Heartburn
Eczema
Piles
Flu
Night Sweats
Alcoholism
Infected Nose
Insomnia
Ruined Nerves
Chronic Cough
Aching Teeth
Shortness of Breath
Falling Hair
Cramps in Feet
Tingling Feet
Constipation
Cirrhosis of the Liver
Stomach Ulcers
Depression and Melancholia

Faced with that lot, it's small wonder that almost all of the drunk writers achieved their best work young and, if they lived long enough, saw their work, as with Hemingway, Sinclair Lewis, and Raymond Chandler, descend into weaker versions of former glories. Most denied drinking whilst actually working, although Faulkner once said that 'I always write at night. And I always keep the whisky bottle near.' His story 'Golden Land' opens with a man waking up:

If he had been thirty, he would not have needed the two aspirin tablets and the half glass of raw gin before he could bear the shower's needling on his body and steady his hands to shave . . . He didn't waken sick. He never wakened ill nor became ill from drinking, not only because he had drunk too long and too steadily for that, but because he was too tough even after the thirty soft years.

It is obvious that this is a chosen way of life, even a way, in using the word 'tough', of reinforcing the perceived masculinity of hard drinking. The glass of gin may have become necessary to stave off the shakes, but it is also taken as a ritual, as part of a willed life. There is an implication in Faulkner's earlier statement about the whisky bottle and his work that a drink, then the next drink, and so on, will enable the writer to open the gates of perception, to see further, rise higher, and perhaps to fall harder. It is a Romantic view and the Romantic Movement came later and lasted longer in America than it did in Britain and Europe. It is a view that caused these American writers to be so grievously damaged by alcohol that in some it drowned first their gifts, then their lives.

The youth and early adulthood of those born at the end of the nineteenth century (Fitzgerald and Hemingway) and in the earlier years of the twentieth (Cheever and Williams) happened to coincide with an enormous change in drinking habits in the United States. The ratification in 1920 of the Volstead Act, prohibiting the manu-facture and sale of alcohol, turned off the legal supply and immediately created a gigantic illegal industry to meet a demand that had not gone away. The economics of this industry meant that the greatest profit could be made by distilling the most concentrated spirits: whisky, gin and rum, or by importing these. The proof strength of the home-produced drink varied but was usually very high and the great symbol of the Jazz Age of the 1920s was the extremely potent hip flask in a young man's pocket.

We forget sometimes how young Hemingway and Fitzgerald were when they wrote their greatest work. Fitzgerald wrote *The Great Gatsby* in his mid-twenties, and had published two other novels and three books of stories by the time he was thirty. He completed only one other novel; *Tender is the Night*. Hemingway's career as a great writer was effectively over by the time he was forty. There were some superb stories and fragments of novels after that, but the posturing drunken Papa Hemingway was a coarser and lesser artist than his younger self.

The body can take a lot of punishment and recuperate swiftly when young and alcohol does, at first, deliver a powerful charge to the imagination. The cool and gleaming beauty of Fitzgerald's early work comes partly at least from a sense of a world washed clean by the wrecking excesses that came before and after spells of hard work. But alcohol, like other drugs, demands more and delivers less as time goes by. Writers may be stimulated by the slanted perspectives alcohol gives on life, but picking up a pen, or switching on a word-processor, are actions very like walking on stage to perform; occasions for fear, and rightly so, and any drug takes away that fear, that necessary stage fright. Fitzgerald admitted that parts of *Tender is the Night* were flawed by being written with the aid of drink and he bitterly regretted the damage it had done to his marvellous talent. It is only a few years from the completion of *Tender is the Night* to the appalling picture of the alcoholic writer in his story 'An Alcoholic Case'. The 'bottle' in this passage is a bottle of gin broken in a struggle with his nurse:

He was looking at the corner where he had thrown the bottle the night before. She stared at his handsome face, weak and defiant – afraid to turn even halfway because she knew that death was in that corner where he was looking. She knew death – she had heard it, smelt its unmistakable odour, but she had never seen it before it entered into anyone, and she knew this man saw it in the corner of his bathroom; that it was standing there looking at him while he spat from a feeble cough and rubbed the result into the braid of his trousers. It shone there crackling for a moment as evidence of the last gesture he ever made.

She tried to express it next day to Mrs Hixon:

'It's not like anything you can beat – no matter how hard you try. This one could have twisted my wrists until he strained them and that wouldn't matter so much to me. It's just that you can't really help them and it's so discouraging – it's all for nothing.'

III

So why do intelligent men and women even start? Why does anyone – plumber, lawyer, doctor – drink in a way that leaves them physically and mentally wrecked?

Whatever the eventual consequences, the reason most people drink alcohol is because they like it. When they start to drink in youth they may not enjoy the taste at first; for some with a palate just out of childhood alcohol has to be sweetened or smothered by other flavours. Many, having got over the problem of taste, find that they like the effect that alcohol has. Those who enjoy neither taste nor effect generally leave the stuff alone.

It seems to be the case that for most alcoholics drinking starts very young and accelerates rapidly, once the company of other like minds is found. In the case of the educated and literate (not always the same thing) the discovery of drink is often accompanied by early creative efforts, usually the writing of poetry. The cultural heroes of young writers are likely to be along the lines of Arthur Rimbaud, Dylan Thomas, or Kurt Cobain; boozers and junkies, rather than grave and sober and *old* artists such as Hardy or Tolstoy. The drinker's companions are chosen for their shared tastes in music, other intellectual (or not) interests, and their ability to drink.

It is from this choice of like-minded associates that one of the chief difficulties arises for any drinker encouraged to cut down or entirely abandon drink. The drinker's friends are usually drinkers of a similar capacity. Not many sober people would choose to spend an evening in the company of people who seem to be going out of their minds in front of them. The particularly intense sodality of male drinkers in particular, the progression from lively conversation to a maundering exchange of witless confessions or outright nonsense, repels any sober person. But it is the social aspect of drink and drinking that some drinkers (not all, not the committed solitaries) find hardest to relinquish. This is when, in the pub, the party, or alcoholic tête-à-tête, there comes that gradual relaxation, the escalation of hilarity and good will, the final release out of one's self. It is illuminating to see the way an earlier generation viewed it. The progression was coldly detailed in the 1911 edition of the *Encyclopaedia Britannica*, in the article entitled Drunkenness:

> [alcohol's] action on an average individual is first to fill him with a serene and perfect self-complacency. His feelings and faculties are exalted into a state of great activity and buoyancy, so that his language becomes enthusiastic, and his conversation vivacious if not brilliant. The senses gradually become hazy, a soft humming seems to fill the pauses of the conversation, a filmy haze obscures the vision. The head seems lighter than usual, the equilibrium unstable . . . judgement is abolished, secretiveness annihilated, and the drunkard pours forth all that is within him with unrestrained communicativeness; he becomes boisterous, ridiculous, and sinks at length into a mere animal.

With the plain speaking customary in its era the article goes on to state that the habitual drunkard:

> . . . must be regarded as temporarily insane . . . and ought to be placed in an inebriate asylum till he regain sufficient self-control to enable him to overcome his love for drink.

In fact this incarceration in an asylum (now a shelter, hostel, hospital, or private clinic) is very unpleasant, but is in a way the easiest part of owning up to drunkenness; the drinker is taken out of his or her accustomed world and the habit treated as an illness. The problem comes with the return to the outside world as a sober person.

To succeed, the renunciation of drink entails the permanent loss of all the companions, friends, lovers, fellows and handmaidens of the drinking cult, the loss of shared rituals, of the hours and hours spent in convivial company. It means no more anticipation of the first drink, or relish of the subsequent glasses, the pain of the hangover (a sort of built-in but hard-earned retribution in the curious logic of the drunk), the recovery, the beginning again. To lose this is to abandon a whole world, a way of life, and to be cast into a psychological desert with only the sober as companions. The act of will necessary to giving up drinking is colossal, and the resultant feeling of loss is akin to that described by outcasts and apostates of the Communist Party or Catholic Church; that they are deprived at once of a life-defining belief system and its accompanying and sustaining society. The sad fact, insufficiently recognised by those determined to treat alcoholics as medical cases, is that for many, even the most dilapidated, drinking is the thing they most want to do in the world, that, indeed, it *is* the world.

And, for writers above all, their world is largely one they create for themselves. Despite boasts of producing thousands of words a day, most writers are more likely to resemble the novelist 'shit in a shuttered château' in Larkin's poem 'The Life with a Hole in it', with his daily five hundred words. They write, sure, but whatever they may say, most don't sit down at nine and write until five. A lot of time is spent looking out of the window or thinking of other things (Dylan Thomas's manuscripts have the names of horses to be backed that day, sums adding up debts, and shopping lists scribbled in the margins). Writers do not have the welcome opportunity to attend meetings or pop off down to Human Resources to have a chat with good old Mike, or answer the busy phone, or have a hundred emails waiting to be dealt with. They have a few hours each day trying to make things up, things that they then try to sell to people who don't really want them. The writers then have to endure a wait before their work is published, and it is then reviewed by people who do not like it or say they like it because they know the author. After a brief flurry of activity there falls complete silence. They begin to write another book. They like to drink socially, it takes the edge off mixing with other people; it is a social solvent. Very soon some of them will get stuck at about three in the afternoon and sit in utter despair. It's then that they hear the 'singing of the bottles in the pantry' that John Cheever described in his journals. A quick snort may get them going again. It does sometimes, but then it doesn't and another snort seems to be called for. They don't drink while they work, they say – so when unable to work they just drink. If they have an alcoholic friend – and this is the only real kind of friend an alcoholic has – they will pass time with them.

This indeed is the opening of Olivia Laing's *The Trip to Echo Spring:* the meeting of kindred spirits, Raymond Carver and John Cheever. They are in a beat-up old car, waiting at just before nine in the morning for the state liquor store to open. When it does they buy half a gallon of Scotch and immediately begin to drink it. At the time Cheever, author of some of the greatest short stories in American literature, was sixty-one years old and newly out of hospital and straitjacket after an attack of delirium tremens. Carver was thirty-five, just starting on a literary career. Both men were spending a year teaching and working on their own stories at Iowa University and had bonded immediately on meeting, over a drink. Their teaching must have been uneven to say the least and they never managed to get any of their own work done. What they wanted and what they did was to drink to excess. All the time.

In his book, *The Myth of Addiction*, John Booth Davies wrote that 'most people who use drugs do so for their own reasons, on purpose, because they like it, and because they can find no adequate reason for not doing so.' And so Carver and Cheever continue to drink although they know that it is damaging to their health, their personal relationships, their ability to perform a job, and that it will most probably shorten their lives. Some drunks are suffering from mental and psychological difficulties that render them unable to deal with life, but some, like Cheever and Carver, are highly intelligent and outwardly successful professional people. The only thing they have in common is drink. To the outsider the persistent, repetitive intake of alcohol, given the overwhelming medical and social evidence of the harm it causes, is extremely puzzling and annoying. But to the drinker, the answer is not based in logic, but in desire.

The word 'love', that is, love of drink, as used in the *Britannica* article above, was replaced in later literature on drunkenness by 'craving'. But 'love' is the correct word for the first stages of the drunkard's life: he or she is infatuated, and looks forward to a long and warm relationship with drink.

For, like lovers, like suicides, alcoholics seek the cessation of time's flow. Unlike suicides, drinkers at first seek this on a strictly temporary basis, hoping to be able to recreate the pleasures of the experience rather than suffer a permanent obliteration of all the senses. The illusion of the cessation of time is accompanied by a feeling of euphoria – all drinkers know the exact point at which this is reached: they do not realise when it topples into drunken unconsciousness, or social disaster. All they want is to be able to repeat the rare moments when they feel elevated and free. In the later stages of drunkenness the drinker wants this state to become permanent; it is in the nature of the drug that this desire is pursued and endlessly lost, over and over again.

IV

But surely these are only 'ordinary' drunks we are talking about? Not people blessed with great talents, genius even, whose craving for booze must come from some deeper motivation, some conscious disordering of the senses to free their vision? They are not the mental weaklings and physical wrecks propping up the bar in pubs that have half their windows boarded-up, are they?

If we regard persistent drunkenness as a weakness of personality then certainly not many writers could be described as being altogether mentally robust. That most outwardly confident of writers, Anthony Burgess, was a heavy drinker who did not develop into a self-destructive alcoholic. I do not think that Burgess, Graham Greene, Evelyn Waugh and other heavy drinkers fit the 'alcoholic' pattern. It goes against the grain of modern medical opinion, which says that anyone regularly drinking even a quite small amount of alcohol above the recommended limit is likely to become at first dependent then an alcoholic, but it does seem possible for people to drink heavily and at a constant level and live to a more or less healthy old age. Burgess crammed his life with work, some of which in his later years he surely did not need to undertake, seemingly unable to turn down any hackwork offered however much it might take time and energy from his novels. Drink was an accompaniment to all of his tremendous activity, but it seems to have been mainly taken as a source of energy, an aid to work that lubricated the great machine.

Burgess seems never to have suffered the feelings – or at least never expressed them – of self-doubt that plagued others such as Malcolm Lowry and Dylan Thomas and John Cheever. If Burgess drank to give himself energy, others did so to bolster what they perceived as inner weakness. The worst and most damaging form this took was in self-accusations of fraudulence and unworthiness. Cheever, for instance, born into a lower middle-class family and without a university education, formed himself into the very image of a New England gentleman. But all of his life he was, as he once accused himself, 'a helpless mixture of fraudulence and honesty'. His 'feigned patrician origins', his promiscuous but well concealed homosexuality, his love for his wife and the destruction of that love by his drinking, the tension created by all these gave him his subject matter and the extraordinary quality of his writing. A feeling of fraudulence haunted others.

11

A young man in New York who asked for an autograph was informed by Dylan Thomas that he was only posing as the poet. Thomas had been disturbed earlier in a bar by someone saying to him that if Thomas had not written a few good poems no one would ever have heard of him. His adult work was highly original and could be mistaken for that of no one else, but his first printed poem, published in a local newspaper when he was twelve years old, had been directly plagiarised with no alteration from a poem in a boys' magazine. Accusations of plagiarism could hardly be made about his own later work, but charges that he was bogus and a charlatan were common among academic critics and becoming more widely voiced towards the end of Thomas's life. To a man who was highly sensitive such doubts must have struck home badly.

So, did the doubts of self-worth cause the rush to the bottle, or did the drink produce the doubts, or at least greatly exacerbate them? Thomas, in common with Malcolm Lowry and Patrick Hamilton, also seems to have had a certain sexual timidity. And he shared with Charles Jackson, John Cheever, and Richard Yates a feeling of intellectual unworthiness because of his lack of a university education.

Writers, by the nature of their trade, must be highly sensitive to social and emotional states. In their work at least. No one sober would have seen the drunken Kingsley Amis or Lowry or Thomas or Cheever or Yates as anything but foul-mouthed bores. When they were drunk, that is. Because, by other reports these men could be, when sober, sensitive and charming. But then again, as John Sutherland has written, 'It is a peculiarity of alcoholics that when things go well, they sabotage themselves . . . My personal view is that drunks do not want the responsibility of a successful life.'

V

One of the difficulties people have with drinking and drunken behaviour is what to call it. As we have seen, many doctors would say that anyone drinking regularly above the officially sanctioned drinks limit is an alcoholic, or potential alcoholic. At the same time, doctors and psychiatrists declare that alcoholism is a 'disease'. But, as Donald B. Douglas, an American doctor who rejects the disease concept, says:

> . . . what kind of a disease can coexist with the best of health? . . . Is it a 'disease' of the will? If so, we must enter the field of addiction to understand it. 'Disease' may be more acceptable to the majority, more respectable than addiction but what does it explain? Is it a mental disease? If so, does the alcoholic have it when sober? If so, what disease? If not, why does he drink again after achieving sobriety? What if the alcoholic decides not to drink? What kind of disease, mental or not, can we decide not to have?

It's a strange disease that can be dismissed or summoned up by the will or acts of its sufferer. This is not to deny the physically injurious aspects of drinking; the heart disease, circulation problems, cancers and dementia that can come with heavy and sustained drinking. But these are the symptoms of poisoning by the direct chemical action of alcohol: they are not caused by the wish to drink.

The prevailing and not wholly disinterested view of the American psychiatric industry is that alcoholism is a disease and that it can be treated if not cured by the use of psychotherapy, drugs, or the intervention of a body such as Alcoholics Anonymous. The American psychiatric bible, the *Diagnostic and Statistical Manual of Mental Disorders*, attempts to pin down this mental and physical disorder. The problem with this is that the *DSM* is about as useful a guide to humanity as the *A–Z Guide to London* is to the lives of the inhabitants of that city. The *DSM* enumerates symptoms of alcoholism, their possible causes and consequences, but treats the matter as one of generalised addiction, not differentiated by individual personality or circumstance. Another researcher in the field, quoted by Olivia

Laing, Mary-Anne Enoch, makes the claim that 'It is well established that the heriditability of alcoholism is around 50%'. This seems to suggest that alcoholism is caused by genetic inheritance, but not by everybody, or perhaps by familial acceptability, but again not by everybody. In fact, as far as I know, none of the children of the writers under discussion here became an alcoholic and some reacted with disgust to the degraded state of their parents. There may well be some genetic predisposition to the drinking of alcohol, but certainly as strongly affecting is the nature of the upbringing of the future drinker, the world they are brought into and what they witness on an intimate and hourly basis. Childhood is an extremely long part of our lives in the sense the child has of being confined into a small world at the most impressionable stage of life for what seems an interminable amount of time. So, cue the unhappy childhood. But, with the exception of Elizabeth Bishop, the problem with the writers looked at in this book is that they seem not to have had childhoods any more miserable or happy than most of us have had to put up with. Millions of us have had difficulties with parents; only a tiny number turn into a Hemingway or a Fitzgerald.

And after all, the business of the writer is not in the generality of the human condition, or of sorting human beings into types or groups. It is in the description of particularity – of one human mind, one room, one love affair; the affairs of one or more individuals in one house can do equally for a huge novel or a short poem. It is the setting down of individually unique lives, not the exemplification of psychological theories that concerns the artist. This is why, in the records of those drunken writers referred to psychiatrists we find they share an unkind contempt for those trying to help them. The hard fact is that good writers, however they may dissimulate and conceal, do usually know far more about what ails them than any psychiatrist attempting to isolate what troubles his recalcitrant patient. The writers *know* that they are harming themselves. The alternative proposed by the physician is to be a *different* person. In the case of Dylan Thomas, it was not an unhappy childhood that haunted him, but the memory of a too happy one; one that he tried to return to endlessly for material, with inevitably diminishing returns as he grew older. For him, drink's job was to stave off marriage, children, money, to reverse time, to relieve of him of the responsibilities of adult life, to preserve him as childish and the recipient of doting love and care. Thomas was a considerably more intelligent man than he made himself out to be. He saw the paradox of his desire, rejected an alternative persona, and allowed his way of life to kill him.

Were these writers so hopelessly locked into disease that they can be regarded as passive victims? The moral ambivalence in the treatments urged by Alcoholics Anonymous is that while saying, 'You cannot really help yourself. Alcoholism is a disease. It's not really your fault at all,' this is accompanied by an insistence that the alcoholic face up to the mental, emotional and sometimes physical damage his or her conduct has caused to others and make full amends.

Did these writers know what damage they were doing to their families and friends?

Dylan Thomas fought with his wife, Caitlin, and sometimes came off the worse for the combat. Richard Yates's relationships with women were ruined by his boozing, and he alienated many friends through boorish and stupid behaviour. The diminutive Jean Rhys attacked her husbands and initiated fights in pubs and public places while intoxicated. Malcolm Lowry drunkenly attacked both his wives. Patrick Hamilton was boorish and insulting when drunk. And so on and on.

Most of these writers had periods of sobriety and these tended to coincide with increased and enhanced periods of creation – so why, as John Sutherland put it, 'sabotage' themselves? We go back to the 'love' of drink, and no man or woman was ever cured of an infatuation by the moral injunctions of others. If the thing that an alcoholic loves more than any other is drink then the only way to replace that object of desire is by another and greater one: for a lover, for family, or work. But the thing about alcohol is that it is so undemanding.

It does not requite the love invested in it, but it never refuses an advance. It requires no education or previous experience to be admitted to its profession. It does not clamour like a child for attention, but quietly invites one to play. It is endlessly forgiving to backsliders. It is very easy.

VI

The advice of V.S. Pritchett (who lived to the great age of ninety-six) was to 'smoke like a fish and drink like a chimney'. Pritchett was a distinguished writer and by all accounts a settled and amiable personality, but as the novelist Philip Hensher has pointed out, most 'writers aren't normal, and if they became normal they might lose what Juvenal described as a disease, the itch to scribble . . . a few grow to value what medical science sees as abnormality.'

The question of whether alcohol is a spur to an artist's creativity is a long and much debated one. It does seem that the use of alcohol in the early stages of the career of a writer who may be emotionally and sexually repressed or socially ill at ease can be a valuable and powerful liberator. In the case of Dylan Thomas it undoubtedly helped to fuel his first youthful burst of great productivity and to diminish his sense of personal worthlessness.

There is another important point to bear in mind when considering in the deepest sense why writers drink – the writer may not consider that the direct use of drink inspires creativity, but he or she may feel a very great fear of the inhibition that may result from conscious restraint, that a constant sense of being on guard *against* drinking may have the effect of altering the writer's personality from being open to becoming closed and costive: that the sheer emotional and physical diversion of giving up drink might well become a perverse incentive for the writer to decide to continue on a path that to outsiders is obviously self-destructive. The alcoholic artist strikes a bargain between the bottle and the work. In the end, if persisted in, it will be a devil's bargain, but then, such highly intelligent men and women know that and must reckon that whatever misery is entailed is balanced by some reward. It is not enough to say that the creators of *Under the Volcano* or *Tender is the Night* or *The Swimmer* were helpless in the grip of a devouring disease. These works exhibit the highest signs of intellectual and artistic control: if their authors were drunk in the street at night, they were, for some years at least, sober at the desk in the morning.

VII

We return in horror and fascination to the man in the bathroom in Fitzgerald's story. For him, this is the end of a long process and the picture is drawn from Fitzgerald's own experience. Fitzgerald was an alcoholic in the accepted sense, but it is a difficult word, easy to throw around, describing a condition that, at least in its early stages, is a disorder of the personality rather than an irreversible medical condition. It can be easy to use it as a catch-all definition, much in the way the word 'depression' is used to describe a variety of emotional conditions from mild anxiety to the deepest grief. Each of the writers discussed in the later chapters of this book drank heavily, sometimes almost insanely. One of their abiding attractions for some of their readers is that these writers dared to do it, to go the whole way in a manner that they would be too scared to even contemplate. But they are mistaken and the writers were too. They were the victims of a seductive, contrary and ultimately destructive Muse, the one described with deadly charm in 'A Drunkard's Address to a Whisky Bottle' by the nineteenth-century Irish writer J.S. Le Fanu:

> Oh terrible darlin',
> How have you sought me
> Enchanted, and caught me?
> See, now, where you've brought me
> To sleep by the road-side, and dress out in rags.

Chapter 1

'The feverish magic that alcohol can work'

Patrick Hamilton (1904–1962)

I

PATRICK HAMILTON is a writer's writer. That is, his books come into and go out of print, writers contribute introductions to reissues that lament the fact that Hamilton remains so neglected, and a scent of fugitive importance hangs about his name. He is not taught in universities and his name does not appear in some standard reference works to English literature, but every now and then a young writer will happen on his books and write excitedly about them, asking why they are not better known, and so he is rediscovered by each generation and his books refuse to die.

To the first-time reader, the novels of Patrick Hamilton appear highly accomplished, full of mordant humour and sharp observation, but sometimes repellent in a way that may explain his neglect as a writer. His characters are dwarfed by the world that surrounds them, a world which is almost always cold and inhuman to the individual, with no hint of redemption and little love. The men and women in these books torture each other verbally and emotionally in a thousand ways, or suffer such torture masochistically, accepting it as their due and rarely rebelling. Like tiny insects imprisoned in the works of a large clockwork watch, time passes above them, what it is measuring is outside their comprehension, and they scurry hopelessly about, looking for an exit – while we gaze down on them with a mixture of fascination and horror.

II

Anthony Walter Patrick Hamilton was born on St Patrick's Day, the seventeenth of March 1904. His father, Walter Bernard Hamilton, was well off (he had inherited a sum worth about £3 million in today's terms), a minor historical novelist, and a drinker. His mother, Ellen, also a writer, gradually found herself running the household single-handedly as her husband ran through his fortune. Both parents had been briefly married before: Ellen had rapidly divorced her first husband; Bernard had been more bizarrely married to a prostitute he hoped to reclaim from a life on the streets. She later threw herself under a train. The marriage of Bernard and Ellen was more conventional, but as Bernard spent his fortune, the family descended from a solid and prosperous life to living in lodgings in London and Hove. Patrick attended a preparatory school in Hove until 1918 (except for two disastrous terms at Colet Court in Hammersmith in 1915, from which he was withdrawn after coming out with details of its aggressively homosexual dormitory life). His stay at Westminster School lasted only one year, his education cut short by an attack of the Spanish influenza that killed many millions worldwide after the end of the First World War.

Hamilton's career as a writer started early; he was only nineteen when his first novel, *Monday Morning*, was published. He published two further novels in his early twenties and in 1929 his play *Rope* (later filmed by Hitchcock) was a huge and lucrative success on the London stage. This, and later plays, including *Gaslight*, were well constructed and popular melodramas that displayed some of the interest in emotional cruelty and frustration that inform his novels. What the plays could not contain was the depth of introspection and the minutely observed particulars of the inner lives of the characters in the novels. A life-long and doctrinaire Marxist, Hamilton wrote: 'I was trying to present a "black" social history of my times. There were so many "white" portraits of the twenties and thirties that I wanted to show the other side of the picture.' And certainly the socialist in Hamilton seems to have made him portray precisely those people the novel usually ignores, or uses as the backdrop to what more 'interesting' characters are doing. Typically, a Hamilton character is a clerk, barmaid, prostitute, petty crook, a spinster or bachelor in an unsatisfactory job or living on a small private income; people who are of little interest to the world outside of themselves, but within whom emotions rage and die. Perhaps the secret of why Hamilton's work has lasted is because of his instinctive recognition of the value of every human life. For each one of us the world is constructed individually inside our minds and emotions and when even the pathetically comic and boorish Mr Thwaites dies, in *The Slaves of Solitude*, a world dies with him. Always greatly influenced by Dickens, Hamilton seems to have taken on those who might have been fleeting bit players in Dickens and to have constructed a whole and often tragic world where they occupy centre stage as heroes and heroines.

III

Hamilton followed in his father's footsteps in two ways: in his early twenties he fell in love with a prostitute, Lily Connolly, and at the same time he began to drink heavily. The affair with Lily did not get as far as marriage and what went on can only be known now through the fictionalised version Hamilton offers in *The Midnight Bell*, the first of three early novels that make up the trilogy entitled *Twenty Thousand Streets Under the Sky*. All three parts are concerned with the failure of love, the inability of men and women to communicate in any meaningful way, and the use of drink as both a friend and a destroyer.

The Midnight Bell deals with Bob, a barman, Jenny, a prostitute, and Ella, a barmaid. As Bruce Hamilton writes in his biography of his brother, 'Many of the incidents in this beautifully contrived tale were taken straight from personal experience.'

The title of the novel is the name of the pub where much of the action takes place. If later writers such as Kingsley Amis and Anthony Burgess use the pub as one dramatic location among others, for Hamilton it is the centre of his characters' world; they may go home to eat and sleep, or visit relatives or friends, they may go on the occasional trip away, but the pub is where they *live*.

It is astonishing how very little has been written about pub life of the last hundred years, despite the many incidental references in novels and biographies and a few sociological surveys by people who write as if they have never taken a drink in their lives. Even the buildings, so ubiquitous in cities, are rarely mentioned. In the whole of Nikolaus Pevsner's monumental multi-volume survey of the Buildings of England there is scant mention of any pub. Perhaps this is because most were built in the Victorian period and for Pevsner this was the Dark Age of Architecture; the extraordinary ornamentation of Victorian gin palaces was not to his taste. Hamilton, above all novelists, is the anatomist of the pub; the places are described in lingering detail and if all of the older pubs in their original state and purpose were lost – as may be the case in the next few years – we would know what they were like from reading his novels.

The Midnight Bell opens with Bob the barman waking up with a bad head. For a few moments he thinks that it is the dark early morning, then realises that it is in fact nearly five in the afternoon, that he has 'got drunk at lunch again' and that in a few minutes he has to open the pub for the evening. The room next to his is that of Ella, the barmaid, who is hopelessly in love with him. The landlord, nicknamed the Governor, and his wife are little seen; their duties rest mainly in the ceremonious unlocking of the doors at opening time, relocking them at closing time, and, in between, talking to those customers deemed worthy of the honour. Ella and Bob do most of the work of serving drinks.

The pub is of classic design. The Saloon Bar is entered 'through a large door with a fancifully frosted glass pane'. The Saloon is thirty feet long and 'a comfortable and continuous leather seat' runs the whole length behind a row of tables. The Saloon Bar 'opened out into the Saloon Lounge'. This is the best room, with smaller tables each surrounded by three or four wicker armchairs. There are prints of 'moustached cavalrymen in a variety of brilliant uniforms'. There is an open fire but 'the whole atmosphere was spotless, tidy, bright, and a little chilly. This was no scene for the brawler, but rather for the principled and restrained drinker.'

There are two other bars, the Public and the Private, 'dreary, seatless, bareboarded structures wherein drunkenness was dispensed in coarser tumblers and at a cheaper rate' to lower class customers.

The first eight chapters of the book describe the workings of the pub from the sliding back of the door bolts, to final lock-up. First there is the empty pub, a stage waiting for its first actor to appear, for the pub is a place in which people perform roles and speak parts. At just after five the door is pushed open and Mr Sounder, a regular, comes in. Mr Sounder is middle-aged, bearded, a very part-time journalist and a full-time bore. He likes to indulge in slightly leering innuendo with Ella, the highly respectable barmaid, and is a man who regards his first drink as the price of admission, hoping that others will buy him further drinks. He is rewarded when Mr Brooks, owner of the local hardware store, comes in and buys him a second beer. A middle-aged couple sit down. It is quiet, but then 'three rough males had entered the Public bar, and were talking in loud voices, and the Saloon door again creaked open, and another couple entered . . . They were followed by two men, who came and stood at the bar. With a sudden burst the place was awake.'

By eight all the bars are full, with a constant hubbub of conversation. Mr Sounder is getting drunk and showing everyone a letter he has written to a newspaper. Two young women come in. Their good looks and clothes and a 'certain hard and unrelenting self-sufficiency' make them instantly recognisable as prostitutes. The quieter, and prettier, of the two, Jenny, is the woman who will drive Bob almost insane with her emotional waywardness and cruelty. Jenny does not at first want an alcoholic drink but her friend pesters her into accepting a gin and peppermint. There is a sense of relief when she relents and joins in. The whole conversation devoted to persuading Jenny to have a 'proper' drink is an indication of the outwardly jovial but coercive nature of the drinking crowd. They are a pack and hunt together and all must have the same prey. The evening warms up. Bob forgets his resolve not to drink that evening and has several beers. At their very first meeting, when he serves her table, Jenny manages to charm him into 'lending' her ten-bob towards her rent.

Hamilton conveys with deadly accuracy the various rhythms and sudden shifts in intensity in the tides of activity in the pub's night. From eight the pub gradually fills up; some of the early evening drop-in drinkers have gone; the ones who remain are becoming pleasantly tipsy. By half-past nine the place is filling rapidly and 'the noise was tremendous, and Ella was off her head with work.' Bob has made almost five shillings in tips waiting on the Lounge tables; at five to ten:

. . . he perceived that the climax of the evening had been reached.

Apart from a few at the back of the lounge, there were now no women in the place, and it seemed as though their disappearance had relaxed the last bonds of equability and restraint.

A horrible excitement was upon everybody and everything. Indeed, to one unacquainted with the feverish magic that alcohol can work there could have been only one way of accounting for the scene. This house must have been the theatre of some tremendous conference, in which some tremendous crisis had arisen at the moment of adjournment, and the individuals had gathered into frightened but loquacious groups to discuss the bombshell.

. . . They thrust their hats back on their heads; they put their feet firmly on the rail; they looked you straight in the eye; they beat their palms with their fists, and they swilled largely and cried for more. Their arguments were top-heavy with the swagger of their altruism. They appealed passionately to the laws of logic and honesty. Life, just for tonight, was miraculously clarified into simple and dramatic issues. It was the last five minutes of the evening, and they were drunk.

This could well describe any pub until fairly recent times, that is, not one encumbered with shatteringly loud music, or remaining open all night; no, this is the classic London pub, open in the 1920s in legally straitened hours, facing closing time. The only perfectly sober person, observing all of this, is Ella, the barmaid.

The first sign of collapse, a distant rumour at first, is the first call by the Governor of 'Now then, gentlemen please! Last orders please!' This is not taken much notice of; the crowd are after all 'just beginning to enjoy themselves'. This is one of the great attractions of the pub, of course: its granting of warmth and company, its promise of relaxation and good grace, and its threat of the withdrawal of those things. It is the reason people, especially men, used to go to the pub and not simply sit at home getting soused. At a time, before the Second World War, of lesser domestic comfort in most homes, perhaps the presence of wife and children in cramped rooms, or dreadful loneliness in one room, for many the pub held the promise of a sort of luxury. It was a version of peace that drew men and, to a lesser extent, women to the public house. And alcohol gives the illusion of stretching time, that this warmth and enclosure and granting of friendship and love are going to last forever.

But then, in the Midnight Bell, comes the next, and louder shout, 'Now then gentlemen! *Time*, please!' And the final flinging open of the door to the cold dark night and the stentorian, 'NOW then, gentlemen! TIME, please!'

The Governor now makes himself busy, going from table to table, snatching up glasses; he gives another terrible shout:

> And now a kind of panic and babel fell upon "The Midnight Bell".
> A searching draught swept in from the open door, and suddenly
> the Governor lowered all the lights save one above the bar. At this
> a few realized that the game was up, and left the place abruptly:
> others besieged Ella madly for last orders. Some of the groups
> dispersed with bawled farewells: others drew closer protectively,
> and argued the louder and more earnestly for the assault that was
> being made upon their happiness.
> "NOW then, gentlemen, please! LONG PAST TIME!"

Indeed it is. They go, reluctantly, even the most grossly drunk who can barely speak. The whole passage describing closing time calls to mind those paintings of the expulsion from the Garden of Eden in which a stern God's finger appears from between clouds, pointing to the exit, and the half-covered, wretched mortals hurry away. The difference of course is that the pub, unlike Paradise, is open again tomorrow and innocence, in all its varieties, can be re-invented and experienced anew.

The Midnight Bell is one of the very best novels of the late twenties and it has not dated. Hamilton describes a world of secular hedonism, a world of forgetting and delusion. If not already an alcoholic at this time, he was a very heavy drinker, obsessed with the world of the pub and the people it attracted. The landlord calling 'Time' is literally that – a man who has the magical power to suspend time, and to enable us to ignore the progression of time in the streets outside and, most dreadful of all, the clock ticking in whatever passes for home. We rarely see into homes in Hamilton's fiction: these are modern city dwellers who seem to have no antecedents, no friends or connections outside the pub.

Ella is revealed, in the third novel of the trilogy, *The Plains of Cement*, as having a mother who lives with Ella's grotesquely boorish stepfather. The events in this novel occur over the same time period as those in *The Midnight Bell*. Ella is half in love with Bob. She sees nothing of his tortured relationship with Jenny the prostitute; the effect of the two books taken together is of one novel describing parallel events with the protagonist of each separate narrative not having any idea of what goes on in the other's life, although their lives are separated by only a thin wall between their rooms in the Midnight Bell. This is a very important characteristic of Hamilton's writing: the extreme loneliness and solipsism of his characters who seem unable to relate in any way with each other except through the medium of drink. Conversation is at the most basic level of idle chit-chat, relatively civilised while the drinking is still moderate, inclining to argument, more or less vicious, when too much has been drunk. In the Saloon Bar of the Midnight Bell it consists of a ritual exchange of clichés. The insanely inconsequential conversation between Ella and her middle-aged suitor Mr Eccles rises to a sort of repetitious mad poetry. Like Pinter, Hamilton achieves a threatening undertow in Mr Eccles's teasing questioning of Ella, which rings virtuosic variations on the interrogatory 'what?' to which he is addicted.

But Ella is that rare figure in Hamilton's books, a non-drinker. She is virtuous and sober, and she immediately recognises the threat that Jenny poses to Bob. The downfall of Jenny is the whole of the short novel that serves as an entr'acte between the other two full-length works.

The Siege of Pleasure opens with Jenny at the age of eighteen. She is a domestic servant, and a teetotaller and virgin at that point. Apart from the masterly depiction of the two ghastly elderly sisters and their senile brother for whom Jenny works, there is nothing much else in the book apart from the set-piece description of her first drunken night out and her presumed seduction by a charming, feckless, and alcoholic 'gentleman'. It is good, but it reads almost like a piece of material that Hamilton could not quite fit into the *The Midnight Bell*, but did not want to waste. It lacks the intense psychological insight of the other two parts of the trilogy, and sometimes reads like a temperance tract in its direct correlation between the first drink taken and Jenny's fall into prostitution.

IV

These tales of thwarted infatuation and habitual drunkenness came directly from Hamilton's own experiences in the late 1920s. Outwardly, he was riding high with the financial and critical success of his play *Rope*. In 1930 he married his first wife, Lois Martin. His brother, Bruce, gives us a portrait of his brother just before this marriage. Bruce had not seen Patrick for three years: when they met at Paddington Station, 'he looked more than three years older. His brown hair was thinner, his face bore marks left by experience, suffering – and perhaps dissipation.' So, despite his success, all was not well. His only sexual experience before he married had been with prostitutes and it appears, from what he told his brother, that he was 'quite unable to manage a satisfactory sexual relation with Lois'. They lived in London for a time, and he completed *The Siege of Pleasure*, while continuing to drink heavily. The difference in quality between that book and the masterly *The Plains of Cement* that followed may be due to the couple moving out of London to a cottage in Norfolk. The drinking eased off, Hamilton's health improved, and he was, in Bruce's words, 'in the fullness of health, energy, and good equable spirits'. Then, early in 1932, Hamilton and his wife went up to London for a few weeks to stay with his sister, Lalla.

The three of them went out for a walk one evening; Hamilton had only been drinking a couple of pints of beer a week and he was perfectly sober. In a narrow street he was hit by a car being driven at speed by a young man. His injuries were described as 'serious'. They included compound fractures to both arms and the right thigh, and multiple cuts, contusions and abrasions to the head and face. Part of his nose had been almost torn off and the scars of this and other facial injuries are clearly visible on photographs and remained so for the rest of his life.

The effects of the accident were devastating and far-reaching in ways other than the physical. He was in hospital and a nursing home for some weeks, but the fairly good physical recovery he made has to be weighed against the psychic trauma caused by his facial injuries. A physically slight and not particularly handsome man already sensitive to his lack of success in attracting women, he must have felt on his release from hospital almost grotesque in appearance. One might, like Byron, carry off a mysterious limp, but not a deformed nose. It was to be two years before Hamilton began writing again and a longer time before his next significant novel. He filled those two years of recovery with convalescence at the Norfolk cottage and a course of study that led him into a narrow and rigid adherence to Marxism. A new novel was beyond his powers at the time, but he did write two radio plays, one dealing significantly with the themes of sadistic revenge on a bully. The other, even more pertinent to Hamilton's life, was the story of a quartet of drunks who run down and leave for dead a cyclist. Perhaps it was remarkable that he did not take heavily to drink at this time; there were times when he got drunk, but more often he lived quietly with Lois.

When he did go up to London on business, he stayed at the Wells Hotel, in Hampstead. It was in the hotel's saloon bar that he first met the writer Arthur Calder-Marshall. At first, until introduced to him, Calder-Marshall took the quiet, slight bespectacled figure sitting on his own in a corner of the bar to be a commercial traveller. The truth was that Hamilton often looked for anonymous, seedy drinking places where he would not be known. The acute awareness of his facial injuries had severely affected his emotional life. It was hardly surprising that when Hamilton fell in love the outcome was a disaster.

Geraldine Fitzgerald was a beautiful young Irish actress who had the same theatrical agent as Hamilton. They met each other socially at dinners and parties and she knew him as a playwright, older than her by ten years, and they became friends. Hamilton's behaviour towards her changed abruptly when he learned that she had become engaged to be married. She would see him standing in the street below her flat, gazing up at the windows. Sometimes, when she was with her fiancé, Hamilton would ring and demand to know if the man was still there. On other occasions, she was sure it was Hamilton on the phone when she answered and there was only silence at the other end. His conduct became so threatening that she was at last forced to leave the flat and move, without telling Hamilton, to another address.

Hamilton never forgot, nor, it seems, forgave what he saw as her treachery. His obsessive, one-sided and undeclared love for Fitzgerald provided the structure and animus for his novel *Hangover Square*, published a few years later, in 1941. If Bone, the hopelessly and endlessly spurned and humiliated lover in that book, is a murderous and exaggerated version of Hamilton, then Netta, the woman pursued by Bone, is a cold, promiscuous and cruel tart. It seems a poor reward for being nice to Mr Hamilton.

Geraldine Fitzgerald went away to Hollywood. A year later, in 1938, Hamilton scored another huge theatrical success with his play *Gaslight*. Again the theme was one of cold and cruel mental torture, this time of a wife by her husband. It struck many chords with audiences at the time of the Munich Agreement: Hitler's incessant gross demands and smaller surrenders were unnerving; the Führer screamed on the wireless, and then was photographed shaking hands with and smiling at Mr Chamberlain. The sadistic toying of a man with his wife, the sinister lowering and raising of the gaslight on the stage in Hamilton's play, must have struck a powerful subconscious note in those anxious times. The money from the play and subsequent film treatments enabled Hamilton to fund a growing expense, his drink bills.

V

His brother, Bruce 'did some quiet arithmetic'. The results were astonishing.

There were two sorts of Hamilton consumption: town and country. Up in London, Bruce reckoned, his brother would begin the day in his Albany apartment with several large measures of whisky. Leaving the flat for a pub or restaurant, he would have 'at least four doubles . . . in the evening perhaps the score would be eight or ten. His daily consumption can seldom have fallen far below the equivalent of three bottles.' In the country he eased off somewhat, substituting pre-lunch beer for scotch, but still averaging a bottle of scotch a day, every day.

Bruce estimated the considerable monetary outlay. Whisky was hard to come by during the war and the official price for a bottle was a little over a pound, although the black-market price could be more than three pounds. Assuming an average daily consumption at two bottles a day, Hamilton was laying out about two thousand pounds a year for just his basic intake. When the costs are added of individual drinks bought in bars, meals, sixty cigarettes a day, tips to bar staff, waiters, taxi drivers and others, a conservative budget of four thousand pounds a year would probably have to be allowed for. It is difficult to put this into modern terms – spirits have not increased by anything like the rate of general inflation, by only about ten times, whereas general inflation rises are nearer thirty times – but a total of something like forty thousand pounds a year must be nearly equivalent.

Hamilton was often hopelessly drunk by late evening and it would seem that on his heaviest days little if any work could be accomplished. For his last two major works, *Hangover Square* and *The Slaves of Solitude,* Hamilton evolved a routine of writing in bed for six or seven hours a day, only drinking in the evenings. The results were probably his finest works.

VI

The subject matter did not change: the analysis and its results grew increasingly disturbing – even more than those of *The Midnight Bell*, the characters of *Hangover Square* are imprisoned physically, spiritually and emotionally, by drink and its distortions of their lives.

Its protagonist, George Harvey Bone, is hopelessly infatuated with Netta, a part-time actress. She has a floating cast of other male hangers-on and occasional lovers. Bone is not among her lovers: his role is to buy drinks for Micky and Peter and the rest of Netta's court, to be the butt of their jokes, and the object of Netta's cool torturing of his emotions. Life is lived in pubs and drinking clubs; to Bone, Netta is 'an awful little drunk . . . She never got up till half-past twelve: just chain-smoked in bed till it was time to drop over and into the nearest pub (only she had to have a man to take her over, because she didn't want to be taken for a prostitute).'

The emotional bind in which Bone finds himself is similar to that of Bob in *The Midnight Bell*: that of infatuation with a woman who despises and toys with him, granting tiny amorous favours and then withdrawing them, accepting money with a pretence of gratitude and then practically demanding it. But the humour of the earlier book is altogether darker in this later one; the easy going and good-looking Bob is replaced by Bone, physically awkward, socially inept, and crucially, a schizophrenic who finally becomes murderously violent.

The novel was written in his relatively quiet periods at home with Lois. She was kept in the background and many people who met Hamilton in London were not aware that he was married. There seems little doubt, from what Hamilton told his brother Bruce, and his close friend Claud Cockburn, that this marriage, though close in terms of enduring affection on both sides, had remained a sexless affair. Hamilton indulged in various minor affairs, but was always conscious of his scarred face, and his main sexual outlet was once more with prostitutes. With these women he was able to buy the sado-masochistic sex he preferred, a taste he transferred to the character of Ernest Gorse, in a later novel *The West Pier*: 'He liked to tie women up in order to get the impression that they were at his mercy . . . and to be tied up by women and to feel he was at theirs.' Bone goes one better in *Hangover Square* when, in one of the most bizarre scenes in fiction, he ties up an entire sitting room and bathroom containing the bodies of Netta and her lover, Peter, with several reels of thread, making a completely protective net around them, so that they shall not 'be disturbed'.

Hangover Square is set immediately before the Second World War. The book is pervaded by anxiety and a sense of the imminent ending of a way of life in defeat: Peter is openly a fascist and Netta is secretly thrilled by 'the uniforms, the guns, the breeches, the boots, the swastikas, the shirts'. The macabre scene when Bone is 'protecting' their bodies is accompanied by the sound of Neville Chamberlain's voice on the wireless announcing the declaration of war on Germany. Oddly, Hamilton's next book, *The Slaves of Solitude*, though set in the middle of the war, sees a return of Hamilton's sense of comedy, which while still dark, is not as utterly black as in *Hangover Square*.

Miss Roach in *The Slaves of Solitude* demonstrates a further development in the evolution of the public house. When Jenny uses the Midnight Bell at the end of the 1920s, she is brazen enough to do so as an obvious prostitute; when Netta goes to a pub at the end of the 1930s she is careful to be accompanied by a man so that she is not taken for a prostitute, but by the middle of the war, the highly respectable Miss Roach has got used to entering pubs alone:

> The blitz in London, with its attendant misery, peril, chaos, and informality, had already introduced Miss Roach to this habit . . . the war . . . had succeeded in conjuring into being yet another small population . . . of respectable middle-class girls and women, normally timid, home-going and home-staying, who had come to learn of the potency of this brief means of escape from war-thought

33

and war-endeavour. Without any taste for drink, and originally half-scandalised by the notion of drinking in public at all, these women would at first imagine that the pleasure they received from the new habit lay in the company, the lights, the conversation, the novelty or humour of the experience: then, gradually, they would perceive that there was something further than this, that the longer they stayed and the more they drank the more their pleasure in this pastime was augmented, reaching, at moments, a point, almost, of ecstasy.

Certainly, Miss Roach is in need of some escape from her room in a dingy boarding house, and even more so from her torments in the dining and sitting room of the boarding house. The house is dominated by the large and loud Mr Thwaites, who has the bully's eye for the slightest weakness in his victims. He is both ludicrous and menacing, and his horribly 'humorous' way of speaking, with much use of mock-antiquities such as 'by my troth' and 'verily' and needling references to 'her friends' (the Russians and their forces), brings Miss Roach to the point of rebellion. There is much drinking in the book, but this is Hamilton's most perfectly balanced novel and for once the subject is not drink, but human loneliness. For all of the inhabitants of the Rosamund Tea Rooms are profoundly alone. They are disturbed by the outside world in the large and jovial form of a heavy-drinking American officer, but we know that he is only an interruption and that when he is gone, the worlds of the hypochondriac Mrs Barratt, the arty Miss Steele, and Mr Prest, an unemployed music-hall comedian, will relapse into their separate darknesses in the boarding house. Things may appear to change: Mr Thwaites, 'this cruel, harsh, stupid, inconsiderate, unthinking man', as Hamilton describes him, dies; Mr Prest appears successfully in a pantomime; Miss Roach comes into a small legacy. It is the nearest Hamilton ever came to a happy ending. But the book ends with Miss Roach going to bed alone in Claridge's hotel; we know that she will always go to bed alone and the very last words of the book are 'God help all of us, every one, all of us.'

VII

The Slaves of Solitude is generally thought of as Hamilton's finest novel. Certainly, he never again achieved anything of comparable range and quality. The rationing of energy and drink that enabled him to write it were now dissipated in a long alcoholic decline. There were three more novels, the trilogy dealing with the criminal psychopath Ernest Gorse. The first, *The West Pier*, starts promisingly, but the material wears thin and becomes progressively more threadbare in the other two books, *Mr Stimpson and Mr Gorse* and *Unknown Assailant*. The problem is that the central character, Gorse, is so deeply unpleasant and mean-spirited that one cannot summon up very much interest in his fate. The richly black satire of his earlier works was based on Hamilton's powers of observation and his ability to retain fleeting pub conversations and personal characteristics, almost as an artist uses a sketchbook. But in the Gorse trilogy, Hamilton seems to take a curious delight in Gorse's mean-minded tricks, and in creating a character such as the snobbish Mrs Plumley-Bruce solely in order to torment her.

Given the state of Hamilton's emotional and physical health in the early 1950s it is remarkable that he could write anything. He had begun an affair in 1947 with Lady Ursula Chetwynd-Talbot, known to her friends as 'La'. For several years Hamilton oscillated between London life with La and out-of-town life with Lois. He also stayed for some time on his own in a dingy boarding house in Reading. The drink was taking its toll, making him loud, coarse, and repetitive. It was as if he had stopped writing about such characters only to start to become one.

Lois divorced him and he moved in with La at her Chelsea flat. He told his brother that he hoped that the new happiness he had found would mean an end to his heavy drinking. It did not. In 1955, the year *Unknown Assailant* was published, he at last sought help; first from a hypnotist, and then from a Dr Dent, who specialised in treating alcoholism. Although appearing to cooperate and take the drugs the doctor prescribed, Hamilton continued to drink in secret. To escape the temptations of the London pubs and clubs, La took a house for them in Blakeney, Norfolk. Bruce joined them and for a while they recreated their old routine of walking and chess, regular meals and very little alcohol. This was one of those periods that every alcoholic recognises: elation at the apparent return of health and self-confidence, at having 'beaten' the craving for booze. It is the most dangerous point for any addiction because this new sense of power wears off, life begins to appear to be a series of routines on one constant mental plane. The drinker feels oppressed by 'goodness' and 'duty'. Life is not so interesting as before: he has become an ordinary person, a 'civilian' in the drinking wars. How can he meet his old boozy friends – those who never seem to come to harm with the stuff – and refuse to join in with them? He is held prisoner by kindly, well-meaning bores. What more do they want of him? He has shown he can conquer the drink. The thing is to be able to drink responsibly. So it was with Hamilton – he was cured; he could take it or leave it alone. He persuaded Bruce to have a couple of whiskies with him. Bruce wrote later: 'Thus did Patrick throw away what was, I believe, his last chance.'

VIII

The story of Patrick Hamilton's last few years of life is a pitiable one. There were small recoveries, which did not last long, and the progress of his alcoholism was one of steady decline. A cure involving electro-convulsive therapy (ECT) was tried and he experienced a slight lift in his spirits. It did not last, however, and he plunged into a deep depression. He now read only trash and had little interest in any of the other arts. Another brief window of health was given by a course of vitamin B injections (very heavy drinking can lead to the destruction of thiamine in the brain and severe long-term problems of memory loss and motor control). His old London friends were ageing or dying off. He could no longer write; the only literary projects he thought up were tired versions of old plots and concerns. He rarely went to London; life in Norfolk was dreary and monotonous, but that seemed to be what he wanted. His daily routine was now completely ruled by alcohol. He would start the morning with a bottle of Guinness for breakfast. A few more half-pint bottles of that, then gin until lunch; the afternoon and evening were spent consuming a bottle of whisky. As he became progressively drunker, his speech would become slurred, and what he did say was endlessly repetitious and tedious.

Hamilton was in a very bad way physically. He had cirrhosis of the liver, could barely walk, and spent much of his time in bed, sleeping in the day and suffering insomnia at night. He was still drinking whisky and La was warned that unless he stopped he could die within months.

His last months were grim indeed; when he did manage to get up he fell easily. He became incontinent and had to have constant nursing attention. At last his kidneys failed and he died in his sleep on the third of September 1962.

La wrote to Bruce that she knew when her husband had died. There was suddenly no longer any sound of breathing from his room; only silence: 'It seemed to be filling the whole house, engulfing it – the silence of snow.'

Chapter 2

'As soon as I sober up I start again.'

Jean Rhys (1890–1979)

I

J EAN RHYS is almost as difficult to place in literary history as she was in life. Born in 1890, she did not come to real literary fame until 1966, with the publication of her novel *Wide Sargasso Sea*. She greeted the critical acclaim and awards with which the book was garlanded with a typically mordant comment – 'It has come too late.' She had gained a moderate amount of attention in the 1930s for four novels, all of them remarkably original works, but none a popular success. Then she disappeared from view. After the Second World War, if her name came up at all, it was assumed that she was dead. Julian Maclaren-Ross, resident gossip of the Soho pubs in which Jean Rhys had drunk many years before, maintained that she had expired in a French sanatorium in 1950.

This was horribly ironic, as she was haunted all of her life by the feeling that she did not belong or fit in anywhere, and that there was indeed something terribly uncertain and unreal about existence itself. In the immediate post-war period virtually all that was known of Jean Rhys was what could be inferred from the novels she had written in the 1920s and 1930s.

On the surface, the life she led and wrote about in London and Paris in her youth has a lot in common with that of the part-time 'actresses' and full-time prostitutes in Patrick Hamilton's fiction. But where the women in Hamilton's novels are, in the end, pathetic, vulnerable and doomed creatures, the women in Jean Rhys's books have a stubborn residual pride that will never quite allow them to surrender completely. Rhys was a superb writer of great insight (often wounding to herself), a conscious and conscientious artist, and a woman of great courage and determination. She was in poor health for much of her life, often cold, hungry and virtually penniless, an inveterate and often violent drinker, and, as in most things, she contradicted the expectations of others by living to a great age.

II

'Jean Rhys' was the pen name invented for his protégée and mistress, Ella Lenglet, by the writer Ford Madox Ford when he published her first stories in his magazine *Transatlantic Review* in 1924. Ella was at the time married to a Dutch journalist and con-man, Jean Lenglet; her full name before marriage was Ella Gwendolen Rees Williams and she was born on the twenty-fourth of August 1890 in Roseau, the capital of the West Indian island of Dominica.

Dominica was the largest of the Leeward Islands and lies between the French islands of Martinique and Guadeloupe. At the end of the nineteenth century it was probably the least British of the colonial islands: the black population spoke a French-Creole patois, and the white community was in a tiny minority. Ella's father was a doctor and an incomer; her mother's grandfather had been the owner of a sugar plantation worked by more than two hundred slaves.

This small world was one of invisible but impenetrable barriers between different classes and colours. A black nurse called Meta told Ella stories of zombies and werewolves. Meta was 'the terror of my life' and showed the young girl 'a world of fear and mistrust'. Despite her nurse's petty cruelties, Ella envied the life of the black islanders:

They had a better time than we did, they laughed a lot though they seldom smiled . . . Every night someone gave a dance, you could hear the drums . . . They were more alive, more a part of the place than we were.

At twelve she was one of the few white children at the local convent school; most of the others were what was then called 'coloured', that is, of mixed race. When she tried to make friends with one of these girls she was met with 'implacable hatred' – 'white cockroaches they called us behind our backs'. With few friends, a father of whom she saw little, and a mother who was emotionally distant, she became a withdrawn bookish girl, in love with words and the Catholicism of her convent school. She discovered the 'facts of life' in a book in her father's library and not unnaturally refused to believe them. Her sense of adolescent sexuality may have been further confused at the age of fourteen. In her short story 'Goodbye Marcus, Goodbye Rose', she describes a 'Captain Cardew', who tells the adolescent girl narrator that she is old enough to take a lover and reaches inside her dress to caress one of her breasts.

In 1907 she was shipped off to England, to the Perse School in Cambridge. She found England repellent: cold and grey and endlessly depressing. When she left school, she was still a 'colonial' abroad. She wanted to be an actress, but still spoke with a strange outlandish accent that prevented her finding work. She signed up at a theatrical agency and began work as a chorus girl. Her career in musical comedy and pantomime lasted only two years. It was the last 'real' job she would have for some time. At the age of nineteen she became the mistress of Lancelot Smith, a stockbroker.

Ella visited Smith in his rooms: warm, well furnished, with ample food and drink before going to bed with him. In the early morning she would let herself out and return to the small flat he had rented for her. Smith was a bachelor, but did not offer to marry this rather odd and beautiful young woman. Then, to her immense distress, he ended the affair. In the autobiography she dictated when very old, she said: 'why I came to worship him I don't quite know', and she blamed herself for the failure of the affair by saying that she realised, after reading about sex in novels of the 1950s and 1960s, what a naïve and wooden lover she must have been: 'a passive, dull girl'. Again hard up and homeless, she moved in with a Madame Hermine, a self-styled 'Swedish masseuse', and drifted into a series of relationships with men.

Sleeping around, she became pregnant and was forced to appeal to Smith for money. He was willing to help her have the child although it was not his, but another family member persuaded her to have an abortion. She was more than four months pregnant. Bearing in mind Rhys's own statement that she wrote about nothing but her own life, the only picture we have of her in this period is in the story of Anna Morgan, in her third novel *Voyage in the Dark*, published much later in 1934.

The novel had been at least partially drafted soon after the near fatal abortion of 1913. In the published version, Anna Morgan is nineteen years old, a chorus girl in a touring musical comedy, playing in a dreary seaside town. She rooms with Maudie, a fellow 'artiste'. Maudie's conversation is about men and clothes and the drab lives of the two are ameliorated by dreams of the 'right man' and drink. But Anna is profoundly alienated from her surroundings. She cannot get used to the cold of England after her island home. 'Not just the difference between heat, cold: light, darkness: purple, grey.' She is picked up by an older man, Walter Jeffries, and becomes his mistress in London. She drinks at his house:

'You've learnt to drink whisky already, haven't you?' he said.

'It's in my blood,' I said. 'All my family drink too much . . . '

I finished the whisky. The paralysed feeling went and I was all right again.

After a while, Anna worries that Walter will grow tired of her and thinks about how odd her life is compared with that of other people:

> But in the daytime it was all right. And when you'd had a drink you knew it was the best way to live in the world, because anything might happen. I don't know how people live when they know exactly what's going to happen to them each day. It seems to me it's better to be dead than to live like that.

Inevitably, Walter tires of her, and a cousin is sent to pay her off with an allowance so she won't have to 'worry about money (for a time at any rate)'. Now all that Anna has to console her are sleep and drink. She falls into a deep depression:

> It's funny when you feel as if you don't want anything more in your life except to sleep, or else to lie without moving. That's when you can hear time sliding past you, like water running.

She drifts into affairs with pick-ups, her life not far short of outright prostitution. As Maudie says, 'Have you ever thought that a girl's clothes cost more than the girl inside them?' She becomes pregnant and is forced to write to Walter for help in paying for an abortion. After what was then an illegal operation, a friend has to call a doctor:

> He moved about the room briskly, like a machine that was working smoothly.
> He said 'You girls are too naïve to live, aren't you?'
> Laurie laughed. I listened to them both laughing and their voices going up and down.
> 'She'll be all right,' he said. 'Ready to start all over again in no time, I've no doubt.'

III

And start again Ella did. She worked occasionally as an artists' model and appeared as an extra in a couple of silent films. During the First World War, she helped out in a canteen for soldiers at Euston Station. Lancelot Smith continued to pay her an allowance for a number of years and she became engaged to a journalist, but continued to have affairs with other men in London. In 1917 she met Jean Lenglet and married him in 1919.

Characteristically, in a life full of legend and fiction, Ella lied about her age on the marriage papers, giving 1894 as her date of birth, instead of 1890, and, for his part, Lenglet neglected to mention that he was already married to another woman. For the next few years they lived a rackety life in Europe, alternating between enjoying plenty of money and near destitution. Ella gave birth to a son in Paris, but the baby died after only three weeks. They moved to Vienna, and Lenglet became involved in black market dealings in currency. Whatever Lenglet was up to, they had to keep moving, often literally on the run, from Vienna, to Budapest, then to Prague. Their second child, Maryvonne, was born in Belgium, but again they had to get out hurriedly, leaving the unfortunate infant in a clinic. It was in this year, 1922, that Lenglet's bigamous past caught up with him in Paris. The two separated and Ella was once more alone, once more without money.

It is in Paris in 1924 that Jean Rhys the writer appears for the first time. A friend sent some of the sketches she had been writing to Ford Madox Ford. Ford was an editor remarkably open to new talent, and he had been an early champion of D.H. Lawrence and Hemingway. An object of reverence to the aspiring writers of Montparnasse, who addressed him as *cher maitre*, Ford derived considerable complacent pleasure from their adoration. He began an affair with this new, pretty young woman and printed her first published work, a story called 'Vienne', changing the author's name from Ella Lenglet to Jean Rhys.

Her style was already remarkable, highly original in its choice of the poetic image, economical in cutting swiftly from one scene to another, and with a gift for presenting the inner thoughts of her characters in a way that held both the past and present of their lives. There is no doubt that Ford was exactly the right editor for her; he contributed an introduction to her first collection of stories, *The Left Bank*, published in 1927, in which he describes how they had worked together on her writing. Always a natural writer, she took what she needed from him and rejected what she instinctively felt was wrong for her. But she was in the studio of a master writer, with whom she also happened to be in love. The other member of the trio, Stella Bowen, Ford's resident mistress, was alarmed for her own position. In her autobiography, *Drawn from Life*, she complained that:

> . . . here I was cast for the role of the fortunate wife who held all the cards, and the girl for that of the poor, brave and desperate beggar who was doomed to be let down by the bourgeoisie. I learnt what a powerful weapon lies in weakness and pathos . . .
>
> All her virtues, in her view, were summed up in "being a sport," which meant being willing to take risks and show gallantry and share one's last crust: more attractive qualities, no doubt, than patience, honesty or fortitude. She regarded the law as the instrument of the "haves" against the "have nots" and was well acquainted with every rung of that long and dismal ladder by which the respectable citizen descends towards degradation.

A fair enough analysis from Bowen's point of view, but then Jean Rhys had never been exactly 'respectable' and for a great deal of her life she continued to be one of the 'have nots'.

When the affair was broken off by Ford in 1926, Rhys was desperately unhappy. She began to drink heavily. She was briefly reunited with her husband and daughter in The Hague, but the marriage was over by June 1928. Rhys left for London and her daughter Maryvonne remained with her father.

IV

Jean Rhys's first novel, *Quartet*, published in September 1928, is a barely fictionalised account of her affair with Ford and the break-up of her marriage. It is told largely from the viewpoint of a young woman, Marya Zelli, who, at the start of the book, is living with her husband Stephan. When he is sent to prison for fraud, Marya moves in with Hugh and Lois Heidler. She has an affair with Hugh; she loves him; he in the end rejects her with great cruelty. Her husband returns, but Marya confesses her affair to Stephan and he leaves her.

Quartet is the most conventional and tightly plotted of Jean Rhys's novels. The style is still a little awkward and the viewpoint wobbles unconvincingly about between characters, but Marya is the first of Rhys's heroines, the first in a series of increasingly harshly drawn self-portraits. There is a reference to Dominica, when Marya lies in bed in a Paris hotel room after drinking too much Pernod and half-dreams the 'dark trees growing close together with thick creepers which hung down from the branches like snakes. Virgin forest. Intact. Never been touched', and a remembrance of English concert party days and 'bottles of gin in the dressing room'. To Marya, drink is a means of escape from the oppressive self. Each of Rhys's heroines has a profound sense of dislocation, as if she is forever in the wrong place, the wrong bed, the wrong body even; what Marya calls 'the essential craziness of existence'. What this realisation breeds is a sense of irresponsibility, a passivity in the face of whatever life throws at her. 'If I went to the devil it would be because I wanted to, or because it's a good drug, or because I don't give a damn for my idiotic body of a woman, anyway.' The only time Marya comes to any sort of accommodation with herself is when she is drinking, preferably alone: 'It was astonishing how significant, coherent and understandable it all became after a glass of wine on an empty stomach.' After visiting Stephan in prison she goes to a café:

> How terrifying human beings were, Marya thought. But she had
> drunk two fines and a half-bottle of something which the *patron*

called champagne ... Then she saw Lois standing near the doorway with her coat on. She beckoned and Marya got up with reluctance.

Lois is beckoning her to come and have a drink with her husband, Heidler. And so Marya's affair begins. She and Heidler sleep together at a hotel, where it is impossible, looking at the bed, not to imagine 'the succession of *petites femmes* who had extended themselves upon it'. The peculiar lassitude she feels when she makes love with Heidler is part of her generally fatalistic attitude to life; it does not occur to her that she can be anything else, or that she has any other purpose than as Heidler's mistress. Happiness is a fleeting thing, not to be expected from life, but to be snatched occasionally from sex and drink. Heidler ends their affair brutally and abruptly. When she leaves the hotel that night Marya gets half-drunk in a café and is picked up by a young man and goes home with him.

It seems that Marya needs to be possessed by a man, but she often rejects happiness as if it were a debilitating illness. Her real moments of energy and sense of belonging occur in bars, drinking on her own: 'the unvarying background, knowing waiters, clouds of smoke' after a couple of Pernods, 'the stuff mercifully clouded her brain'. It is the illusory sense of time standing still, of a suspension of life that makes the bar and café so attractive. It is the one constant that, at a price, will never let the drinker down.

V

In 1928, after her return to London, Rhys moved in with Leslie Tilden Smith, her literary agent. They married in 1934 after she had divorced Jean Lenglet (her daughter, Maryvonne, remained with Lenglet). She again lied about her age: it is given as thirty-eight on the marriage certificate; she was actually forty-three.

The return to England, the onset of middle age, and a steady and loving partner should perhaps have meant a more settled life; it was anything but that. By 1930, Tilden Smith had been forced to close his literary agency and the couple were extremely hard up. Their relationship had become stormy, with the diminutive Rhys physically attacking her husband, leaving his face scratched and his eyes blacked. The novel she was writing at this time, *After Leaving Mr Mackenzie*, shows very clearly her self-knowledge of the place that alcoholic addiction now played in her life.

The plot of the novel is simple. Julia has parted from her lover and is living in a cheap hotel in Paris, on a weekly allowance from her ex-lover, Mr Mackenzie. She has no man at the moment and her landlady disapproves of her 'habit of coming home at night with a bottle'. During the day she lies in her room, reading and sleeping. If she does go out, she still makes herself up carefully, knowing that she is beginning to look old. The weekly cheques stop coming after six months, she rejects Mackenzie's final pay-off of fifteen hundred francs, but another man, Horsfield, meets her when she is half-drunk in a café and gives her money. She buys some new clothes and moves back to London. Julia's way of life has always been funded by 'living on the money given her by various men. Going from man to man had become a habit.' She does everything on impulse and only moderates her behaviour when she needs money.

The final pages of the short novel deal with a single night in the city. She has dinner and wine. At a larger café she has brandy. Outside in the street a young man, little more than a boy, tries to pick her up but then veers away when he sees her face, older than expected, in the lamplight. Another café, and more brandy. The following evening, Mr Mackenzie, seated outside a café, sees her and persuades her to have a drink for old times' sake. As she drinks a Pernod he looks across the table at her:

She looked untidy. There were black specks in the corners of her eyes. Women go phut quite suddenly, he thought.

She asks him to lend her a hundred francs. He gives her a little more:

> Julia put the money into her bag without counting it.
>
> Mr Mackenzie fidgeted. 'I'm afraid I must be getting along now. Will you have another drink before I go?'
>
> 'Yes, another Pernod, please,' she said. And then: 'So long.'
>
> 'Goodbye,' said Mr Mackenzie.
>
> The street was cool and full of grey shadows. Lights were beginning to come out in the cafés. It was the hour between dog and wolf, as they say.

The last two of her 1930s' novels, *Voyage in the Dark* and *Good Morning, Midnight* (from a poem by Emily Dickinson that sounds as if it should have been a lyric sung by Billie Holiday) are related in the first person, heightening their seemingly autobiographical nature. But, if Ella Williams, Ella Lenglet, or Ella Tilden Smith led a life similar to her fictional counterparts – amoral, promiscuous, irresponsible, increasingly drunken – there is one major and over-riding difference. Their creator was an artist who had sufficient genius to portray this world of men and women in a way that is not self-pitying, and whose sordidness is illuminated by sudden perceptions or poetic images. In the end, she seems to say throughout her work that no one is to blame, except existence, and that is to be shunned and escaped from in all its obviously ordinary terms. Read in the chronological order of their subject matter, the tales of Rhys's heroines grow darker and darker. The consumption of alcohol rises progressively, from the very young Anna, in *Voyage in the Dark*, drinking to cheer herself up, to the much older Sasha, in *Good Morning, Midnight*, drinking resolutely to get drunk.

VI

Sometimes Jean Rhys was able to stop drinking, although the reason often seems to have been from want of cash, rather than any moral or medical reason. A letter in 1933, to the writer Evelyn Scott, says that she 'hasn't touched a drop for a month'. But the letter carries on more ominously: 'Won't it be fine when I do. It ought to give me a kick.' In another letter Rhys says about the writing of *Voyage in the Dark*: 'I don't know what I feel about the blessed thing. I had the horrors about it and about everything for a bit . . . But I expect that was my liver and lights giving way under the strain of two bottles of wine a day.' Drinking made her aggressive and uncontrollable and led to ruptures with most of her friends. As Carole Angier says in her biography of Jean Rhys, 'It was now the second half of 1935, at the latest early 1936 . . . The miracle Jean had hoped for hadn't happened . . . her slide had not stopped. On the contrary, she had become an irretrievable alcoholic.'

In 1936 her husband inherited some money and for the first time in almost thirty years Rhys was able to return to Dominica. She found the island as beautiful as ever but was depressed by visiting the old family estate, Geneva, which had largely been destroyed by a fire. She argued terribly with her friend Evelyn Scott at a party in New York and returned to London, from which she sent a letter of apology that was about as unapologetic as could be. She admitted that 'as a well trained social animal I'm certainly not the goods', and went on to say, 'I do not agree that my way of looking at life and human beings is distorted. I think that the desire to be cruel and to hurt . . . is part of human nature. Parties are battles . . . a conversation is a duel.' And if there were the slightest suspicion on her part that anyone was being cruel or unkind to her, Rhys would attack, verbally or even physically.

But the marriage endured. Tilden Smith made a slim living as a freelance editor. He helped Rhys with her work, typing up handwritten drafts of her new novel, *Good Morning, Midnight*, the most radically modernist of the novels and formally the most perfect. Every page is dotted with ellipses to denote cuts that are like cinematic dissolves in their effect, passing us from past to present and back, from one thought or memory to another.

The drinking is now extreme. The Rhys heroine, Sasha, is older and not very much wiser. Once more we are in Paris, but Sasha remembers living alone in London:

It was then that I had the bright idea of drinking myself to death. Thirty-five pounds of the legacy had accumulated, it seemed. That ought to do the trick.

I did try it, too. I've had enough of these streets that sweat a cold, yellow slime, of hostile people, of crying myself to sleep every night. I've had enough of thinking, enough of remembering. Now whisky, rum, gin, sherry, vermouth, wine with the bottles labelled 'Dum vivimus, vivamus . . . ' Drink, drink, drink . . . As soon as I sober up I start again. I have to force it down sometimes. You'd think I'd get delirium tremens or something.

Sasha is the first of the women in the novels to have a job, as a saleswoman in a fashionable Paris dress-shop. It doesn't last long, as she is soon dismissed for a mixture of insolence and incompetence. Now, armed only with her four hundred francs severance pay, she has her hair dyed and buys some new clothes. Instead of attracting an older man she becomes the prey of a young gigolo who assumes that she has money. In a café she asks herself:

Will I have another little Pernod? I certainly will have another little Pernod. (Food? I don't want any food now. I want more of this feeling – fire and wings.)

So it goes, from café to café, from Pernod to whisky. 'If I have a bottle of Bordeaux at dinner I'll be almost as drunk as I'd hoped to be.' The confusion of tenses is used in a masterly fashion throughout the book to bring the past into the present, and to oppose it to a threatening and probably hopeless future. A long section dealing with her first marriage and the death of her infant son melds seamlessly into the

Paris of the novel's action. She forms a bond with the gigolo, which comes to an end with a miserably awkward and humiliating sexual encounter. He leaves, and in the closing scene of the book the man who has the next room in the hotel to Sasha, a commercial traveller she has been trying to avoid, comes into her room in his dressing gown. The book ends with Sasha extending her arms in an embrace and whispering the words, 'Yes – yes – yes . . . ' – a parodic echo of Molly Bloom's ecstatic sexual release at the end of *Ulysses*.

Some critics see *Good Morning, Midnight* as Rhys's masterpiece. Carole Angier calls it 'a very great novel'. It is certainly a brilliant portrait of the final ageing and burning out of the Rhys heroine. But the overwhelming solipsism of Sasha almost veers into sentimentality, close to self-pity on occasion. There is also a sense that the material is wearing thin and some is being recycled. But it may be, as Carole Angier says, that the four early novels should be taken as one whole chronicle, endlessly circling back on itself and using the same obsessive memories and experiences, 'slowly spiralling up the same circular staircase'.

With the publication in 1939 of *Good Morning, Midnight*, the first part of Jean Rhys's life as a public writer came to a close. The reviews were good, though mixed as usual in their appreciation of her style, which was commonly supposed to be influenced by Hemingway, and disapproval of the moral weakness of her heroine and her sordid way of life. But the Modernism of the 1920s was dead; modified and simplified in the neutrally voiced realism of Isherwood and Greene. It was not the best of times to be publishing a novel of any sort: the outbreak of war eclipsed the literary world of the 1930s and the affairs of Mr and Mrs Tilden Smith.

VII

In 1940, Jean Rhys was fifty years old. She had been through a lot and was to go through an awful lot more. Her husband went into the

RAF and her first husband and daughter were in occupied Holland. She drank, made rowdy and violent scenes in public and appeared in court on charges of being drunk and disorderly. In 1945 her husband Leslie was taken ill and died suddenly of a heart attack. Rhys soon married again, Leslie's cousin, a solicitor named Max Hamer, but life became, if anything, even less stable. Hamer was not a success in his career and they were soon in financial difficulties. They moved out of London to a house in suburban Beckenham.

Mrs Ella Hamer, as she was now known, was frequently drunk and a public nuisance. To her neighbours she was not a famous writer, but simply an ageing alcoholic woman of the sort who might be lost in the vastness of a city, but who in a small town or suburb rapidly gets into trouble. And trouble came from her aggressive behaviour when drunk. Several times in the late 1940s she was arrested for assault or other drunken behaviour, once being remanded to Holloway Prison a medical report. But there was a gleam of light in the darkness.

In 1949 an actress named Selma van Diaz placed an advertisement in the *New Statesman* asking for news of the whereabouts of Jean Rhys. Van Diaz had made a radio play version of *Good Morning, Midnight* and needed copyright permission. Rhys was flattered, but this new recognition, or at least acknowledgement that she still existed, did not temper her behaviour. She continued to get drunk and annoy, or be annoyed by, her long-suffering neighbours. But worse was to come. In 1950 her husband Max was arrested and convicted of obtaining money under false pretences. He served two years in prison and on his release the couple were in near destitution.

The radio play version of *Good Morning, Midnight* was not broadcast until 1957. One of her neighbours now went around telling everyone that mad Mrs Hamer was pretending to be a dead author called Jean Rhys. Rhys wrote to a friend, 'It's a weird feeling being told you are impersonating yourself, you think: perhaps I am.' But the broadcast awoke interest in Rhys and her work. Jennifer Ross, then married to Alan Ross, the editor of *London Magazine*, lent a copy of *Voyage in the Dark* to Francis Wyndham, an editor at publisher Andre Deutsch, and he wrote to offer Rhys a contract for her next novel. It took a further eight years of great effort for her to finish *Wide Sargasso Sea*.

It seems barely possible, given her husband's continual ill-health after prison (which he had left at the age of seventy) and her own alcoholism and violent temper and occasional mental disturbance, that she should have still been writing. The tale told in her letters, of an elderly woman battling against poverty, drink, and cold gives some idea of her bloody-mindedness and devotion to her art. When she got a little money, it was 'never mind I intend to spend my last penny on a spree soon. Taxi to Tiverton where Pernod, vodka, not bad vin rouge and Penguins can be bought.' She was seventy-one when she wrote this and deep into her revision of *Wide Sargasso Sea*.

She and Max settled, in 1960, in a miserable bungalow in a small village near Crediton in Devon. Relations between Rhys and her new neighbours settled rapidly into the familiar pattern of mutual loathing. The strain of looking after Max was overwhelming after a time. He needed constant nursing and was admitted to hospital in 1963. Rhys herself underwent treatment for depression and suffered a heart attack. But somehow her book had been revised and completed and it was published in 1966 to huge acclaim.

Jean Rhys was now seventy-six years old. She lived, in some comfort from the earnings of her new book, the reissue of the earlier novels, and from literary grants, for a further thirteen years. She had many friends and admirers, with some of whom she was charming and charismatic, although others were alienated by her foul temper and sudden changes of mood aggravated by alcohol.

Her stubbornness and courage had at last found their just reward, but she was now an old woman; a state of affairs that enraged and depressed her. Drink, clothes, and attention were craved, and given in some measure. From the photographs of the late 1960s and 1970s we see extraordinarily beautiful huge eyes staring as if lost behind a mask of make-up and old age. There were two further collections of her remarkable short stories and a posthumously published autobiography, *Smile Please*, written with the aid of the novelist David Plante.

VIII

It is entirely possible that, without the intervention of Selma van Diaz, Jean Rhys would have ended her days as Ella Hamer in a hospital or institution, leaving carrier bags full of disordered manuscripts under the bed in the bungalow to be disposed of as rubbish by the neighbours. It is also possible that the earlier novels would have disappeared forever into the great heap of unread novels from any period; though it is not likely that work of such quality would ever have been wholly lost. But, unlike her fictional alter egos, Jean Rhys had her ultimate triumph. If I have concentrated on her early life and work it is not to slight that wonderful later novel, *Wide Sargasso Sea*, but because her earlier work, so radical and original, has been overshadowed by the remarkable story of her rediscovery.

To those who saw Jean Rhys in her long and tortured years of obscurity, she sometimes appeared as simply a mad, drunken old woman. She could be manipulative, cruel, violent and, at times, endlessly self-justifying and self-pitying. But, unlike the rest of us, who share some or all of these faults, she was also capable of seeing herself quite clearly and coldly. Perhaps she needed drink to ward off her feeling of the sheer terror of existence, and of non-existence as a whole person, but it is inconceivable, however it may have wrecked her life, that she would have changed her behaviour if that would have cost her the unflinching truth expressed in her novels and stories.

Chapter 3

'Delirium is a disease of the night'

Charles Jackson (1903–1968)

I

IN 1945, the actor Ray Milland felt that he needed to gain some background for his role as Don Birnam in the film of Charles Jackson's novel *The Lost Weekend*, and he spent a night in one of the alcoholic wards of Bellevue Hospital in New York. He found himself in

> a large whitewashed ward containing about twenty other beds . . .
> Three tough looking male nurses . . . were in charge of the ward.
> They seemed more like jailers than hospital attendants. The place
> was a multitude of smells, but the dominant one was that of a
> cesspool. And there were the sounds of moaning and quiet crying.
> One man talked incessantly, just gibberish, and two of the inmates
> were under restraint, strapped to their beds.

Milland goes on to describe how paraldehyde was issued at night to sedate the inmates, but he was woken in the night by the admission of a new patient:

> He kept up a high, keening wail, and when they got him to the bed
> he started screaming that it was on fire. They finally got him strapped

down, but the screaming didn't stop . . . Then from across the room
a long ululating howl started . . . Suddenly the room was bedlam.

II

The Lost Weekend was Charles Jackson's first novel: it gave a new
phrase to the language and has never been long out of print. It tells
the story of five days in the life of Don Birnam, would-be writer and
alcoholic. For a long weekend, from Thursday to Tuesday, Birnam
drinks enormously, his binges punctuated only by periods of
unconsciousness or blackout. Virtually no other action takes place
except for drinking and its results, culminating in a terrifying attack
of delirium tremens. There had been plenty of liquor in American
literature of the previous forty years, and even more in many of the
writers, but this was the first novel to deal in such a detailed, almost
obsessive way with an alcoholic's life. The book was a sensation; a
critical and popular success. The author admitted it was based on his
own experiences, and it was painfully revelatory of his character; the
man recalled by his friend Dorothea Straus, in her book *Showcases*, as
'many Charles Jacksons . . . the warm, proud father, the occasional
companionable husband, the unbridled alcoholic, the famous author,
the clown, the irrepressible homosexual.'

Charles Jackson was born on the sixth of April 1903. His early
childhood seems to have been happy and uneventful in Newark,
a village in New York State, renamed as 'Arcadia' in his short stories
– a change that gives a sense of the settled happiness as a young child
that recurs throughout his writing, but it is also an ironic choice of
name for a place whose corruption and hypocrisy become plain as he
grows older. The first disturbance in his life came when Jackson was
twelve years old and his father deserted the family. A more terrible
disaster followed with the deaths of his sister and baby brother in a car
crash in 1916. Jackson graduated from high school in 1921 and the
following year enrolled at Syracuse University on a business course.

He was there for only two semesters of his first year. One of the few records of his stay is captured in a photograph of a group of students; he is a good looking young man with a sensitive face oddly reminiscent of the great jazz player Bix Beiderbecke, a man born in the same year as Jackson and one also plagued by demons of sexuality and alcoholism. Quite early on in the autobiographical *The Lost Weekend* there is a potted version of its hero Don Birnam's life:

> . . . when his father left home and left him . . . the fraternity nightmare . . . leaving home, the Village and prohibition . . . the TB years in Davos; the long affair with Anna; the drinking . . . Juan-les-Pins . . . the pawnshops; the drinking, the unaccountable things you did . . . the books begun and dropped, the unfinished short stories; the drinking the drinking the drinking . . .

The manuscript of the novel contains the phrase 'the homosexual incident, excursions that were linked so peculiarly with drinking'. This was omitted in the published novel, but there are other clues to Birnam's (and Jackson's) sexuality in the passages that clearly describe adolescent homosexual experience.

What remains in the published text seems to accord pretty well with what we know of Jackson's early life. A personal statement he gave in his entry to Stanley Kunitz's *Twentieth Century Authors* contains some of his hero's experiences, but for obvious reasons omits the drinking and, significantly, the 'fraternity nightmare'. Jackson's statement says that he graduated from high school in 1921 and that that was the end of his formal education. He clearly wanted not only to forget the year at Syracuse, but also to conceal any evidence of his stay. We probably shall never know why he left college so abruptly, but in his writing he was so often scathingly honest about his own life that the shame and disgrace that seems to have attended his early exit from Syracuse is present in several forms in his fiction.

In *The Lost Weekend*, Don Birnam goes over and over the disgrace of being expelled from his fraternity house for developing a homosexual crush on an older student and writing passionate letters to him. In a terrifying dream Birnam is chased from the campus by the massed student body acting as a lynch mob. None of this was included in the Billy Wilder film of 1946: the hero was issued with Jane Wyman as a girlfriend. But it also has to be remembered that even in the 1920s most American writers had had a college education and Jackson's expulsion can only have added to the sense of isolation and exclusion that seems to have marked his whole life.

In the early 1920s he took jobs in a jigsaw factory and in bookstores in Chicago and New York. In 1927 he contracted tuberculosis. The disease was, Jackson said, 'very serious'. So, at this date, we have a sensitive young man who had probably had a number of homosexual encounters, perhaps emboldened by drink. The terror of contracting tuberculosis, a possibly fatal disease, must have been exacerbated by his knowledge of the theory held by many psychiatrists at the time that the disease was caused psychosomatically by the repression of 'forbidden and hystericised emotions'. These are the words of Dr Krokowski in Thomas Mann's *The Magic Mountain*, published in 1924. The novel is set in a sanatorium in Davos, Switzerland, and it was to Davos that Jackson came for treatment in 1929.

There was no effective treatment for tuberculosis until the discovery of streptomycin during the Second World War. Before that, it was thought that the symptoms could be alleviated by fresh air at altitude and by rest and solitude. The theory was attractive, if clinically ineffective. It was however extremely lucrative as a business: by the time Jackson went to Switzerland there was a score of sanatoriums in Davos alone, some of them huge buildings more akin to luxury hotels than hospitals. It appears that Jackson had money sent to him from America ('from a rich old man', according to his friend Dorothea Straus).

He stayed in Davos for some months. It was clean, beautiful and bracing and the mountain air may have prolonged some lives, but there were still many deaths amongst the mostly young population. All the hectic diversions of dances and concerts, flirtations and affairs were overshadowed by the constant and morbid attention paid to the X-rays and temperature charts that monitored the progress of each patient. Sometimes the disease cleared spontaneously and patients went back to the outside world, sometimes, as was the case with Jackson, the administering of a pneumothorax puncture to collapse a diseased lung was presumed to have checked the disease. The result was that Jackson was judged well enough to leave, although he suffered from problems with his lungs for the rest of his life. After a short stay in the South of France, once more paid for by the same elderly patron, he returned to the United States in 1931.

There are now long gaps in the record of his life. Some clues to these missing years were given by Jackson in interviews; he said that he read a huge amount and 'over many years' wrote stories and novels, all of which remained unpublished. He was for the next five years in and out of dead-end jobs and presumably drinking more and more, culminating in a crisis in 1936 when his brother, Frederick, had him committed to Bellevue Hospital.

The oldest free hospital in the USA, originally established in 1736 as a 'Publick Workhouse and House of Correction', Bellevue was by 1936 an enormous complex of twenty-five buildings, comprising 102 wards. It served the poorer East Side of Manhattan and in the mid-1930s handled something in the order of three quarters of a million admissions and outpatient appointments a year. Because it dealt with many of the least nourished and worst housed of New York's poor the hospital had a very high death rate. Jackson was admitted to one of the alcoholic wards (in the same year, Malcolm Lowry was treated in the same part of the hospital).

The treatment of Jackson does not appear to have differed much from that dispensed in the notorious Ward 30 of earlier days, described in 1920 by an ex-nurse, Ernest F. Hoyer:

The first sight to greet one was over a dozen delirium tremens cases, securely tied down with sheets . . . All stark, raving mad: singing, cursing, laughing, crying . . . From that room we came to another ward-section . . . here the patients were bed-patients, either surgical or medical, mostly fractures and alcoholic pneumonia . . . I have seen as many as seventy [patients] admitted in one day. The rank and file of an alcoholic ward is, in reality, the scum – the flotsam of a city.

Between the years 1902 and 1917 there was an average of some 8,500 alcoholic admissions a year. But before and during the First World War, the temperance movement had a significant impact, as did wartime prohibition from 1917. By the time of Hoyer's article, the Eighteenth Amendment prohibiting the sale and consumption of alcohol had been passed in January 1920, and admissions that year fell to a record low of 2,091. Hoyer was optimistic: 'Now that John Barleycorn is dying a lingering but sure death, we can bid good-bye, I hope forever, to the many alcoholic wards scattered all over the dear old USA.'

His optimism was horribly misplaced: from 1921 onwards the rate of alcoholic admissions increased steadily until, by the time Jackson was committed, it was running at its pre-First World War levels.

The medical treatment described by Jackson in *The Lost Weekend* is fairly rudimentary. Conditions in a crowded hospital ward where patients, often exhibiting extremes of mental and physical distress, are constantly being admitted and released (in Don Birnam's case, after only one night) are not likely to be particularly or sensitively tailored to suit each individual. Drunks are often violent and have to be restrained and the sort of men and women who then undertook to deal with such patients were not likely to have been of a tender disposition. The brutal sarcasm of Bim, the male nurse in *The Lost Weekend*, is that of a man who has seen it all, has heard every conceivable excuse, a man who has in his own mind reduced each of his patients to the denominator common to them all: 'a lush'.

Treatment consisted of physical restraint of those likely to hurt themselves or others, administering of sedatives, and, for a few deemed likely to benefit, some psychiatric treatment. It was a far cry from the regime of expensive nursing homes for the rich with their carefully chosen diets, and individually administered weaning procedures.

Despite the horrors of the alcoholic ward, the treatment worked – up to a point – for Jackson. He did manage to give up drinking for the next dozen or so years, but he became heavily addicted to the drug Seconal. This barbiturate was prescribed to aid sleep and was thought to be particularly effective against the awful insomnia and nervousness that affected those undergoing withdrawal from alcohol. Soon after his release from Bellevue, Jackson felt confident enough to present himself as writer and to ask for a staff job at CBS Radio in New York.

Jackson had actually published nothing at that date but as his calling card he gave his interviewer, Max Wylie, the manuscript of a novel he had written about his time at Syracuse University. On the strength of some 'great pages' in this, Wylie gave him a job at $80 a week. Despite Wylie's amused description of his new employee as somewhat 'effete' and 'effeminate', Jackson married in 1938. His wife, Rhoda Booth, was an editor at *Fortune*, the business magazine. Jackson adored the two daughters they had together and the marriage seems to have been at first a success.

How far the marriage was a deliberate strategy, part of a self-imposed regime of emotional stability and sobriety, and an attempt to deal with repressed homosexuality, we cannot know. Many homosexual men at that time sought a way out of their true nature by marrying – sometimes with disastrous results. In Jackson's case, marriage does seem to have steadied him and enabled him to concentrate on his creative work and his first major publication came in 1939 with a short story 'Palm Sunday' in *Partisan Review*. By 1940 he was earning $500 a week as the writer of a radio soap opera,

Sweet River. This work came to an end in 1943 when he gave Max Wylie the first part of *The Lost Weekend* and Wylie took it to Stanley Rinehart of publishers Farrar and Rinehart. Another publisher had previously rejected it on the grounds that in the middle of a war, 'nobody cares about the individual'. It was snapped up, and reprinted six times before the year was out.

The Lost Weekend has often been compared unfavourably with Malcolm Lowry's *Under the Volcano*, as if critics feel they have to heavily mark down Jackson's book as some kind of rival. Well, as a work of art it is not in any sense a real rival. It has little of the complexity and force of Lowry's work. The chief character, Don Birnam, is endlessly self-centred and self-pitying; the smell of shame that comes off the book is almost suffocating. The few other characters – Birnam's woman friend, Helen, his brother, Wick, and assorted barflies and pawnbrokers – are ghosts who hover in the background, never springing to life. Birnam's remorseful speeches to himself are repetitious and embarrassing. And yet, the book survives as a study of a type of man who is an extreme alcoholic; not a hectic, heroic drunk leading his followers on a tragic but also merry dance as Lowry's Consul does, but a pathetic addict. Don Birnam's drunken binges are suicide on the instalment plan by someone who has tried to kill himself before but has never had the courage to follow the act through to the end. But he is not a contemptible man. He knows what he is doing and there is some attempt at creating a philosophy of the way of life as a drunk, much as Lowry was to do:

How is it he could take it over and over again and yet again?

What capacity, vitality, or resilience did he have that others did not? Was it that his imagination laid hold of that suffering and transmuted it to experience . . . a realization of who and what he was, a fulfilment of self? Was he trying to find out, in this roundabout descent to destruction, what it was all about; and would he, at the final and ultimate moment, know?

The major difference between the two authors in their lives and work is that Lowry actually liked booze and boozing and all the paraphernalia of bars and fellow drinkers and adventures that come with the drinking life. Jackson, like his protagonist Don Birnam, seems to have been a solitary drinker by preference. Birnam does not even like the taste of whisky, while getting through more than a quart a day. His preparations for a binge have an almost religious air about them, a complex preparatory ritual that begins solemnly with the raising of the first glass to the lips. If this seems to identify the character in the book too closely with his author then one can only say that the descriptions of bars and the ways that drunks have of measuring out their drinks and days are too exact not to have been based on anything but extensive and repeated personal experience.

The publication of his first novel changed Jackson's life considerably. It also seems to have gone to his head for a while, especially after Billy Wilder's film version was released in 1946. The film won four Oscars and Jackson became a minor Hollywood celebrity for a while. He made a lot of money and spent it freely. By 1950, he was speaking scornfully of Hollywood and New York's 21 Club, but this was when his fame had dissipated and the money had started to run out. Success meant also that he could publish widely and his stories appeared in most of the leading journals – presumably some of them stories that had been resolutely rejected a few years earlier. Indeed, Jackson said in an interview that the stories in *The Sunnier Side* (1950) represented the life of 'Don Birnam as a kid ... The stories have a continuity with the novel.' Jackson had toyed with the idea of a sequel to *The Lost Weekend*, a novel in which Birnam embraces sobriety, and some of these stories may have been fragments of this unfinished work.

III

In January 1945, an article in *The Grapevine*, a journal issued by AA, reported that at a meeting in Hartford, Connecticut, Jackson had

'explained his remarkably understanding portrayal of Don Birnam
by saying simply "I have a good memory." Listeners drew their own
conclusions.'

Photographs of him taken in the early 1950s show an impeccably
dressed and groomed man who might, with his neat moustache and
bow tie, be a small-town businessman or academic. If one looks
closer it is not fanciful I think to see tiredness and melancholy in his
large eyes and the darkening of the skin beneath them, and in
the deep lines running from the nose to the edges of the mouth; it is
the face of someone who has been profoundly hurt. An interview by
Harvey Breit in *The New York Times Book Review* in 1950 seems to
bear out this underlying melancholy. The impression one got, said
Breit on first meeting Jackson, was of a 'terrible and moving effort in
the man to be deeply honest at each and every turn'. Jackson spoke of
his unhappiness at the success of *The Lost Weekend*, its 'ballooning to
a success out of all its proportion to its real value. You feel a fraud.'
When asked how he had started as a writer, Jackson said that it had
happened in his adolescence. 'When I was fourteen and fifteen I was
writing poetry. When I'd finish a poem I'd look into the mirror to
see if I looked different, if my face had changed.' This is virtually
indistinguishable from the passage in *The Lost Weekend* in which
Don Birman remembers doing exactly the same thing. In fact,
Birnam is forever looking in mirrors to study change in himself, in a
mixture of disgust and alcohol-fuelled narcissism.

The book itself has a far more powerful impact on those who have
shared some of its experiences; it too acts as a mirror, and a highly
unsettling one. A copy I borrowed from a public library years ago
had obviously been read by a fellow alcoholic; passages had been
heavily underlined and anguished exclamations of 'God', 'This is Me'
and 'No, no!' appeared in the margins.

The financial success of the book, coupled with the film deal,
enabled Jackson and his wife and two daughters to move to a large
house in New Hampshire. The house was one that he and his wife

had long coveted and the money from his novel enabled him to fill it with pictures and antiques. Instead of the cramped flat in which he had written *The Long Weekend* he now had a library. Dorothea Straus describes his desk as

> equipped with an assortment of pens, well-sharpened pencils, and the typewriter ... that had been used for *The Lost Weekend*. The window overlooked the single drowsy street of Orford and the Vermont hills beyond. But the tragedy of the library was that its owner was producing nothing there.

His interests outside of writing were 'reading, music (especially Beethoven and Mozart), and my children'. After his death, his wife said that at this time he was also a binge drinker in a 'cycle of relapses and periods of sobriety'. He was a patient of several psychiatrists, including Lawrence S. Kubie, a leading New York practitioner, who had made something of a speciality in treating eminent literary drunks; his patients included playwrights Tennessee Williams and William Inge. The figure of the 'foolish psychiatrist' is a target for ridicule and anger in *The Lost Weekend* and given the generally auto-biographical nature of the book it is reasonable to assume that Jackson had had earlier encounters with the profession, perhaps during his stay at Davos. He had said in his AA lectures that 'most alcoholics, like Don Birnam, suffer some underlying neurosis that is responsible for their addiction.' It seems clear that at least one of Jackson's underlying problems was his homosexuality, which he needed to embrace intensely in a physical way but of which he felt ashamed, at least in the earlier part of his life. One great difficulty writers have when seeking psychiatric help with their conflicts and problems of addiction and sexuality, is that it is almost inevitable that most imaginative writers will know more about the origins and symptoms of their complaints than most psychiatrists are able to discover and successfully treat. The writer will think that he or she is permanently one or two steps ahead of the psychiatrist and often take some delight in trying to outwit and outscore someone they see as a well-meaning fool who is only telling them what they already know all too well. Nonetheless, whatever the degree of their cooperation, Kubie assembled enough from his clients to produce a book entitled *Neurotic Distortion of the Creative Process*.

IV

The distortion in whatever drove Jackson may account for the long delays between books in the last decade of his life and the choice of topics – alcoholism, homosexuality, and mental sub-normality – uncommon in the novel at that time.

There is little doubt that Jackson saw alcohol, the source of his one successful novel, as the driving force of his own creativity. The long letters he wrote to friends, letters that, like Lowry's, became a substitute for the grind of stories and novels, were often composed at night when he had been drinking. Many contained ideas for stories and novels he was going to write when he got the chance. They read much like the wonderful flush of ideas that overwhelms Don Birnam as he stands at a bar. He has the images, the ideas, the dialogue, the whole story in his head . . . until the next drink, and it goes.

Like the fictional Birnam, Jackson often drunkenly threatened to commit suicide. Inevitably, as his literary career dried up in the early 1950s, so did his income. The house in Orford was sold and the family moved to a smaller one. Jackson continued to drink; an evening typically progressed from 'beer . . . to whisky and soda . . . to straight whisky'. He would disappear for lost weekends of his own, checking into cheap hotels for a few days of a drunken jag. He made a return visit to Bellevue after an unsuccessful suicide attempt. He recovered and once more pulled himself together. He made a short-lived conversion to Roman Catholicism and a rather more long-lived one in coming out as openly gay.

His last substantial work to be published was the novel *A Second -Hand Life*, in 1967.

The book was not a commercial success, though it gained some respectable reviews. Jackson himself reviewed *The Selected Letters of Malcolm Lowry* at about this time. The tenor of his review was begrudging. Jackson said that Lowry had written only one major work, *Under the Volcano*. But, by dying young after writing a complex and obscure work with which critics could wrestle to their hearts' content, Lowry had scooped the pool of posthumous fame and enduring legend. The not so subtle sub-text of Jackson's argument was that he himself had lived too long to gain that sort of reputation and fame.

He didn't have long to go. By now he was living in an apartment at the Hotel Chelsea, with a young man he had picked up at an all-night diner. The last time Dorothea Straus saw him he looked 'shockingly old and shrivelled'. He had recently undergone an operation on his lungs and was forced to carry an oxygen inhaler everywhere. The last encounter of the old friends at the Strauses' Westchester home was not a success. 'The evening was lifeless,' said Dorothea. Jackson returned to the city alone and on the twenty-first of September 1968 took another overdose of pills. This time he did not wake up.

Like Lowry, Jackson is famous for one book. Unlike Lowry, he did not see himself as the creator of a personal and poetic vision of the artist as a Promethean doomed hero. Rather, Jackson rendered as fully and frankly as he could a picture of a fairly common figure, the artistic, sensitive would-be writer, but one who is afflicted by a craving for alcohol that he wishes to control but cannot; from which he can sometimes absent himself but to which he must return in an endless cycle: the classic 'binge' alcoholic. He was never to approach the power of *The Lost Weekend* in his later books; the writing of his life story had literally consumed that life.

Chapter 4

'I love hell. I can't wait to get back there.'

Malcolm Lowry (1909–1957)

I

IN APRIL 1944, Malcolm Lowry wrote from his lakeside shack in Dollarton, Canada, to his friend Gerald Noxon: 'Have you read a novel *The Lost Weekend* by one Charles Jackson?' Lowry went on to describe the subject matter as 'admirably about a drunkard and hangovers and alcoholic wards as they have never been done before . . .' and said that the book had dealt him 'a somewhat shrewd psychic blow'. In fact the blow had been dealt weeks earlier when Lowry first read a review of the book. It must have been a worrying time waiting for *The Lost Weekend* to arrive in the post, and wondering if it would confirm his worst fears – that it anticipated, perhaps even bettered, his own almost completed novel *Under the Volcano*, on which he had laboured for many years. The coincidence of the two books being so close in subject matter appalled Lowry.

II

A deep concern with the sometimes threatening nature of coincidence went back a long way with Lowry. In another letter, he recalled that in the 1930s a friend, John Sommerfield, had written an unpublished

novel called, bizarrely enough, *The Last Weekend,* which featured
Lowry as a young drunken genius. Another friend, Charlotte
Haldane, had included him as a character in her novel *I Bring Not
Peace,* published in 1932. The legend of the feckless, perpetually
drunk young genius from whom great things were imminently
expected was firmly in place in the early 1930s.

His letters of the time, particularly to older writers such as
Conrad Aiken and John Davenport, certainly often sound as if they
were written when he was drunk; comparing them with earlier
quite conventional letters, one hears already the voice of 'Malc'.
Both of these correspondents were drinking companions: Aiken
was twenty years older, also a solid drinker, an established poet and
novelist, to whom Lowry had written a fan letter; Davenport survives on the fringes of literary history mostly in the footnotes of
biographies of Dylan Thomas and Kingsley Amis and other writers,
where he features as a formidable personality, acute literary critic,
and dedicated boozer.

'I drank a lot of whisky with Charlotte Haldane last night . . . and
was nearly sick in her mouth,' Lowry wrote to Aiken in 1930. He
became very close to his mentor, who was at one time paid a retainer
by Lowry's father to stand guard over the young man. Lowry was
always dependent on money from his father; if the income was
sometimes uncertain and fluctuating it enabled him to live and travel
widely: a remittance man. (Malcolm's father, Arthur, was a teetotaller
who died, ironically, of cirrhosis of the liver.)

His son was born, in 1909, in Liverpool. He was sent to preparatory
school and then to Ley's, a public school. He began to drink there,
but in no other way did he seem anything but a rather rowdy, well-
built boy with an unfortunate penchant for playing the ukulele.
The first sign of the incessant wandering that was to mark his life
came at the age of eighteen when Lowry left school and insisted
on joining a ship, ominously named the *Pyrrhus,* as a deck hand.
His Melville-inspired romantic notions of life at sea took a lot of

knocks. His fellow seamen regarded him at best as an oddity and interloper – not helped by the fact that his father's Rolls-Royce delivered him to the quayside to join his ship. It was on shore leave that he began to drink extremely heavily; certainly when he returned from this long voyage to England and went up to Cambridge he was drinking most of the time.

Well, students have always drunk heavily, usually beer in England and usually socially, but Lowry's drinking was even then seen as excessive and abnormal. There are several reasons why young men and women choose to drink themselves into a state of intoxication over and over again. They may feel that drink helps them to overcome shyness in meeting and mixing with others, though this also implies that they feel themselves somehow different and apart from others. They may be sexually insecure and find that drink leads them into situations they would normally lack the courage to enter. The unfortunate corollary of this for men is that alcohol taken in sufficient quantity often destroys sexual potency. In this case, alcohol can provide a handy device for avoiding sexual relations, and very heavy drinking serves as a replacement for and suppressor of sexual desire.

Lowry seems to have always been sexually insecure. Some of the crew of the *Pyrrhus* had twitted him on the smallness of his penis during a visit to a Japanese brothel. His first wife, Jan Gabrial, also remarked in her memoirs on the 'very small penis' although she also says that they had a passionate and fulfilling sexual relationship. Lowry himself once bitterly remarked that he had been the butt of jokes about his penis all his life. This may account for the manner of his courtship of both of his wives; a bombardment of passionate letters on first meeting, sudden alcoholic withdrawals from their company, and tearful reconciliations. It would seem that he needed to be very sure indeed of his ground in a relationship with a woman before exposing himself to any possible ridicule. Although physically attractive to women and charming in his manner – at least, when sober – he was no womaniser. A lover who has to sing 'The Star-Spangled Banner' in an attempt to retard premature ejaculation is likely to have a limited career in that direction. All this may seem prurient and irrelevant, but if we are searching for a reason for excessive and habitual drinking it may lie in a quite simple wish to avoid hurtful humiliation. But there was another factor that may have caused him to carry on drinking in an abnormal fashion.

The suicide of a close friend at Cambridge, Paul Fitte, left him with overwhelming feelings of guilt. Lowry later intimated that the friend had made homosexual advances to him. Probably drunk, he was with Fitte when his friend announced his decision to commit suicide. One account has Lowry helping Fitte to prepare his room to gas himself and then lurching off to the pub, saying, 'Now, do it.' The suicide is alluded to in several works that remained unpublished until after Lowry's death.

So, by his early twenties, adding intense remorse to his ragbag of insecurities, he was drinking whisky in the mornings and often continuing to drink throughout the day. In London he drank in the pubs of what has come to be known as Fitzrovia, an area reaching roughly from south of Euston Road to the North of Soho and named after Fitzroy Square. Here he met the very young Dylan Thomas and other writers and artists and their inevitable hangers-on. He wrote short stories and poems that were not published; but he was also working on his first novel, *Ultramarine*, a fictionalised account of his voyage to Japan.

Ultramarine was published in 1933 and it was in that year that Lowry's more or less continuous exile from England began. He travelled to Spain with Conrad Aiken. In 1934, in Paris, after a swift courtship, he married a young American actress, Jan Gabrial. Never a good linguist, he did not understand the marriage service and had to be prompted in his responses. He had met Jan in London the year before and wooed her with a series of passionately written letters.

Until the end of her long life (she died in 2001 aged eighty-nine), Jan believed in Malcolm the writer but not 'Malc' the almighty drunk. Six months after the wedding, following one of Lowry's monumental benders, she walked out on him for a brief time.

Jan Gabrial has had a bad press from Malc's friends and drinking buddies. The impression they give of her in various memoirs and fictionalised accounts is of a promiscuously unfaithful and shallow young woman; Margerie Bonner, Lowry's second wife, caused Jan to be virtually air-brushed out of the *Selected Letters* she edited with Douglas Day in 1967 and Day's biography of Lowry says that Jan had dropped from sight and was untraceable. It was not until 1995 that the letters Lowry wrote to Jan were printed and her interviews with Gordon Bowker enabled him to give a much fuller picture of the writer in his biography *Pursued by Furies*. She published her own account of her life with Lowry in *Inside the Volcano* in 2000.

What is plain in all accounts of his life is that Lowry's first recourse at any time of stress was to the bottle. Generally, over time, alcoholics withdraw from relationships with family and friends and become paranoiac, secretive and solipsistic. The alcoholic's world shrinks and shrinks; habit becomes ingrained – the anonymity of bars, the bottle, 'the drink, the drink, the drink' become an existence that is sufficient and in an odd way safe from interruption by Life. Grand intellectual dreams may be entertained; the booze means they can be put on hold endlessly, or instantly forgotten. There is much of this in Lowry's mental make-up, but it is remarkable how he managed to retain until the end an openness to others and an ironical self-awareness as to what he was doing to himself. The barrel-chested man with a brick-red face is described over and over again by friends as lying on a floor or a couch or bed in a state of extreme intoxication. A little later he would be on his feet again and relatively sober, beaming and full of charm and humour.

A rapprochement with Jan came in New York in 1936 and for a while things went happily for the couple, but this time it was Lowry who left her, without explanation. He moved in with a homosexual friend from whom, he said, he had caught syphilis in circumstances he could not, or did not want to, remember. When Jan tracked him down he gave his venereal disease as the reason he had stayed away from her. Not long afterwards he entered Bellevue to be treated for alcoholism and syphilis; whatever his dilapidated state, he emerged after two weeks with the material in note form for one of his finest works, the novella *Lunar Caustic*.

In *The Lost Weekend*, Don Birnam feels only disgust and shame at his stay in the alcoholic ward. But, for Lowry, his fellow inmates were fallen and damaged angels. The stay in Bellevue had a profound effect on him; for all its horrors he now felt himself to be one of the fallen; for the first time perhaps he had begun to develop, as his biographer Gordon Bowker says, 'a sense of himself as both deviant and yet representative of suffering humanity'. The hell of the alcoholic ward gave Lowry an odd sort of courage he had not possessed before – a sense that he was embarked on a voyage that would certainly be forever on his terms and told in his way.

When he was declared clear of syphilis he returned to Jan and shortly after they embarked on the trip to Mexico that was to be the basis of his one indisputable achievement, the novel *Under the Volcano*.

III

The couple arrived by boat in Acapulco on All Saints' Day, the first of November 1936; the next day was *Día de los Muertos* – the Day of the Dead.

They moved into a room at the Mirama Hotel and it was here that Lowry's journey into a self-induced Hell began. They had lived relatively soberly since their arrival until, on a visit to the studio of a local painter, Lowry discovered a new drink – mescal – to add to his already impressive list. Mescal is derived from the flowering heads of the peyote cactus; its principal active ingredient is mescaline, which is related to adrenaline and which directly affects the nervous system, producing a sense of calm at first, but then often inducing hallucinations and confusion. That night, he went missing and was brought home by the police. After a few weeks they moved to the town of Cuernavaca. This is the original of the town of Quauhnahuac in *Under the Volcano*: the town, that as the very first page of the novel states, has fifty-seven *cantinas*.

Lowry would set out in the morning to work in one or other bar. Many of these – and the sort most favoured by Lowry – were little more than one room with a counter and a few tables; shelves of glasses in front of a large mirror, and sometimes a small, more private room at the back, a kitchen, living quarters and a primitive toilet. Others were more extensive and might have rooms for lodgers or prostitutes at the back. And he *did* work, jotting down thoughts, impressions and sights, until the drink took over. He stayed out all day and sometimes most of the night. He became impossible to track, moving from one bar to another, sometimes slipping surreptitiously out of the back door as Jan or some acquaintance entered the front. This went on until a visiting English friend, who acted as drinking companion to Lowry and their interpreter, suggested to Jan that she put veronal in Lowry's drink at home, to slow him down or knock him out for a while. The sleeping draught was secretly administered; it had no effect whatsoever. Jan was fervently grateful when Lowry's friend left to return to London.

Lowry now entered one of those quiet periods of steady and hard work of which he seemed capable only when alone with a protective and loving companion. When not writing the first version of *Under the Volcano*, he and Jan would walk and ride, exploring the landscape and ruins of the Zapotec civilisation. His paranoid suspicions of being followed by secret agents and police may not have been so ill-founded. His father had once gone so far as to instruct his lawyer to hire a private detective to report on Lowry in Mexico and he may well have been an object of suspicion for the local police and, even worse, for the fascist paramilitaries who plagued the country at that time. The Spanish Civil War and German Nazi influence in Mexico had exacerbated feelings of tension against intellectuals, especially against a gringo writer. But, mostly sober, Lowry managed to keep to his work throughout the spring of 1937. Then, on the twenty-third of May, his old friend Conrad Aiken, 'that bottle-a-day bard', as Jan scathingly called him, rang from Mexico City to say that he was coming to visit them

Lowry greeted his old friend enthusiastically and they were soon off to Charlie's Place for a celebratory drink. This began a series of intensive drinking bouts. In an interview given to Charles Montgomery shortly before her death, Jan put the blame squarely on Conrad Aiken for 'dragging' Lowry back to the cantinas and re-starting the round of heavy drinking. She decided she had to get away if only for a few days. She was seen off on the bus by a semi-penitent Lowry and the detested Aiken.

When she came back the Lowry/Aiken carousel was again revolving at high speed. The details she gives of his drinking are harrowing enough and Lowry sometimes sounds barely sane in his addiction. 'He would drink anything,' Jan wrote. Anything included tequila, mescal, whisky, gin, beer, rubbing alcohol, after-shave lotion, and hair tonic. She describes his hands as shaking so much in the morning that he had to contrive a hoist using a towel so that the hand holding the glass could be raised by the other hand to his lips. (The severity of the shakes in later years meant that he could no longer hold a pen and had to dictate his work.)

It was only when Aiken left that Lowry was able to return to work. Life returned to some normality. He and Jan visited one of their servants in a grim penitentiary and came back to find that an earthquake had struck Cuernavaca. In Lowry's world of super-stitious coincidence this was regarded as an omen of worse things to come.

Sure enough, they did – in the form of the English novelist Arthur Calder-Marshall and his wife Ara. Birds of ill omen indeed to Jan, and it does seem sometimes that Lowry's friends were not averse to deriving amusement from helping 'Malc' to destroy himself. His life in the next couple of months amounted to a huge alcoholic siege of his body and mind. Even when his friends departed he spent all day and most of the night in the cantinas and when he did come home his rows with Jan were intense and often violent.

They had been in Mexico for a little over a year when she decided to leave him for good and to return to America. As she says in her memoir of their life together: 'we had so much: freedom to work without restraint, to travel when and as we wished, and to explore our love. But it had never been enough.'

IV

The following Mexican period is the most obscure of all of Lowry's life. When Jan finally left in 1937, Lowry was alone for several months. The evidence for what happened to him in those months is supplied largely from later letters to friends. We know that he travelled to Oaxaca, spent Christmas in jail there, travelled on to Acapulco and Mexico City, and was back in the United States in Spring 1939, where he tried, unsuccessfully, to patch things up with Jan.

For any more information on Lowry's life we have to turn to the great novel he made out of his experiences in Mexico. Modern literary critics frown on identifying an author with his work but in the case of Lowry he *was* his work; if he had been able to he would have crowded every second of his real life between the pages of an impossibly huge book. And indeed a great deal went into this one novel, written between 1937 and 1946: his drunkenness in Mexico, politics, the state of the world, his youth, Jan, Margerie his second wife; even the cabin in Canada where he wrote the final draft is woven into the novel as an aspiration, a hoped for Paradise.

The plot is simple enough: It is the Day of the Dead in November 1939 and two friends, Doctor Vigil and Jacques Laruelle, sit drinking and talking about their friend Geoffrey Firmin, Consul in the Mexican town of Quauhnahuac. The book then goes back, to the Day of the Dead the year before, when the Consul is waiting for his wife Yvonne and his half-brother, Hugh Firmin, to arrive. When they do, at seven in the morning, the three will spend the next twelve hours drinking, talking, and taking a trip to a nearby town. By seven in the evening both the Consul and Yvonne will be dead.

There are twelve chapters for the twelve hours of the book's life. This is but the first sign of Lowry's obsession with numerology and the occult, and of the complexity of the book's construction. He was always a keen and knowledgeable film watcher with friends in the industry and the book uses all the devices of the silent cinema – cross-cutting, flash-backs, simultaneous actions by two characters, close-up and landscape shots, even captions and titles in the forms of glimpsed signs and posters – together with the overlapping dialogue and voice-over narration of the sound film. Lowry was also famously well read and the book is littered with quotations and echoes from Sophocles, the Elizabethans, the Romantics and a host of others. The whole novel is built around interlinked and repeated symbols and images from classical mythology, the Bible, and the Cabbala. What could have been a confused farrago is in fact a highly organised work that builds in power and meaning until its shattering and tragic end.

There are weaknesses, of course. The conversations between the Consul and his estranged wife Yvonne are sentimental and even novelettish. Monologue, not dialogue, was Lowry's forte. Hugh, the half-brother, only intermittently comes to life, and seems to be the continuation of Lowry by other means – his interior thoughts contain much barely disguised Lowry autobiography. But if Hugh uses quite a lot of Lowry's more conventional experiences, it is the Consul who bears the burden of his alcoholism.

The Consul is a genuinely tragic hero who is destroying himself. Yvonne meets him first, at dawn, in the Farlito, a bar where he has spent most of the small hours drinking. He is alone but for a peasant woman:

' . . . what beauty can compare to that of a *cantina* in the early morning? . . . And, by the way, do you see that old woman from Tarasco sitting in the corner, you didn't before, but do you now?' his eyes asked her, gazing around him with the bemused unfocussed brightness of a lover's, his love asked her, 'how, unless you drink as I do, can you hope to understand the beauty of an old woman from Tarasco who plays dominoes at seven o'clock in the morning.'

What the Consul is describing here will be familiar to many heavy drinkers; it is that feeling of great calm and clarity, particularly early in the morning when one has not slept, and before the hangover supervenes, when the world appears a particularly vivid place, the faces of strangers can take on an almost hallucinatory glow, and there is a wonderful sense of the world being washed afresh.

For, whatever else *Under the Volcano* is – and that 'whatever else' has filled many books and theses over the past fifty years – it is also a record of twelve hours in the life of one alcoholic. I say *one* alcoholic because both the Consul, as a fictional character, and his author, Malcolm Lowry, are utterly unique as individuals whatever physical and nervous symptoms they might share with fellow dipsomaniacs. As Dylan Thomas said when someone asked him why he got drunk so often, 'Because it's different every time.' In other words, he was using alcohol as a device to change the way he thought and felt and, presumably, because he enjoyed it. A woman alcoholic once told me how much she loathed the first drink of the day, 'You can feel yourself change,' she said. This is self-knowledge and control giving way to impulse and desire and it rather contradicts the tendency by some doctors to view the alcoholic as a walking assemblage of physical and mental symptoms rather than as an individual human being who has arrived at this stage of dependency by his or her own route. Alcoholism may well be classified as a disease (although, as has been said, there is considerable controversy about this definition), but it is in part at least, and for some people, a willed affliction. There is no doubt that many alcoholics arrive at their final dreadful destination by a process that they found, at least at the outset, highly enjoyable.

So, let us see what the Consul does on the day Lowry has organised for him in pursuing his peculiar vocation. (I have omitted the chapters and passages dealing with Hugh and Yvonne's thoughts and actions.) This is the Consul's day in terms of drink taken.

He leaves the bar with Yvonne and they walk home. There, breakfast awaits in the form of a tray bearing glasses, a bottle half-full of Johnny Walker whisky and a glass of a strychnine mixture, a remedy concocted by his half-brother Hugh (suitably diluted, strychnine was in the past given as a stimulant to patients suffering from the palsy from lead poisoning, beriberi, and the shakes induced by alcoholism). The Consul has a glass of this mixture as his first self-consciously virtuous drink of the morning – remember that he has already been drinking non-stop for some hours. He is very drunk but does not feel so, and when he goes back into the street he falls flat on his face. A passing English motorist offers him a reviving drink and he takes 'a long draught' from a bottle of Irish whiskey. He goes back to the house and picks up his strychnine mixture again. The stranger's whiskey has made him long for a proper drink and he complains to himself that Yvonne 'could not know the perils, the complications, yes, the *importance* of a drunkard's life'. A sense almost of glee possesses him at the thought of the secret world that is his own, the world of the cantinas. He wants to be there *now*, to see the early sun 'falling like a lance straight into a block of ice'.

Next he drinks from the whisky bottle, and then, by mistake, takes another dose of strychnine. Seconds later, in drunken optimism, he hopes that the strychnine will act as an aphrodisiac so that he can at last make love to Yvonne. He pours another slug of Johnny Walker, but does not drink it. He falls asleep in the chair.

He wakes a whole chapter later (in which Yvonne and Hugh have gone out riding) with a terrible hangover. He totters down through his garden to where he has hidden a bottle of tequila. A voice – imagined – warns him to put down the bottle. He sees a snake in the grass at his feet. But as he drinks he begins to feel more in command of himself. He drinks more tequila and becomes aware of his American neighbour, Mr Quincey, observing him. In a passage of exquisite humour, Quincey asks the Consul if he would mind being sick on his own side of the garden fence. They are interrupted by Dr Vigil, a drinking friend; a fellow adept 'in the Great Brotherhood of Alcoholics'. Now the Consul's consciousness begins to take on a kaleidoscopic confusion of scene and time. Yvonne is seen to return, her arms full of bougainvillea. And then suddenly he comes to, alone and sitting in the bathroom.

These confusions in the order of events and jumps and cuts in the normal progression of things are exactly how a drunk experiences the disjunction of the normal flow of time. The Consul does not know if it is day or night. It is just past noon. He studies the wall beside him; its cracks and stains terrify him. He calls to Hugh for help. He has the shakes very badly. Before Hugh can stop him he seizes a bottle of bay rum, takes a large swig, and is promptly sick.

A little later, with Yvonne and Hugh, dressed and shaved 'a figure of complete respectability', the Consul sets out for the bullring at Tomalin. On the way to the bus they meet Laruelle who invites them in for a drink. The Consul finishes off the contents of Laruelle's cocktail shaker. It is now that Yvonne asks him the question that puzzles all who are not alcoholics: 'Don't you think of anything but how many drinks you're going to have?' His answer, fumbling and awkward, is, 'Yes . . . Yes, I do.' And indeed he does. Now Laruelle and the Consul decide they have time for a quick one in a cantina before the bus comes. They drink tequila. Laruelle attacks what he sees as his friend's weaknesses and asks if he realises quite what 'extraordinary allowances are being made for you by the world which has to cope with you . . . ?' The Consul gazes out of the bar and ignores him, intent on his own dreams. Laruelle pursues him with *'Facilis est descendus Averno* . . . It's too easy.' He tells him that 'even the suffering you do endure is largely unnecessary . . . You deceive yourself.' The Consul makes no answer and when they leave the bar he is very drunk.

On the bus he drinks habanera, Cuban rum, from Hugh's bottle. After the bullring they go inevitably to another bar. Here the Consul's mind is in a magnificent whirl, concocting a monologue of great erudition, charm and diversity. What actually comes out of his mouth is a rambling political rant, which winds up in accusing Yvonne of having an affair with Hugh. Suddenly, now in the middle of his ranting, he finds that 'in this room, matter was disjunct'. A clock is ticking behind the bar. It is half past five. He makes his escape.

'I like it,' he called to them, through the open window, from outside. Cervantes stood behind the bar, with scared eyes, holding the cockerel. 'I love hell. I can't wait to get back there. In fact I'm running. I'm almost back there already.'

And he flees into the night.

Hugh and Yvonne hunt him through the bars. He has in fact returned to the Farolito, the bar where he had started to drink in the early morning of this day. He is accused of being a spy by sinister policemen. They bully and goad the Consul. At the last, in the almost unbearable end to the book, he is dragged outside and shot, and in the final terrible sentence, 'Somebody threw a dead dog after him down the ravine.'

This, though it leaves out most of what makes the book of lasting value, does show the bare bones of the Consul's drinking day, and probably can be taken as fairly representative of Lowry's own day to day existence in 1937 to 1938.

In 1939 he crawled back to the States and attempted to get together with Jan. But divorce proceedings were put in hand and later that year Lowry met the woman, Margerie Bonner, who was to become his second wife and amanuensis, secretary and collaborator for the rest of his life.

V

If ever there was an advertisement for solitude, poverty and relative sobriety it was in the years between 1940 and 1944 that Lowry and Margerie spent in their lakeside shack at Dollarton, near Vancouver, shaping and re-shaping his one great work.

By 1944 Lowry was reaching the end of the third draft of *Under the Volcano* and it was then that the news came of the publication of Charles Jackson's *The Lost Weekend*, and that it was an immediate critical and popular success.

Lowry had feared accusations of plagiarism for all of his writing life. Conrad Aiken had accused him of borrowing much too freely from his novel *Blue Voyage* for Lowry's first novel *Ultramarine*. Even given the overwhelmingly autobiographical nature of all of his work, what Lowry was afraid of was the unconscious appropriation of other writers' mannerisms, styles, and even words in his attempts to render his own life as fiction. Lowry had a formidable memory for what he had read and for the details of his own life; the difficulty sometimes lay in the confusion between the two, a confusion hardly helped by the state of extreme drunkenness in which he spent much of his adult life. But his book *Under the Volcano*, the one he now feared would be compared with *The Lost Weekend*, that book was the product of his soberest years, his most unremitting labour, and his strictest artistic control.

What did Lowry see in *The Lost Weekend* to so concern him? It was not simply the subject matter and the usual writer's fear that a rival has queered his pitch by getting first to an important subject. What concerned Lowry was that, for all the obvious stylistic differences, there were many structural similarities between the two books. Each takes place over a limited time scale – five days in Jackson's book, a single twelve-hour period in Lowry's. Both make extensive use of flashbacks and cinematically influenced cutting. There are three main characters in each book: Birnam, his brother, and Helen in Jackson's; Firmin, his half-brother Hugh, and Yvonne in Lowry's. The two books share much else in common: the use of flashbacks full of guilt and remorse; the leitmotivs of cinema posters (in Jackson, *Camille* starring Greta Garbo; in Lowry, *The Hands of Orlac* with Peter Lorre); the endless looking into mirrors and questioning of self-identity; a shared hero-worship of Scott Fitzgerald.

There was also the fact that both books are full of quotations from other authors. *The Lost Weekend* opens with an unacknowledged quotation from James Joyce's story 'Counterparts': 'The barometer of his emotional nature was set for a spell of riot.' There are many other quotations in Jackson's book, triter than those in Lowry. Jackson's are mostly taken, not always appositely, from Shakespeare and have a rather hackneyed look. But by the time that *The Lost Weekend* reaches its last pages, Lowry must have wondered what he himself had left as untouched subject matter.

The Bellevue episode in particular worried Lowry. Don Birnam, the drunk in *The Lost Weekend*, wakes up in the alcoholics' ward in Bellevue Hospital after collapsing in the street. To establish that he is sufficiently lucid to leave he is asked by a doctor what day and month and year it is. He answers that it is 1936, that he is thirty-three years old. (Jackson was born in 1903.) But 1936 was also the year in which Lowry spent two weeks in Bellevue as a voluntary patient, drying out. If we presume that he read the whole book in his shack at the water's edge in Dollarton the following must have seemed especially uncanny:

> The shack he had rented at the tip end of Whoopee Wharf and no longer had the money to pay for (but who cared? who even knew?) was as isolated from the world as the lonely melancholy bell-buoy that rang dolefully all night long somewhere out in the bay.

It could be one of Lowry's autobiographical personae, Ethan Llewellyn or Sigbjørn Wilderness, both obsessed by the sea.

In June 1945, writing to his agent, Hal Matson, he feared that people would regard his book 'as nothing but a pale reflection of that excellent study'. Worse, his other work, *Lunar Caustic*, would, with its description of Bellevue, be seen as even more directly indebted to Jackson. He went more fully into the matter in the famous and very long letter to Jonathan Cape that explained the structure of his novel. Lowry takes several pages to establish his precedence in the matter of writing *Under the Volcano*, starting back in the late 1930s, even saying that he has removed one passage that, although written much earlier, was too close in spirit to a passage in Jackson's book

In June of that year a fire destroyed their shack and most of Lowry's manuscripts; only *Under the Volcano* was literally snatched from fiery oblivion. Finally finished in 1945, it was despatched by Lowry's agent to publishers in New York and London.

What happened next seems bizarre even by Lowry's standards. He visited Los Angeles late in 1945, and then in late December took ship with Margerie to Mexico. With ghastly irony the film of *The Lost Weekend* was playing in Acapulco that week. Did Lowry see it? He would certainly have seen the posters advertising it.

Lowry and his wife spent Christmas and New Year in Cuernavaca. Why did Lowry return to the scene of his torments? Bearing in mind Lowry's curious belief in the circularity of time, he may have felt that to revisit the scene of his suffering was to resurrect and revalidate that experience. Perhaps he needed in some peculiar way to prove that this place existed and that the life recounted in his novel had indeed occurred there. It is quite possible that he was still unnerved by the publication of *The Lost Weekend* and wanted fresh confirmation of what *he* had seen and done.

It was on the second of January in Cuernavaca that he received news simultaneously of acceptance of his book by Reynal and Hitchcock in New York, and provisional acceptance by Jonathan Cape in London. But the rest of the second Mexican adventure was a disaster. Some spring had been released in Lowry that once more set off his incessant drinking. The couple were eventually deported from the country and fetched up in Haiti in a hotel inhabited by what a fellow guest described as 'international white trash'. Here Lowry distinguished himself by descending the main staircase of the hotel, fully dressed, drink in hand, and walking slowly and steadily to the side of the swimming pool and stepping in to the deep end, to sink gracefully down, holding his glass resolutely up. In a state of alcoholic collapse he spent a couple of weeks in hospital. Some notes he scribbled there reveal his disturbed state of mind: 'What do you fear? Being found out. Then why do you always give yourself away? What do you seek? Oblivion.'

And sink, really, is what he continued to do for the rest of his life until his death in 1957. The publication and critical success of *Under the Volcano* in 1947 was a very great disaster for Lowry and one from which he never recovered. He appeared red-faced, drunk and silent at literary parties; he travelled and he drank and drank. He and Margerie returned to Dollarton, but the paradise he had tried to create was forever irrecoverable.

VI

Under the Volcano was intended to be a part of a grand sequence of novels, or perhaps one huge novel, called *The Voyage that Never*

Ends. Perhaps over time, as it grew and spread in mad profusion, it could be more cruelly and accurately called The Novel that Never Begins; the fact is that *Under the Volcano* was the only part he completed as a satisfactory, discrete whole. And after the publication of *Under the Volcano*, his drinking and the accumulated nervous and mental damage it had wrought meant that Lowry was no longer capable of the intellectual task of shaping and organising his materials; he spent years shifting passages and individual sentences and images around like the pieces of an immense chaotic jigsaw puzzle. Drink had given him the character and imagery he needed for one great novel; drink as surely took them away in the following years. The pity of it was that all of his work was autobiographical; scarcely another character but a version of Lowry has any real existence in his writing, but he had used up the most interesting part of his life: himself as tragic drunk beleaguered by a strange society, by history, by personal demons, in the character of the Consul. Not all the wishful thinking of his admirers, or mutterings about 'metafiction', can make the posthumously issued books look other than wrecks and remnants around the proud ship *Under the Volcano*. Assembled from Lowry's mass of manuscripts and notes, *La Mordida* and *Dark as the Grave Wherein My Friend is Laid* have the occasional brilliant and gleaming poetic passage, but these are heartbreakingly set in the surrounding morass. (His fears of *The Lost Weekend* make yet another appearance in the form of a character called Jack Charleson in *La Mordida*.) The last of these posthumous works to appear, *October Ferry to Gabriola*, edited by his widow, Margerie, was published in 1970. It had been described by Lowry's normally faithful editor Albert Erskine as 'tedious beyond belief'. This novel, by which Lowry set great store, contains some wonderful passages, but mostly it is a laboured rehearsal of old themes. Some of the writing is staggeringly banal and one suspects that a lot must have surely been the editorial work of Margerie: 'The Llewellyns, this time avoiding the staircase, gazed about them with interest.' And, 'They gave themselves over to the view again, sea gulls and lighthouses, blue seas and mountains – how grand it was!'

If in the 1950s Lowry was indeed working very hard, he was also drinking almost incessantly. On a visit, his friend David Markson saw the decline in Lowry; his rambling digressive conversation, his inability to settle on any point without endless repetitive elaboration – much the way his manuscripts from this period look. Lowry's later work does contain superb fragments, but too often it circles around events in his own life which had taken on mythic proportions for him, but fail to resonate with his readers; the suicide of his friend at Cambridge, Bellevue, the shack and its burning down, the collapse of the pier he had built at Dollarton, the second Mexican debacle, the trans-American bus journeys undertaken with Margerie. These ideas were elaborated and interwoven and repeated over and over again so that even the most faithful of Lowry buffs must groan at the umpteenth appearance of the song 'Frère Jacques' as a leitmotiv.

Perhaps, in the end, the true legacy of Lowry is the novel *Under the Volcano*, the novella *Lunar Caustic*, and the two volumes of collected letters which reclaim a life from apparent degradation with great intelligence and much humour; as he himself said, 'cheerfulness keeps breaking in'. *Under the Volcano* was a great novel achieved almost despite its author's life. He could not have continued in a career of writing conventional novels and stories as Charles Jackson attempted to. The difference between the two books is the difference in the men's lives – *The Lost Weekend* is indeed a powerful documentary account of an alcoholic, but it could be any one of the depressing life stories recounted in the publications of Alcoholics Anonymous. It should be read once, but it is difficult to see anyone wishing to re-read it for pleasure. If we judge *Under the Volcano* as a conventional novel, it is obviously deficient. It is digressive and sometimes confusing, but it is a book that must be read several times to reveal its true greatness and oddly noble vision. It is the one triumphantly successful part of the great monologue, the Lowrylogue, that Lowry conducted with himself all of his life.

Chapter 5

'A womb with a view'

Dylan Thomas (1914–1953)

I

DYLAN THOMAS died in St Vincent's Hospital, New York, on the ninth of November 1953. He was thirty-nine years old. The post-mortem examination gave the main causes of death as pneumonia and 'acute and chronic ethylism', that is, a recent high intake of alcohol and a life-long addiction to alcohol. There was no mention of the medical incompetence that hastened his death.

It may seem odd to start with a man's death, but it seems apt in talking about Dylan Thomas. From the poems of his adolescence – and half of his published poems were written in draft form before he was twenty – his work is shot through with images of death and decay, of transience and mourning: bones, worms and the grave lie behind the celebration of blood, birth, sex and the natural world. For a long time the general public – when it took an interest in such things – knew him as the poet who drank himself to death.

II

In fact, Dylan Thomas, long known as a complete and hopeless alcoholic, probably drank less than any of the other writers considered in this book. Yet Thomas became the most famous drunken writer of the twentieth century. One reason of course is that his death, just before the great success of his play *Under Milk Wood* and just after the issue of his *Collected Poems*, was seen as tragically premature. It is possible that neither the play nor the poems would have done so well critically and commercially if it had not been for his death, but it was the case that the public saw a poet cut down in his prime. He was the wild Celtic bohemian who was famous as a brilliant reader of his own work and that of other poets, with a rare power to move and captivate his listeners. In a country where poets were popularly viewed as effeminate and anachronistic figures of fun, he was the magnificently carefree lover of booze and women. His reward was an undying fame with the general reading public, and the undying hatred of academia. Thomas was overrated by his contemporaries, many of them friends, but underrated by the next generation of poets and critics. The word 'underrated', as we shall see in a later chapter on Kingsley Amis, hardly does credit to some of the publicly expressed loathing and contempt for Thomas that occurs even in works of literary criticism. There is no doubt that Thomas touched a lot of people in a huge variety of ways; there is also no doubt that his relatively youthful death was, as a cynic said about the death of Marilyn Monroe, 'a smart career move'. He was fixed forever, on the edge of ageing, his work forever youthful. A man in increasingly desperate financial straits, whose drinking had increased immeasurably on his trips to America, a normally robust man whose health had begun to give out, a poet whose work seemed to have reached a creative height from which it could only decline in the coming years, his death cut him away at one stroke and sent the tubby, unruly little man into immortality.

Perhaps he got out just in time. One can hardly dare sketch out a possible picture of later life for him without a sense of awful foreboding. The bad behaviour – the obscene jokes at dinner parties, the capering about pretending to be a dog, the crude approaches to women – may have been tolerated in a charming cherubic young poet. It would have become increasingly ludicrous and pathetic in later years. An increasingly corpulent and balding Dylan Thomas sagging drunkenly in the corner of the pub would have become an object of pity, if not outright derision. After all, what's the point of living on as Dylan Thomas if you're no longer *Dylan Thomas*?

III

Dylan Thomas was born on the twenty-seventh of October 1914 at 5 Cwmdonkin Drive on what was then the western edge of Swansea. The family had just moved into a newly built, suburban, four-bedroom house. His father was a schoolmaster; his mother kept the house and looked after the new baby and his seven-year-old sister, Nancy. Thomas lived in this house until he was nineteen, when he departed for London and fame as a poet. It is worth dwelling on his childhood and upbringing; they are quite strange, not for the completely false image of the Celtic bard that got stuck in his public's mind, but for their very ordinariness. His ancestors were small farmers and farm workers, railwaymen, and the occasional minister and teacher. As a small boy he went to a local private school and then to Swansea Grammar School where his father was English master. He left at the age of seventeen having failed his school-leaving certificate and he received no further formal education. It was quite rare in the literary world of that day for a writer not to be a child of the professional or upper middle-classes. Nearly all of the poets of his generation, or a little older, Auden, MacNeice, Spender, Empson, Day Lewis, and Betjeman, had been to public school and Oxford or Cambridge, and spoke with an Oxbridge accent. Thomas's powerful and orotund voice was one of his major assets as a performer; he pitched it almost an octave lower than his normal speech for his public readings, but even in conversation it had an obvious and rare charm. It was the product of early elocution lessons, his father's precise and beautiful reading of poetry, and his own acute ear as a mimic. What he called his 'parsonical bray' brought him fame and money, particularly on his tours of America, but it can make uneasy listening now. Some of his work seems to be written for the great organ of his voice to perform and it sometimes shrinks, like the lyrics of a great aria, when confronted on the page.

The fierce ambition of Dylan Thomas to be a poet was evident alarmingly early on. His father had a fine collection of books and his son read widely in them. In a way he is a pre-modern poet: most of his formative reading was of the Romantics and Victorian and Georgian poets; his concern for self-invented stanzaic forms and the musicality of his verse are defiantly his own. His contemporaries also worked in the traditional metres – Auden was a master of them all – but Thomas was different. His models and influences were odd for the time; he harks back to Thomas Lovell Beddoes, Swinburne, and Francis Thompson, poets for whom the sound and sweep of words and obscurity of vocabulary sometimes seem more important than the sense.

The mention of Auden brings us to another rather peculiar difficulty in writing about Dylan Thomas as a conventional literary figure. No one would dream of writing a biography of Auden that called him 'Wystan' all the way through, but it somehow sounds rather harsh when writing about Dylan Thomas not to refer to him simply as 'Dylan'. Even at this reach in time he has for some of my generation (born in the 1940s) a personally beguiling quality and many of his biographers, even the most recent, refer to him throughout their books as 'Dylan'. In the case of the first major biographer, Constantine Fitzgibbon, this is understandable; he was a friend of the poet. But why should people who were not alive, or were still children when Thomas died, hold him in such affection? It is as if his charm, his insistence on winning over audiences and acquaintances, what someone called 'instant Dylan', radiated beyond his actual work. It was still working powerfully in the 1960s when that other bardic figure Bob Zimmerman renamed himself Bob Dylan in homage to the poet, and The Beatles put him in their pantheon of cultural heroes on the cover of *Sgt. Pepper's Lonely Hearts Club Band*.

But Thomas it must be, however hard-hearted it seems to address by surname one who harked back to his childhood in so much of his adult work. The childhood portrayed is one of radiant happiness, although Thomas himself remarked once that one thing worse than an unhappy childhood is a too happy one. The stories of *Portrait of the Artist as a Young Dog*, written in his mid-twenties, are plainly autobiographical; the life of a boy from early childhood to late adolescence. The stories are beautifully crafted and simply written: they tell of visits to the country, eccentric and drunken country relatives, a fight with another boy, who becomes his best friend, collaborating in writing and jokes, and inevitably the first interests in sex and drink.

But whatever impressions the stories or a poem like 'Fern Hill' give of a childhood idyll, the situation at home was far from the world of the poems. Daniel Jones was Thomas's closest friend for many years and his book *My Friend Dylan Thomas* sheds some light on 'what went on in the Thomas family'. Thomas's mother was largely uneducated and shared none of her husband's intellectual interest; indeed her domestic chatter drove her husband to distraction and rage. The back room in which he read 'smelt of the self-pity of a despondent schoolmaster', Jones wrote. It was obvious that a chair at Oxford was his natural place and not a miserable teaching post at Swansea Grammar School. He despised his pupils and his colleagues and his sharp tongue was greatly feared by both. Dylan rapidly found what a useful asset this was in enabling him to come and go in school as he pleased and skip whatever classes he liked under the assumed protection of his father. His mother spoiled him, his father corrected his earliest poetic efforts, but his sister Nancy did not trust her brother. When he was in his later teens she warned her friends not to leave purses or coats lying about in the house because money and cigarettes were likely to be stolen by her brother. He spent a great deal of time at the home of his friend Daniel Jones. Together they wrote poems, writing alternate lines, creating the name Walter Bram for the poet responsible. They invented fantastic composers – Winter Vaux, Lackety Apps, and the

Reverend Percy – and performed the compositions, with Thomas playing inexpertly but enthusiastically on anything he could bow or scrape. Jones was one of his first drinking companions: 'at first half-pints of mild . . . later, gallons gulped with relish and at speed during pub crawls.' When settled in London, Thomas wrote a sentimental letter recalling their shared days as the happiest in his life. But then, the happiest days for him were always the ones he had just escaped or been expelled from.

His teenage years were the most creatively prolific in the whole of his life. The four surviving notebooks (there may be others that are now lost) that he filled between 1930 and 1933 contain a volcanic outpouring of words. If one knew nothing about Dylan Thomas and came across these notebooks as the work of an unknown young poet no one could surely deny that they are works, however wildly obscure and naïve, with the energy and originality of young genius. Open the notebooks at random almost anywhere and the voice and vision are unmistakeable, 'How can the knotted root/Be trapped in a snare of syllables/The tendril or, what's stranger, the high flower/Caught. Like a ferret though a thought it is,/ Inside a web of words . . . ' This, from November 1931, is an earlier example of Thomas's vision of the world transfigured into words. He saw the world as made of a mysterious energy ('The force that through the green fuse drives the flower/Drives my green age': written in October 1933) that is both creative and destructive, bringing love and flowering, but also decay and inevitable death. And all this magnificent, munificent creation was being set down by someone who was little more than a boy in his bedroom in Cwmdonkin Drive.

Most intelligent and sensitive adolescents go through a phase of writing poems or attempting to play a musical instrument or paint, but with most these efforts die down as first sex and then jobs and family responsibilities redirect their energies. What is interesting about the young Dylan Thomas is the complete concentration on the creative act, on his ambition to be a poet at all costs. Nearly all of his work places the creator in the middle of his creation; most of Thomas's poems are concerned with himself, his body, and the relations of that observed body to the rest of the natural world. And this creation becomes an endless series of Edens from each of which he is doomed to be expelled. It started very early: his mother's womb, indeed his own conception, was a constant obsession. No wonder he called the pub 'a womb with a view'. The analogy was well-founded: both are warm, ill-lit, well supplied with nourishing fluids, and cut off from the outside world. And they both shut us off from and expel us into that outside and infinitely crueller world where we must fend for ourselves and provide for others. Dylan Thomas had little interest in doing either of those things.

After leaving school he was taken on as a junior reporter by a local newspaper and drank with his hard-bitten elders, but it is difficult to believe the claims, largely made by himself, that he was drinking between ten and twenty pints of beer a day. To Daniel Jones, Thomas was 'a steady and habitual drinker, not a heavy hardened drinker . . . his day was a succession of pints of beer, but the first four of these slurred his speech, and each pint after that brought him nearer to sleep.' Jones also points out that Thomas was a robustly healthy young man, despite his gloomy prognostications of TB and an early death.

Portrait of the Artist as a Young Dog ends with the hero, aged eighteen or nineteen, preparing to say farewell to his home town: 'It was understood that he would soon be leaving for London to make a career in Chelsea as a free-lance journalist; he was penniless and hoped, in a vague way, to live on women.' Which is precisely what Thomas did, or attempted to do.

IV

So, it was off to London to become Dylan Thomas, or, rather, to create Dylan Thomas. To Daniel Jones, 'Dylan's life presented an extraordinary paradox. While remaining hidden, he sent into the world a counterfeit image of himself, a fetch.' A 'fetch' is usually defined as the disembodied spirit of a living person that appears to others at the moment of that person's death. What Jones meant was that Thomas projected a contrary image of himself quite calculatingly and then found it gradually overwhelming him. The man described by neighbours in Wales as a 'perfect gentleman', by close friends as a quiet, charming, amusing man, by women as a tender lover, by Jones's eight year old son as 'a man full of generosity, kindness and humour' became, in Jones's words, 'unscrupulous . . . ruthless . . . a liar . . . a cheat . . . and a cynic'.

Settled in London, he soon found, as Constantine Fitzgibbon said:

> In his early days, before the legend had been created, nobody cared much whether Dylan drank or not. In the Soho pubs of the middle thirties there were a great many young people who drank as much as Dylan and quite a few who drank considerably more.

It sometimes seems that, in his odd, compulsive way of lying about almost everything, he learned to act drunk as a way of actually avoiding cripplingly large quantities of beer. All through his life there are stories of a serious Thomas talking quietly to one person in a pub, only to appear instantly drunk when others came in. This is not to say that he did not drink a great deal on a good many occasions, but when he did he invariably ended up completely and helplessly drunk. In his first few years in London, he spent his days in the pubs and drinking clubs of Soho and Fitzrovia. He did little writing. He did not need to – he had more than enough material written in his late teens – the poems from the early notebooks are those that appeared now in the literary magazines. It is a paradox that it was not the bohemian life in London that was the incubator of these remarkable poems but the provincial lower middle-class life from which he had escaped.

Where did Thomas's money to live in London come from? He was becoming adept at borrowing small amounts that it must have seemed mean to demand back. That other great artist, the musician

Charlie Parker, was to boast of his ability to con people out of a few dollars; while neglecting and throwing away the fortune his talents might have brought him. Parker, who died in 1955 aged thirty-four, was often linked with Thomas by the American Beats, who saw both of them as charismatic artists destroyed by an uncaring society. Like Parker, Thomas had a sharp eye for the assets of his admirers and a growing armoury of subterfuges and charms to draw out the small or larger sums he needed.

He was in the right place – London – he was young, and he quickly achieved that most necessary push to the beginner, a scandal. A poem published in *The Listener*, 'Light breaks where no sun shines', contained the lines 'A candle in the thighs/Warms youth and seed and burns the seeds of age'. This image was taken as literally sexual by a number of readers, quite rightly in fact, in view of the blatantly sexual nature of much of Thomas's poetry at that time. Letters of complaint were duly sent into the magazine. More importantly, the poem and the minor furore it had caused were noted by a number of important figures. T.S. Eliot, 'The Pope' of literary London, wrote to Thomas, as did Stephen Spender (a rising Cardinal). The publication of his first book later that year added to his growing reputation. He was writing nothing new, apart from a few book reviews. Every now and then, when particularly broke, he would flee back to Wales – once to nurse the gonorrhoea he had caught off one of his casual girlfriends.

There was no question of Thomas taking a job: he was a poet, who must not be diverted from his work. Poetry was his life, a holy vocation. As Randall Jarrell wrote: 'A good poet is someone who manages in a lifetime of standing out in thunderstorms to be struck by lightning five or six times: a dozen and he is great.' Well, Thomas managed at least six strikes in his life, but there was an awful lot of time to be filled up waiting. Drink and talk, talk and drink, became his main occupations. In the London pubs, Dylan Thomas was a notorious figure, exciting and funny in the early stages of the evening, blustering and aggressive if he felt attention was drifting away from him, or performing stupid and childish acts to regain attention; on one occasion he pretended to be a dog and expected to be patted as he trotted about on all fours. When drunk he expected a bed for the night from any woman who happened to be around; for sex, or simply motherly solicitude.

His life changed dramatically when he met and, in 1937, married Caitlin MacNamara. She came from an upper-class Anglo-Irish family with the usual history of waste and wildness that characterised that class, and if Thomas fancied himself as a bohemian he soon found that he had got himself a wife who was the carelessly ruthless real thing. She could and did drink Thomas under the table. When they fought, as they did ferociously, she gave as good as she got. She was radiantly beautiful and as domestic as a lynx. He wrote to a friend, 'I am lost in love and poverty and my work is shocking.'

The couple were penniless. Lack of money at last forced them to leave London, to live first with Caitlin's parents, and then to move to Laugharne, a small sea town on the Pembroke coast. Here, away from the temptations of the capital, he began to work again, writing the stories that were to be published as *The Portrait of the Artist as a Young Dog*, and the sonnet sequence, 'Altarwise by Owl-Light'.

In 1939 their first child, Llewellyn, was born.

V

'He's in the room with me, making noises to his fingers, his eyes unfocusing . . . ' The birth of a son did not mean that Thomas became a dutiful and home-bound father. Caitlin was expected to cook, keep house, and look after his child. She wrote that she did not remember him being at home for a single evening of their married life. After a lengthy breakfast, the first cigarettes and the terrible coughing that accompanied them, the day proper would begin with a few pints of beer at lunchtime, break for a nap or some work in the afternoon, and then continue back at the pub in the evening. He was offered an advance to write a Welsh travel book but did hardly any work on it. Instead, he dreamed up a scheme whereby a number of patrons would each send him five shillings a week. There were few takers.

The war that began in September 1939 came as a personal affront to Thomas. He joked in a letter to a friend, Desmond Hawkins, 'Being my hero, my chief concern, too, is to keep myself out of death's way. And no, I don't know what to do either: declare myself a neutral state, or join as a small tank.' In a way he did both: he avoided military service, after being declared medically unfit, and the constant intake of beer was beginning to turn him into a paunchy, red-faced figure. The war effectively killed the chances of making much money from the *Portrait*, or another collection of stories and poems, *The Map of Love*. A little money came from America where his work was beginning to be published, some from radio broadcasts, and more from friends. He had written the first ten thousand words of what was intended to be a novel, *Adventures in the Skin Trade*. It was to tell the adventures of a young man coming to London. When he offered the opening chapters to his publishers, a reader's report was devastating: 'unless he pulls himself together he is going to fizzle out as an author quite ignominiously . . . he is slipping into a state of literary irresponsibility'. There was little further work done on the 'novel' although Thomas continued to try and get advances on it for many years. He sold his Swansea notebooks to a book dealer and thus closed off the mine he had worked since the age of fifteen. It became clear as the war progressed that some dramatic change would have to come in his fortunes. In 1942 he took up an offer from Strand Films to write documentaries commissioned by the Ministry of Information.

He moved back to London, taking a large one-room studio in Chelsea. Caitlin sometimes joined him, but for the greater part of the next two years she and Llewellyn and her new baby, Aeronwy, lived in the country with relatives. Thomas was back on the loose on his own in London, ripe for another dose of what he ruefully called 'capital punishment'.

Perhaps surprisingly, he turned out to be a conscientious worker. Strand Films was a pretty easy-going place, but Thomas was horrified when one of his fellow writers, Julian Maclaren-Ross, suggested they keep a bottle of whisky in the office to guard against morning hangovers. There were no such inhibitions after office hours. It was then that 'Dylan' emerged, taking up his old place in the pubs of Fitzrovia and Soho.

It was here that Thomas was to be found every night he was in town; and 'found' is the right word, because people often formed hunting parties to discover where 'Dylan' was performing that night. He moved between pubs, stayed for a while in one and then moved on to another, surrounded, as John Davenport said, 'by cloudbursts of laughter'. His retinue consisted of a few genuine friends and fellow writers, but also of would-be and never would-be artists and hangers-on who had, one way or another, managed to avoid the armed forces. People in uniform were generally despised by the Fitzrovian infantry and the war was regarded as an irritating and occasionally dangerous bore. There were a few famous names, among them the rackety old monster, the painter Augustus John. John had seduced the teenage Caitlin, and also her mother; it was said that some families could claim three generations who had slept with the painter. Sexual relations were no less easy in the Fitrovian pubs and Thomas joined readily in the sexual free for all. The one thing everyone had in common was drink.

And for the first time Thomas had money. He earned ten pounds a week from Strand, at least twice the average wage of the time. Very little of it found its way back to his family. It was mostly spent on feeding the increasingly bulky Dylan, the famous young poet and the funny man in the pub. Others, less affectionately, recall a man who parked himself in their houses or flats, sponged on and stole from them, whose behaviour when refused anything – once defecating on someone's floor – was that of an embittered and damaged child. He did his work, got drunk every night, and only when he returned to Wales, in 1944, did he begin to write poetry again.

VI

This was to be the pattern of his life: Wales and relative sobriety; London and drunkenness with friends and others; and then the visits to America.

With the end of the war, he had begun to put out feelers for an invitation to read in America; his poems had been well received there, it was an opportunity to widen his audience and also to earn a great deal of money. He was now in demand as a broadcaster, but after several broken commissions the BBC was reluctant to advance him money on any more projects. The fifteen or twenty pounds he could earn for a broadcast often necessitated a trip to London and there was little but small change left when he returned home.

A brief respite came with the award from the Society of Authors of a Travelling Scholarship that took the family to Italy. Settled in a villa above Florence, Thomas suffered with the heat, disliked the attention Caitlin got from Italian men – which she revelled in – and was unhappy drinking wine instead of his usual beer. When he saw a party of Italian poets coming up the hill to the villa he hid in the lavatory until they had gone away.

On their return to England, a new patroness, Margaret Taylor, appeared and the Thomas family moved to a summerhouse in the garden of her house near Oxford. Margaret Taylor was besotted with Thomas; her husband, the historian A.J.P. Taylor, was less impressed and the whole affair eventually broke up their marriage. Often the last of Thomas's money earned in London went on a hired car back to Oxford, depositing a sodden and penniless breadwinner before an increasingly unforgiving Caitlin.

He took on more film work and was commissioned to write three feature-length films for Gainsborough Films, a production company that became famous in the post-war years for a succession of bodice-rippers that usually involved the loutish Stewart Granger, the heaving bosoms of Margaret Lockwood, and the gloomily handsome James Mason. Thomas was now earning very well indeed, but he had never filed a tax return and a sudden demand for estimated back payments plunged him into financial difficulties. Llewellyn was at boarding school, and Thomas had a wife and two other small children to support. Why was he always so broke? Of course, to have demonstrated an ability to handle his finances sensibly would have been to remove the poet from having to depend on others and thrown responsibility for providing for himself and his family on to him. And that would have been the end of the Dylan who must be looked after; he would turn, like his father, into Mr Thomas, the dour provincial bookman. It was his duty therefore, as a poet, to remain as poor as possible: to be poor was to be helpless, and to be helpless meant that others must help, must pay attention. So the film money was thrown away, on drink and friends, to preserve 'Dylan'.

Margaret Taylor intervened once more, at Thomas's urgent request. This time she bought a house at Laugharne, where the Thomases had lived before the war. The Boat House came to them rent-free, it overlooked the sea, and there was a shed set a little way off on the cliff side where he could work. It seemed, at last, an ideal solution. They moved there in early 1949.

VII

Thomas was thirty-five years old. His days in Laugharne fell into a routine. When his parents moved to a house in the town he would visit them in the mornings to do *The Times* crossword with his father, then go to Brown's Hotel for a few quiet beers, catching up with the local gossip, perhaps playing cards with locals, then back for a leisurely lunch at the Boat House. In the afternoons, 'blown up with muck and somnolence', he would make his way to the shed to work. Here he slowly pieced together some fine poems. These poems have a sense of landscape and the outer world not present in the earlier self-obsessed poems. But every poem was only achieved by an agony of endlessly redrafting word by word, line by line. In the last six years of his life, Thomas wrote six poems: 'Fern Hill', 'A Winter's Tale', 'In the White Giant's Thigh', 'Poem on His Birthday', 'In Country Sleep', and 'Over St John's Hill', and all of them are superbly crafted lyric poems. Accusations of sentimentality are very occasionally justified, but the poems have a human range and warmth unmatched in any of his other work. It would have been better for Thomas and us, his readers, if he had never stirred again from Laugharne. He might still have been poor but he would have settled into a routine of work, a routine that he found necessary to achieve anything good, or indeed anything at all. As he wrote in a letter in early 1950, 'When I am here, or anywhere else I like, and am busy, then drink's no fear at all, and I'm well, terribly well.' He could have lived on the commissions he received, but didn't complete, or even start. For Thomas the debts that he continued to run up, and the debilitating trips to London, again only indicated the necessity of escape. Rescue was looked for once more: his begging letters were now almost as carefully drafted as his poems. Then, at last, on the twentieth of February 1950, after many negotiations, he flew to America to undertake a lecture tour.

VIII

The figure the Americans encountered was far from the luminously eyed slim young poet of Augustus John's famous portrait. This Dylan Thomas filled out his buttoned-up jackets in bulges and rolls of fat, his once thick and curly hair was balding at the crown, his teeth were embarrassingly broken and yellowed. The poet Robert Lowell gave a very good description of how Thomas struck his fellow writers:

> Somehow he was kept on beer most of the time, but he'd begin at 7 in the morning and end at 12 – no meals except breakfast. About the best and dirtiest stories I've ever heard – dumpy, absurd body, hair combed by a salad spoon . . . a great explosion of life, and hell to handle.

The welcoming party given for him, attended by most of the leading literati of New York, saw a man who 'by a loud and awkward entrance, seemed to demand considerably more attention than the party was disposed to grant him.' This is from John Malcolm Brinnin's *Dylan Thomas in America*. Brinnin acted as Thomas's manager and agent in America; not an easy task, and his book is an odd mixture of what seems to be sometimes an almost sexual infatuation with Thomas and rather prissy horror at his antics. However, the unprepossessing start of the New York party was followed by huge success with audiences.

It was Thomas's voice that conquered all reservations about his personal appearance and behaviour. For the next hundred days he toured the campuses and lecture halls of America, filling them to capacity while he read his own and others' poems. He was sometimes drunk before and always after readings; he was enchanting and boorish by turn; his legend went before him, snowballing across the continent. As Brinnin wrote:

> If Dylan had done and said all that was reported as truth, he would
> not have been tolerated in even the most liberal of surroundings; if
> his rumoured carousals and lecheries had been as outrageous and
> consistent as they were said to be he would have been hauled off to
> jail or committed to an asylum.

But the reality was that there was always more than enough to talk about when Dylan Thomas hit town. After a reading, glass of scotch in hand, he would regale academic company with dirty stories, booming quotations, or indulge in awkward fumbling approaches to his hosts' wives. As ever, Thomas felt intellectually unsure of himself with academics and he responded by behaving especially badly in their company. The habit of his hosts in serving him large measures of spirits rather than his normal beer often resulted in him drinking himself into insensibility before the party came to an end. It was only when he was with old friends or staying in some household where he could relax and not feel threatened that he became the quietly spoken, endearing – and sober – man that his closest friends recall.

He made his way alone across the continent. 'I'm hardly living; I'm just a voice on wheels,' he wrote home to Caitlin. He sent the usual protestations of undying love, accompanied by a warning that he was unlikely to bring much of the promised money back with him, what he called 'my earnings for us'. He was true to his word in this at least. He had earned substantial fees, his board and lodgings were usually provided free, apart from some travelling expenses there was little to be bought, but once again all that he earned rapidly and mysteriously evaporated.

Most of the money probably went when he had finished his tour and remained for two weeks in New York. His headquarters became the White Horse Tavern in Greenwich Village, the nearest thing to a British pub he could find. He visited nightclubs and restaurants and conducted at least two affairs.

He sailed back broke, the voyage no doubt leaving time for much sober and sombre reflection on the reception he could expect to receive from Caitlin.

IX

Drink has a very mysterious quality: it dissolves money faster than any acid – and in whatever way we try and add up the cost of drinks Dylan Thomas must have consumed in America the total never remotely approaches the amount of money he actually spent. There were of course all the hangers-on to be treated, and by now Thomas had quite a retinue of women and men who wanted to be with him at all hours of the day and night; there were the taxis, the meals not eaten but paid for, and money lost or, literally, thrown away. In his three months in America Thomas earned almost £3,000, about £40,000 in today's terms. Tax was due on his earnings; nothing had been put aside.

Back in England, he wrote again to Margaret Taylor asking for money, now pitifully and ungraciously blaming Caitlin for wasting what little money he had sent her. The rows and physical fights with his wife intensified in venom. While he had been away she had engaged in casual sexual affairs in Laugharne. It was a small, tight-knit town that Thomas loved; she had come to loathe it and it must have seemed to him that she was fouling his one last safe nest.

He was now writing and endlessly re-writing his play *Under Milk Wood*. Work was briefly interrupted for a trip to Iran to research a commercial film on behalf of the Anglo-Iranian Petroleum Corporation (later British Petroleum). The sights and atmosphere of the country and its poverty, which horrified Thomas, were related brilliantly in a series of letters home to Caitlin. She did not answer them – she was still smarting from news of *his* affairs with women in America. There has been some speculation that Thomas was recruited by the intelligence services to some mysterious end at this time – it can only be said that any intelligence officer who recruited Thomas as an agent must have been mad or drunk or both. Still, as there was no shortage of people in those services who were both of those things there may be some truth to the story.

This was his last good time. On his return to Laugharne he completed two extraordinary and beautiful poems: 'Do Not Go Gentle into that Good Night', addressed to his seriously ill father, and 'Poem on His Birthday' – which might be described as a presumptive elegy for himself. He was still able to convert the chaos of life into carefully ordered and powerful works of art. But both poems are valedictions. His marriage was coming apart. He was consumed by sexual jealousy over the affairs that Caitlin conducted with such little concern for his feelings. For her part, Caitlin was utterly bored by life in the small town and with looking after their children – she once commented on her surprise that, despite her many infidelities, they all 'looked like Dylan'. She accused him of ceasing to be the poet she had married, and of turning into a parody of his former self.

It was just after his trip to Iran that Thomas visited Swansea to read to the University English Society. His meeting with Kingsley Amis is dealt with in the chapter on Amis, but it is worth noting that it was an encounter between someone who was rapidly becoming an ageing representative of the bohemian poetry of the 1930s and 40s and a young representative of a new and more sceptical, academically attached generation. Thomas, whose work for so long had been synonymous with the celebration of youth, was falling out of fashion with the literary world, if not the general public. For so sensitive a man it must have been yet another dreadful worry to add to many others.

The one place he was sure of a warm reception was America. Caitlin insisted on accompanying her husband on his trip in January 1952. Her intention may have been to ride shotgun on her husband's second wild ride across the States, but in public she behaved as badly, or worse, than he did, but with few of his redeeming features: humour, self-irony, and occasional good grace. In New York, Thomas made the first of the recordings that were to widen greatly his audience in the coming years. The two of them were in America for four months and again he earned substantial amounts of money: news came back from England that his son Llewellyn had been expelled from his school for the non-payment of fees. The only money his parents returned with was a few hundred dollars that Brinnin had managed to secrete in Caitlin's handbag.

When they got back the drinking continued. Another of the legends that has grown up about Thomas is that he was reasonably safe in Wales and London, drinking only beer and resting up at home between drinking bouts, and that it was America that broke his health and took his life by encouraging him to drink spirits. In fact it is plain, from Thomas's household bills in Laugharne, that he was now also drinking whisky at home. His health was poor; always a heavy smoker, he had successive bouts of bronchitis, but more worrying were the blackouts he was now experiencing.

On some fronts, things were looking up. In November 1952 his *Collected Poems, 1934–1952* was published. It is still the place to go to read Thomas at his best; he chose and arranged the poems and later editions of his collected poems are bloated by juvenilia and other work he would probably have rejected. The reviews, especially from critics of his own generation, almost all hailed him as a great poet. The first edition of 5,000 soon sold out, and Thomas was awarded the Foyle's Literary Prize of £250. He earned a further £1,000 from royalties and readings in the first half of 1953. But his personal affairs were turning out disastrously. In December 1952 his beloved father died; in January a woman friend who had promised to help him financially committed suicide, the same month Caitlin underwent an abortion, and in April his sister Nancy died, aged only forty-six, of cancer.

In April he sailed once more to America, carrying a heavy load of grief and worry.

X

As soon as he landed he set out to get drunk. He began an affair with Liz Reitell, Brinnin's assistant, at the Poetry Centre in New York. The first stage performance of the as yet uncompleted *Under Milk Wood* was given, with Thomas as narrator; he sounds composed and reads quite brilliantly on a recording. The love affair and the successful staging of his play meant that he remained a little steadier than usual on this visit. But he still got drunk. He fell over and broke his arm and was introduced to a Dr Milton Feltenstein, who treated him with cortisone and morphine injections with what Thomas called his 'winking needle'. He returned to Southampton after only four weeks, on the second of June 1953, in time for the celebrations of the coronation of Elizabeth II.

When he got back to Laugharne, an icy Caitlin informed him that she was ready to leave him. There were now school fees to be found for his daughter Aeronwy, and Margaret Taylor was at last demanding that the Thomases pay rent on their house. The continuing payments of back income tax were now joined by demands for payment of national insurance stamps. His *Collected Poems* was selling well but Thomas must have looked at the cover as if it were a tombstone with his name and dates of 1934–1952. How on earth was he to produce another body of work to equal that of his first twenty years? He was thirty-eight years old and for a writer whose stock in trade was youth and early mortality the future must have looked extremely bleak.

It is clear that the figure that Thomas presented to the world in person and through his letters, of the penniless, beleaguered poet, was not truthful. This is to put it too harshly perhaps, but he was always an accomplished and compulsive liar. Thomas would have answered that he was a lyric poet and that he must therefore be protected however little he produced, like some exotic plant that puts forth one magnificent bloom on one day of the year. It is a position he could defend as a young man producing his first flush of valuable work. But now he was not even producing any worthwhile poetry. In his last year, his worksheets show a man bereft of inspiration, casting about in *Roget's Thesaurus* for word choices, writing over and over again desperately thin variations on the same lines. This was his true horror – the death of the poet in him. Anyone who has ever written anything approaching a half-good poem knows the difficulty and joy of that achievement. It is like no other and when it is taken away or burns out or simply dies gradually it is a failure of both the mind and the sensual body. His last, unfinished poem was intended as an elegy for his dead father: it is heart-breaking for its bathos and the banality of its language rather than for its subject matter.

America still offered various ways out. There were tentative offers of teaching posts at universities, Stravinsky wanted Thomas to write a libretto for an opera, there was a woman, Liz Reitell, who loved him, and perhaps a new and revived life.

XI

The end was merciless.

As we have seen, Thomas had suffered great personal losses in the previous few months and he was in a fragile state emotionally and physically when his plane took off for New York in October 1953.

It was plain from the outset that something was seriously wrong with him. He spent two relatively quiet and sober days with Liz Reitell then went out and got very drunk. He celebrated, if that is the word, his thirty-ninth birthday on the twenty-seventh of October. Birthdays had always been important to Thomas and this one upset him. He was now drinking anything and everything offered. There were rumours of other drugs and Thomas seemed to be sunk into despair at times. Doctor Feltenstein and his winking needle reappeared to administer more cortisone. John Malcolm Brinnin met Thomas at a rehearsal of *Under Milk Wood* and was shocked at his appearance: 'His face was lime-white, his lips loose and twisted, his eyes dulled, gelid, and sunk in his head.' This is not the description of a man who is drunk but one who is seriously ill, probably already harbouring pneumonia. He was drinking whisky in large quantities and his 'friends' were still rushing him from one party to another. He collapsed after he had tottered off alone into the night and returned saying that he had consumed 'eighteen straight whiskies. I think that's the record.' Investigations in the following days found that this figure had been wildly exaggerated by Thomas. He was very ill the next day but managed to go to the White Horse tavern for a couple of beers. Soon after he collapsed again, now raving. Dr Feltenstein was summoned and injected him with half a grain of morphine. A few hours later he passed into a coma and was rushed to hospital. He never recovered consciousness and died there on the ninth of November.

The death has always been mysterious. The accepted 'fact' was that Thomas had died as a result of alcoholic poisoning. David N. Thomas has produced what is probably the nearest to a definitive account of the poet's last days. He has seen a summary of Thomas's medical notes from St Vincent's Hospital, which have until very recently remained inaccessible:

> Dylan had pneumonia on admission to hospital, as well as bronchitis . . . [these] as well as his emphysema impaired Dylan's breathing, and as a result his brain was starved of oxygen, leading to swelling of the brain tissues, coma and then death.

None of these related complaints had been diagnosed by Feltenstein, and an injection of morphine fatally 'impaired Dylan's respiratory system still further'. Although Thomas had obviously put himself in harm's way by drinking wildly, he did not 'die' of drink. It seems that a man who was already ill was egged on to alcoholic excesses by his hangers-on and toadies. He soon became seriously ill and then was the further victim of medical incompetence and the administering of a drug inappropriate to his condition that directly resulted in his death.

Thomas was not a hopeless alcoholic: he could and did go for fairly extended periods drinking relatively lightly. He liked drinking very much indeed, but he seems to have chosen drunkenness because it pleased other people – 'because they expect it,' as he once said. The poetry and stories did not come out of the befuddled mind of 'Dylan', lurching and falling over in drunken buffoonery, but from an exceptionally intelligent and clear-eyed vision. It is thanks to the respites and withdrawals from alcohol in his life that we have his handful of great poems. It's time that the self-generated legend of 'the drunkest man in the world' was put aside in favour of what is unique and valuable in his work.

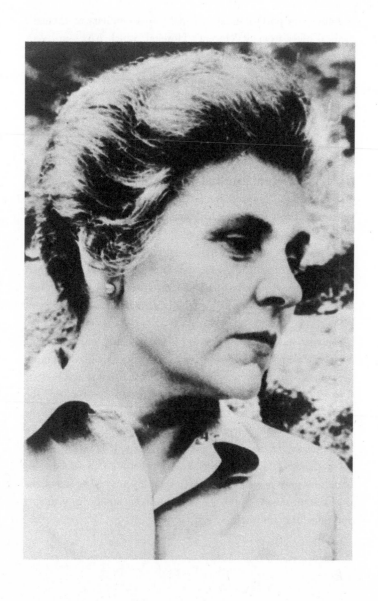

Chapter 6

'I will not drink'

Elizabeth Bishop (1911–1979)

I

O F ALL the writers included in this book, Elizabeth Bishop is probably the most difficult to write about. She did her best to keep her private life as private as possible and much of her heaviest drinking took place when she was alone, in apartments, hotel rooms, and bars and cafés where she could be anonymous – a small respectable-looking woman, getting quietly stewed. She didn't boast about her capacity for drink or celebrate drunken misadventures.

For Bishop, drunkenness was a shameful failing. Is she out of place in this book? She certainly seems to have felt out of place in the world at large for much of her life. Even in photographs there are few where she looks at ease. One famous picture, of Bishop sitting on the front steps of the Square Roof brothel in Key West, shows her puffy-faced and obviously drunk. In group photographs she often looks not one with the company, as if she has been inserted or superimposed on the picture. Wherever she is, in photographs, in the letters or memories of others, in biographies and memoirs, she somehow manages to slip away.

II

Around 1970, Elizabeth Bishop wrote a poem entitled 'The Drunkard'. As with most of her work dealing directly with personal experience it remained unpublished until after her death. The opening lines record her earliest memory, of watching at the age of three a great fire blazing at Salem, Massachusetts, from her home on the other side of the harbour. All her life she remembered her early childhood and youth with great vividness. As well she might, given their nature. Near to the end of the poem she says grimly:

> ... by the age
> of twenty or twenty-one I had begun
> to drink and drink. I can't get enough...

W.H. Auden's prescription for the grown-up human being, at least that for a writer from the upper middle-classes in the early twentieth century, was spelled out in his 'Letter to Lord Byron': 'Let each child have that's in our care/As much neurosis as the child can bear.' This does not appear to have been the case in Auden's own early life; a few stanzas on in the same poem a line states baldly: 'We all grow up the same way, more or less.' But if ever a future poet suffered from neurosis heaped upon her in childhood it was poor Elizabeth Bishop.

She was born on the eighth of February 1911, in Worcester, Massachusetts. Her father, William Bishop, was the son of a rich self-made building contractor; her mother, Gertrude (née Bulmer), who had trained to be a nurse in Boston, came from a family of tradesmen and small farmers in Great Village, Nova Scotia. When Bishop was only eight months old, her father died of Bright's disease. He was thirty-nine. Her mother descended into a state of distraught grief that deepened into insanity. Amongst Bishop's early memories was hearing her mother screaming when they were at her grandparents' house in Great Village: she attributed the breakdown to her mother's reaction to a visit by a seamstress who had come to measure her for new clothes to replace the mourning she had continued to wear for years. Her mother rapidly deteriorated, she imagined persecutions and attempts to poison her, became violent and uncontrollable, and was committed in 1916 to the Nova Scotia Hospital in Dartmouth. She was never to come out again. Elizabeth was five.

She was put in the charge of her maternal grandparents, the Bulmers. Despite its name, Great Village was a small place of a few wooden houses, a shop and post office, a church, and little else. Situated on the shore of Cobequid Bay, which leads into the North Atlantic Ocean, the land behind was of hills and forest, small farms and pasture land, lakes and rivers. The sea and harbours, the life of the small communities that work them, the wildlife of water and land fuelled much of her later poetry and Elizabeth loved Nova Scotia all of her life.

Her grandparents were sober chapel goers, though her Uncle Art was the village drunk. Years later Bishop wondered if her drinking was inherited: she said that at least three of her uncles were heavy drinkers and that drink had contributed to her father's early death. Apart from Uncle Art, there seems to be little evidence that this was the case, and, after all, there are few families that don't possess at least one drunken uncle. The Bulmer family were kind to her and Great Village itself was the first of those places that Bishop regarded as a haven.

But to a child who was remarkably sensitive and observant, her mother must have seemed a living ghost, trapped somewhere near, but never to be visited. Bishop's own health was not good. She had always suffered from a weak chest and frequent colds, and as she moved into her sixth year she began to suffer attacks of asthma and eczema, two complaints in which fluctuations in severity may be linked to emotional upset and anxiety.

There was more of that to come. The Wilson grandparents in Massachusetts decided that the young girl should move down to them and receive the sort of education that the Bulmers could not afford. As Bishop put it in her autobiographical story, 'The Country Mouse': 'I had been brought back unconsulted and against my wishes to the house my father had been born in, to be saved from a life of poverty and provincialism'. Her paternal grandparents meant well, but to the young girl the Wilsons were distant and intimidating figures and she was often left to her own devices. In 'The Country Mouse' she describes the sprawling, large house, set in fifteen acres of wooded land, with its front room, never used, and library used only by herself, the servants who spoke Swedish, the rats who scuttled in the attic, while she 'explored the house like a cat'. The memoir ends, when she is seven years old, with a sudden epiphanic realisation of her own utterly unique personality; characteristically it came as a question to herself: '*Why* was I a human being?'

She returned to Great Village for school vacations, a long journey by trains and ferry: the final train leg in Nova Scotia passed the sanatorium where her mother was confined.

Her childhood became a bewildering shuttling between relatives, most of whom treated her well, with the exception of Uncle George who 'helped' her to bathe and sexually assaulted her, and terrifying Uncle Jack who became her guardian. 'I was scared to death of him and he didn't like me,' Bishop said. There were more pleasurable interludes, but some of Elizabeth Bishop's childhood sounds like a Grimm Brothers tale illustrated by Paula Rego at her darkest.

There were summer camps at Cape Cod beginning in 1924, when she was thirteen, and continuing until 1929, where she could fish and sail and swim with girls her own age. All through her life, water was a saviour; the lake, the river, the pooled water in ports and small harbours, the sea – all represented escape. She knew her possible escape routes from an early age; at seventeen, in a short piece entitled 'On Being Alone' she wrote:

There is a peculiar quality about being alone . . . It is as if being with people were the Earth of the mind . . . but in being alone, the mind finds its Sea, the wide, quiet plane with different lights in the sky and different, more secret sounds.

But the company of others could have its attractions and after all her journeyings between aunts and uncles, she must have welcomed Walnut Hill boarding school as a deliverance from family bonds. The girls were bright and intelligent, the teachers for the most part close to their pupils. There were sentimental crushes between girls and staff, in both directions. The very first letter in the collection of Bishop's letters, *One Art*, includes an extract from a note from one of her teachers:

> Elizabeth my dear, come up the path through the fir trees and white birches to my little cottage by the sea and there by the fireside, where nothing is 'developed' save friendliness and poems and contentment . . .

At Walnut Hill she published poems and stories in the student magazine; when she graduated to Vassar in 1930 she was to co-found and edit a literary magazine and begin to find her way as a writer.

III

If we take her poem 'A Drunkard' as autobiographical evidence, Elizabeth Bishop began to drink at 'twenty or twenty-one', which would be sometime in her first two full years at Vassar. Brett C. Millier, the author of the first important biography of Bishop, said that she 'drank destructively because she was an alcoholic'. This is the theory of alcoholism as a disease that pre-exists in some way before manifesting itself as an urge to drink alcohol. Millier offers further explanations; that alcoholism is caused by a faulty enzyme, by proximity to other drinkers when young, by genetic inheritance. But he does ask the most important question of 'why she drank at all?'

On the evidence, the reason seems fairly obvious. In the free drinking atmosphere of young and fairly well-off Americans in the early 1930s the culture was a drinking one, with wine and spirits readily available even under prohibition. That Bishop drank more heavily then and for the rest of her life than most of her contemporaries seems to me evidence that she must have found in drink something other than a chemical or genetic imperative. An intensely shy young woman, uncertain of her social position, of her sexuality (she knew by now that she was fundamentally lesbian), essentially without close family, she found in alcohol what other socially and emotionally awkward souls have found: an emollient and helpful companion; in more extreme cases, a guide to temporary oblivion. She did get drunk socially, found this intensely embarrassing and demeaning (although outsiders may have hardly noticed) and began what became a lifelong alternation of periods of relative sobriety in public and intense binges of drinking alone.

She left Vassar in 1934. To that date her romantic life seems to have consisted of a few early adolescent crushes and sharing beds with other girls in their mid-teens while at summer camp, and occasional, inconsequential dates with young men when she became a student. She liked men well enough, but only one, Robert Seaver, became very close to her, so much so that they went away for weekends and shared a room. Friends expected them to marry. But Bishop was actually in love with her room-mate at college, Margaret Miller, a promising painter. As Miller was not a lesbian and Bishop never declared her love, this became yet another secret feeling to be hidden away.

Knowing nothing of this, Seaver appears to have remained very seriously attached to Bishop. She liked him as they say 'well enough' but had no intention of marrying (the only man she ever regarded as a possible emotional partner, and in an intense way, was the poet Robert Lowell when they met after the war).

Nineteen thirty-four was a momentous year. In the March, a few weeks before Bishop graduated, her mother died, still helplessly insane, in the Nova Scotia hospital to which she had been committed in 1916, when her daughter was five years old. They had not seen each other since then and Bishop had made no effort to visit her. She had long regarded her mother as dead. As a school friend said, 'Elizabeth didn't talk much about her childhood . . . She really had to grow up all by herself.' And in the same year she first met Marianne Moore, the great American poet, twenty-four years her senior, who became almost a surrogate mother, and a mentor reading and commenting on Bishop's early work.

A Vassar friend, Mary McCarthy, helped her find a small apartment in Charles Street in the Village when she moved to New York. Her family trust fund was enough to live on but she wanted a job. What she found had an odd relationship to the profession of letters, if not to literature. The business purported to be a correspondence college for would-be writers who answered advertisements placed in magazines and sent in their manuscripts with a reading fee. Nothing was promised and there was no hope of publication, so that the whole scam was actually a step down even from a vanity press in that it produced nothing except vague 'advice'. In various accounts, Bishop lasted for between two weeks and a couple of months before leaving in disgust.

IV

Bishop's first serious affair in New York was with a rich young woman, Louise Crane, who was also a heavy drinker. Crane was sexually experienced and multiply unfaithful, a lover of jazz and jazz musicians. The singer Billie Holiday was also seeing Crane at this time and in her autobiography *Lady Sings the Blues* wrote an unflattering portrait of a rich, idle, shop-lifting Louise Crane, disguising her lightly with a false name.

Whatever else happened in their relationship, the most important thing that Crane introduced Bishop to was foreign travel – as travellers and residents, not just tourists.

In June 1935 Bishop crossed the Atlantic by liner. She and Crane lived in Paris for a while, before touring through France, Germany, Spain, and North Africa. In a photograph taken with Crane in France, Bishop looks for almost the first time unselfconsciously happy and very young. They did not return to New York until June 1936.

It seems that Robert Seaver had proposed marriage to Bishop before she left for Europe. She had no intention of marrying anyone and had broken off their relationship. Perhaps he had fresh hopes after her return to New York – there must have been some correspondence or even a meeting, for in November she received a postcard from Seaver. The message was brief: 'Elizabeth, go to Hell.' Shortly after, he shot himself.

In 1937, Bishop wintered in Key West, Florida, and later that year sailed for a second time to Europe, with Louise Crane and her Vassar room-mate, Margaret Miller. A second photograph of Louise and Elizabeth in Paris shows a very different couple from that of 1935. In the later picture, Louise looks grimly long-faced, Elizabeth seems to be masking the lower part of her own face by holding a cigarette to her lips, but her eyes are wide and seem to look blankly through the photographer. This was taken a short while after a car accident. Crane had been driving, they had spun off the road, Bishop and Crane had rolled free from the overturned car, Margaret Miller, with whom Bishop was still in love, had her right arm severed between elbow and wrist. A surgeon later told her that she might be able to resume painting and drawing with her left hand. The party returned to America in December 1937; in January of 1938, Bishop moved to Key West, where she lived off and on for the next ten years.

V

Henry de Montherlant's phrase 'Happiness writes in white ink on white paper' has the air of unassailable truth. Any writer will tell you that tragedy is a great deal harder to write than comedy, and that comedy has a shorter shelf life, but again, like most of such phrases, it is only partially true. Happiness is a pretty little anodyne word that does not venture so far as to contain the sensations of joy, ecstasy, and epiphany conjured up in pages of Tolstoy, Hopkins, and even James Joyce (after all, 'Yes,' is the concluding, life-affirming word of *Ulysses*). De Montherlant had obviously not had the chance to read Elizabeth Bishop letters and poetry on her life in Key West.

Bishop was known in her own lifetime for her few slim volumes of poetry and a handful of short stories, but the many letters she wrote, sometimes several in a day, should be regarded as creative equals to her poetry. When the selection *One Art* appeared in 1994, the poet Tom Paulin wrote that the publication 'is a historic event, a bit like discovering a new planet or watching a bustling continent emerge, glossy and triumphant, from the blank ocean. Here is an immense cultural treasure . . . ' The many letters written from Key West, were singled out by Colm Tóibín as full of 'joy and wonder'.

Of course Key West was a form of exile, but so are most of our self-administered balms. By the very nature of life they do not and cannot last, but for as long as they do they can make us happy and if we are talented enough we can convey that sensation to others. Here is Bishop writing to Marianne Moore soon after arrival: 'Down the street is a very small cottage I can look right into, and the only furniture it contains beside a bed and chair is an enormous French horn, painted silver, leaning against the wall, and hanging over it a pith helmet, also painted silver.'

A typical Bishop observation, so unexpectedly real that it approaches the surreal, or rather, as she said, after dismissing some work by Max Ernst, 'the always-more-successful surrealism of every-day life'.

She was truly happy, living alone, working steadily at poems and stories, drinking and dancing in Sloppy Joe's, a bar named after its owner. Louise Crane came down from New York, bringing with her whisky and wine and new jazz and blues records. They bought a house together, although Crane was more easily bored in Key West and often disappeared back to New York. Bishop wrote to her friends Frani Blough and Margaret Miller: 'One of the reasons I like Key West so much is that everything goes at a *natural* pace . . . as soon as anyone has worked for a week, they 'knock off' for two or so, and drunkenness is an excuse just as correct as any other.'

So, a slightly rackety, happy life in a beautiful port and its back country, for as long as it lasted. That was until her affair with Louise Crane came to an abrupt end in 1940.

Bishop had become suspicious that Crane was unfaithful to her, but did not have to face the proof until the two of them were in New York in 1940. Bishop had returned to the Fifth Avenue apartment to find her lover in bed with Billie Holiday. As she wrote, over thirty years later, about jealousy: 'It's the worst feeling in the world . . . I wish I could be all for promiscuity and free love and ménages à trois and not give a damn whom you sleep with. But I can't.' Despite this statement, and her public demeanour, Bishop seems to have led a full, if discreet sexual life, mainly lesbian, but she had always liked men and there is no doubt that later she loved Lowell deeply and perhaps had the occasional heterosexual affair.

But broken up by the ending of her affair with Crane, she returned alone to Key West. She became deeply depressed and threatened suicide. Friends said that she was 'difficult' at such times; presumably she had started to drink heavily once more.

To add to her misery, her beloved Key West was beginning to change rapidly and for the worse. The navy began to develop the port as a base for submarines and sea planes. The racket of building work and traffic and the influx of many new outsiders disturbed the quiet 'natural pace' of life in the town. But among the newcomers was Marjorie Stevens, the wife of a Boston publisher. Bishop wrote some years later to her psychoanalyst, Ruth Foster, that she had been drunk at the beginning of every one of her affairs. Perhaps she *had* to be drunk to drop her fears and defences, but one night a very drunk Bishop met Stevens in a Key West bar. They moved in together, until they sought greater peace and quiet, first in North Carolina and then Mexico.

In late 1941, Bishop left for New York and stayed for almost a year, again alone.

VI

Now thirty years old, Bishop considered that she had achieved little with her writing. She had a reputation already as a fine poet, but she had not sought to advance a poetic 'career'. Her work was published in leading magazines, but she refused offers to be published in anthologies (particularly those devoted solely to women poets). Unlike other writers who choose exile or reclusiveness and fail to build a reputation in the great metropolitan centres of the arts, Bishop's work had so far succeeded almost entirely on its own merits. She was early on given a 'first view' contract by *The New Yorker*, and throughout her life was awarded a steady stream of prizes, grants and fellowships. Her four slim books of poetry (all that were published while she lived) were almost unanimously praised by her peers. She seems to have been stubborn in denying her reading public any evidence in her poems that would enable them to guess at what their author was like. Michael Hofmann, discussing her dismissal of herself from her poems, rightly called her an 'Eye' poet, rather than an 'I' poet.

A poem might begin as a personal reaction to something experienced or observed, and notes and early drafts might contain autobiographical material, but these personal elements were eroded over periods of months or even years, to an impersonal viewpoint, moving steadily away from the subjective to the objective world. There is no doubt that much of the work she published is marked in some way by her own suffering, by feelings of guilt, grief and early trauma, but we only infer their presence by reading the biographies and letters published after her death.

The wide admiration for her work while she lived rested on its value as poetry, not as some form of confession or by following any artistic credo or programme. She belonged to no school; her only close influence, Marianne Moore, was also idiosyncratic as an artist. Bishop wrote few reviews of other poets, thereby avoiding the flattery or malice common to poetry magazines. Her absence for long periods from any poetry 'scene', and her instinctive avoidance of public utterance and distrust of praise, account for the rare quality that Anthony Hecht saw in Bishop: 'Poets are . . . not noticeably free from small envies and petty jealousies . . . this is so much the rule with us that any exception to it . . . is unsettling and not altogether easy to explain.'

And Bishop certainly is difficult to explain. Even to herself? She lived in two segregated personalities: one that appeared openly in the public literary world and one she thought she had successfully concealed in which she was a drinker and a passionate lover of women. The strain of maintaining an identity that is fundamentally a role is one reason for drinking oneself unconscious. Bishop would drink socially, drink flowed freely at the lunches and parties of her friends, but her binges when she drank enormous quantities of bourbon and anything else available were conducted away from others. She wrote to Ruth Foster that the early morning was 'about the time I normally start drinking, or writing a poem, or, come to think of it, when I like best to make love . . . '

Returning to Key West she did some war work in a factory until falling ill. Pent up at home she was alone much of the day and was often drunk when Marjorie returned home. Now, as even heavy drinkers know, the sight of their beloved partner drunk while they themselves are sober is not an attractive one. There were rows and reconciliations, but the affair was under great strain. In 1944, Bishop returned to New York, once again alone.

VII

Most of this private side of her life was invisible to her friends. She was a popular figure in the New York literary and artistic world. Interviewed for the oral biography *Remembering Elizabeth Bishop*, the poet Howard Moss said of her: 'I adored her because she was so completely interesting . . . Just to take a walk with her was to observe in the most casual way a lot of things that you would not ordinarily notice. Also, she was so terribly nice. She didn't seem to be trying to get anything, or have an idea of a career.'

Bishop would have pulled a wry face and made some crack about being considered 'nice'. But her literary career was progressing well. In 1946 she won a competition run by the publisher Houghton Mifflin, worth $1,000 and promising publication. The company issued her first collection of poems, *North and South*, in August the same year. It met with almost universal praise, even from the notably astringent critic Randall Jarrell. Marianne Moore praised the book in the *Nation*, though rather bewilderingly designated the poems as 'beautifully formulated aesthetic-moral mathematics'. A review by Robert Lowell was mixed; he thought some of the poems failures, or slight, but generally judged Bishop to have produced 'some of the best poems written by a woman in this century'. Whatever her thoughts about being praised as a 'woman poet', the two became great friends when they met the following year and they corresponded (another huge tranche of Bishop's letters) until Lowell's death in 1977. Other rewards followed: a Guggenheim Fellowship, and in 1949, with Lowell's aid, an appointment as Poetry Consultant to the Library of Congress.

Before she took up that post she went on holiday to Haiti. She told her doctor, Amy Hausmann, that everything had gone splendidly in Haiti, that her asthma had abated, that she was not drinking, but she fell back into heavy drinking on her return to Key West. At this low point a visitor described her as looking very much older than her age:

'Her face was puffy . . . very pale . . . almost sickly.' A young woman who lived with them and acted as a companion to the sick woman was instructed by Marjorie Stevens that no alcohol could be allowed in the house, that Bishop was 'a cunning drunk and . . . would call over the place to try and get liquor'. Bishop still managed to get alcohol and hid the bottles about the house. When she could find nothing else she drank a bottle of rubbing alcohol and was rushed into hospital. A spell of treatment for alcoholism in a Connecticut clinic was prescribed.

A fairly disastrous spell at Yaddo followed. Yaddo crops up quite a lot in the biographies of American writers, painters, composers, and others: an invitation to stay there was a mark of honour. It was (and is) an artists' community comprising several elegant buildings on a private estate set in parkland at Saratoga Springs, in New York State. Yaddo's stated mission was to be a place of 'rest and refreshment for authors, painters, sculptors, musicians and other artists'. Numbers were limited to around twenty at a time: some worked there, others did not. John Cheever said that it had 'seen more distinguished activity in the arts than any other piece of ground in the English-speaking community'. Well, Cheever himself spent much of his own time there drinking, and so it seems did Bishop.

Yaddo was not the rest she needed and her distress is plain in the letters she wrote from there (later collected in *One Art*, edited by Robert Giroux). A letter early on in her stay confesses that she has never 'felt so nervous and like a fish out of water'. In a sequence of letters to her friend, the painter Loren MacIver, she set out a distressing picture of her state. She imagined that all the friends she had made in her life now disliked her and that the clinic she had attended for treatment of her alcoholism had destroyed her self-confidence and social skills. 'In fact,' she wrote, 'I JUST DON'T KNOW anything except that I'd like to die quite quickly.' She repeated her fear at taking up the job at the Library of Congress. She drank heavily, although she was not the only guest at Yaddo to do so – one novelist got so drunk that he was removed to a local jail to sober up. One funny and sad image, a quintessentially double-edged Bishop image, occurs at the end of a letter where she says that she has been trying to pull herself together at the end of a stay in which little writing work had been done: 'I've just been out blowing bubbles on my balcony, my chief diversion.'

But at last the much-dreaded post at the Library of Congress had to be taken up. It involved a move to Washington and settling into bureaucratic work to which she was not used or suited. She was awkward and felt out of place with the round of meetings, arrangement of recordings and readings by other poets, and a punishing social round of parties and lunches. She characterised it wryly as 'Poetry as Big Business'. Even worse, as she told a friend, 'It has kind of taken poetry away from me. I had to read so much I didn't like, it absolutely numbed me.' On one occasion, invited by Lowell to dine with T.S. Eliot and W.H. Auden and overcome with nerves, she instead sampled all the bottles in a friend's apartment and passed out. A rare high point was in meeting and talking to Dylan Thomas, whom she liked very much. They locked themselves in the butler's pantry at a busy party and toasted each other: two small curly haired outsiders clinking glasses. Unfortunately, there's no mention of Bishop in Thomas's letters, but then he often hardly knew which city he was in during his American tours, let alone being able to remember any among the host of poets he was obliged to meet. After reading what she called 'a solid year of drivel at the Library' Bishop was grateful when the post ended in September 1950.

In October she was persuaded by friends to return to Yaddo. The weather was cooler in the autumn and she was happy she had finished with Washington. She struck up a friendship with a painter, Beauford Delaney, and the two would sit in rocking chairs drinking and talking before dinner, though Bishop often didn't make it to dinner. Or breakfast, or lunch: at these times she kept to her room, drinking solidly.

The drinking continued when she returned to New York, living in a succession of dingy hotel rooms. To friends she appeared at the end of her tether. But her life, which she often thought of ending at this time, was about to flower again. In 1951 she was awarded a fellowship worth $2,500. Her doctor recommended travel. By what turned out to be a lucky chance, a trip she had booked to Europe fell through. She took the next boat available. That one was going to the port of Santos in Brazil. She sailed in November 1951.

VIII

Any old-fashioned Hollywood biopic dealing with Elizabeth Bishop would probably concentrate on her ten years spent in Brazil and end with a caption saying something like, *The Great Poet Lives Happily on in her New Life, in a New Country,* over a flickering piece of colour home movie showing the real poet smiling shyly at the camera. (Who on earth would have played Elizabeth Bishop? Was there ever a Hollywood biopic about a poet? There was a 1950s film about the Brontë sisters; the only scene I can remember is of two extras passing each other on a wide pavement, lifting their top hats and exchanging the salutations, 'Morning, Thackeray', 'Morning, Dickens.' And my attention was caught years ago by a mention on a BBC radio arts programme that Sylvester Stallone was planning to make a film called 'Rimbaud'.)

Almost as if passing through some horrible initiation into what was to become a new life in Brazil, Bishop fell seriously ill with an allergic reaction to cashew nuts. Her whole body was swollen and her asthma and eczema flared up. She wrote to Amy Baumann, relaying the mixture of drugs she was being given for her ailments, and asking for others only available in the US to be posted by air mail. She sent a forwarding address: c/o Lota de Macedo Soares, Rua Antonio Vieira 5, Leme, Rio de Janeiro.

She was in the care of Lota for the next ten years. They moved together into a house, Samambia, built to the wealthy Lota's design, in the mountains at Petropolis, about 40 miles from Rio de Janeiro. (It is described beautifully in Bishop's letters home to America, and in her poem 'Song for the Rainy Season'.) After a long period of being unable to write anything at all in her dark times in Washington and New York, Bishop again began working – on stories of her childhood. Her letters to friends sound wistful for their company, but she was in love with Lota and the strangeness and beauty of Brazil and its people and, as ever with Bishop, its wild creatures and landscapes. She wrote to Amy Baumann that:

> The drinking seems to have dwindled to about one evening once or twice a month, and I stop before it gets really bad, I think . . . the drinking and the working both seem to have improved miraculously. Well no, it isn't miraculous really – it is almost entirely due to Lota's good sense and kindness. I still feel I must have died and gone to heaven without deserving to, but I am getting a little more used to it.

The good times lasted. Bishop washed Lota's hair and wrote a poem, 'The Shampoo', that Katharine White, her editor at *The New Yorker*, could not understand. In May 1953, she and Lota wrote a joint letter to two musician friends in New York. Lota signed off with, 'Elizabeth . . . is getting used to being happy and sleeping well, and less scared'. The words could be those written about a child who has come to stay.

Bishop's second book of poems, *A Cold Spring*, was published in 1955. In reality she had struggled to have enough new work to justify even a very slim volume. Her publisher solved the problem by reprinting the poems from her first book, *North and South*, with the newer ones. These new poems from the late 1940s and early 1950s contain some of her strongest work, much of it set beside the cold sea of the North American coast she knew so well, or in the darkness and emotional traps of the city of New York. The book ends with her poem to Lota, 'The Shampoo'. Further poems inspired by her life in Brazil had to wait for her book *Questions of Travel* in 1965.

But the trouble with any earthly paradise is that there are always snake and apple waiting to put an end to happiness and innocence. When Bishop found herself rehashing her childhood in stories, she once again began to drink. Perhaps also she felt guilty that in some way she was being kept financially by Lota. And, basically a solitary, Bishop was genuinely alarmed by Lota's host of extrovert Brazilian friends. A drunken spell ended in hospital. Lota took charge of the situation and Bishop was prescribed Antabuse to counter the attractions of alcohol. The combination of the two can cause vomiting, stomach cramps and violent headaches. These effects can be sufficient to stop anyone from drinking while taking the drug – but one of the problems is that it so closely mimics a bad hangover that the drinker prefers to take alcohol after all.

Inevitably, for a woman of Bishop's sensitivity and intellectual curiosity, the charms of surroundings that had appeared exotic and exciting began to wear thin. She was awarded a Pulitzer Prize for *A Cold Spring* in 1956, and valuable fellowships in the next few years. The writing of poems was difficult – what she was writing above all was a great number of letters to friends, particularly to Robert Lowell, of whom she wrote: 'As you must know I love him, next best to Lota, I suppose.'

She complained that 'I can't write at all anymore'. She began a new affair with another woman and moved out from Lota's house. To add to Bishop's already heavy chain of grief and guilt, Lota committed suicide in 1967 after a final meeting in New York.

In 1965 her third collection of poems, *Questions of Travel*, was published, and the praise it received once more encouraged her to write. It was significant that the book was divided into two sections: 'Brazil' and 'Elsewhere'. For most of her life she lived in both a series of actual physical locations in which she took delight and which inspired her poetry, and a constant spiritually dark and emotional 'elsewhere' that inspired little except despair.

That interior world grew darker as she aged. The next dozen or so years saw the suicides of several renowned poets, including Anne Sexton, John Berryman, and Randall Jarrell, and the sudden death of Robert Lowell in 1977. Jarrell and particularly Lowell had been good friends. Sexton she had disliked; she regarded her as one of the confessional poets with whom she was not in sympathy. As she famously remarked, 'Sometimes I wish they'd keep it all to themselves.' She had even taken Lowell to task for including extracts of letters written by his estranged wife, Elisabeth Hardwick, in his book *The Dolphin*. She wrote to him: 'Lizzie is not dead . . . One can use one's life as material – one does, anyway – but these letters – aren't you violating a trust? IF you were given permission – IF you hadn't changed them . . . etc. But *art just isn't worth that much.*'

She was of course aware that such a view was even then out of fashion. Now that the works of poets such as Dylan Thomas and Philip Larkin, originally published as a few very slim volumes, have been blown up by the inclusion of rejected, unfinished, fragmentary, unpublishable work, of inchoate drafts and dimly lit first thoughts, and printed in a rich brocade of notes in enormous tomes as thick as those of Browning and Tennyson, there is little space for any one like Elizabeth Bishop to hide. With our regard for the artist over the art, and the view of craft as 'elitist', it's not difficult to envisage a near and dreadful future when all the unsatisfactory odds and sods that poets rightly rejected are preferred to the free-standing works of art they laboured to perfect.

IX

Bishop kept the darkest parts of her life, her melancholy and terror, to herself. She drank herself into hospital several times in her late fifties and her sixties, but in public to most people she was a quiet, witty, charming, distinguished writer. Although she continued to live in Brazil for part of the year, she undertook a series of teaching appointments, first at the University of Seattle, Washington, then at Harvard from 1970 until 1975. She was not popular with either students or academics. Apart from honourable exceptions, such as the poet Dana Gioia, who found her teaching revelatory, the faculty members regarded her as something of an embarrassment, old-fashioned and not caring less about current teaching methods, or the unsubtle arts of deconstructionism, structuralism, or any other ism. What Bishop tried to teach was how a poem is put together, not how it is taken apart. The simple reason why she put up with years of teaching was because she needed the money, and you can earn a lot more from teaching poetry than writing it.

When her fourth and final book of poetry, *Geography III*, was published it was dedicated to Alice Methfessel, a much younger woman she had met at Harvard, who became her friend and lover and with whom she found great happiness. After Bishop's death in 1979, she became executor of the poet's estate.

As was said at the start of this chapter, there is a difficulty in writing about the private life of Elizabeth Bishop. Bishop's alcoholism was only mentioned in letters that remained unavailable for a long time after her death or in posthumous gossip gleaned by biographers from her friends. This makes her a different case from the rest of the writers in this book; they used, more or less, the drinking in their life in their work. Bishop was scrupulous in not doing so. When she drank self-destructively it was for reasons we can only guess at. Even in her darkest periods, when she seemed bent on drinking herself to death, she wrote hardly anything at all about the hell in which she was living.

Above all, her finest work is about what she saw and what she thought about it. Unlike some other poets, she did not adopt a persona and then create work to suit the public's expectation of that image. Her work represents only those parts of her own life that she could bear to show to others, or even more modestly, the parts that she thought could be of the slightest interest to others.

As Michael Hofmann has written: 'We have rather forgotten we don't make characters or poets like her any more, who flourish in absence and shade.'

Chapter 7

'The singing of the bottles in the pantry'

John Cheever (1912–1982)

I

JOHN CHEEVER kept a close record of his drinking. In the twenty-nine loose-leaf folders containing the typewritten pages of the journals that record his daily routines, ideas for stories, dreams, reading, sexual activities and church-going, there are many passages dealing with alcohol and the circumstances in which it was taken and the effects it had. He considered, like many other writers, that it had a direct relation to his creative force. In 1968, at the age of fifty-six, he wrote:

> I must convince myself that writing is not, for a man of my disposition, a self-destructive vocation . . . It has given me money and renown, but I suspect that it may have something to do with my drinking habits. The excitement of alcohol and the excitement of fantasy are very similar.

II

Drink played an essential part in his life from its beginning. His mother, Mary, confessed to him that, 'If I hadn't drunk two martinis one afternoon you never would have been conceived.' His father, already forty-nine years old, wanted this unwelcome child to be aborted, but his second son was born on the twenty-seventh of May 1912, in Quincy, Massachusetts.

John Cheever was a man highly conscious of his New England roots and most of his work deals, on the surface at least, with the middle-class suburban society into which he was born and in which he lived most of his life. He liked to say that his father, Frederick Lincoln Cheever, was the owner of a shoe factory, and that his paternal line stretched back to Ezekiel Cheever, a famous scholar who had sailed to America in 1637. It was certainly true that Cheever was descended from early settlers, but Ezekiel was a very distant cousin, and his own father was a shoe salesman not a manufacturer. More disturbingly, drink was a hereditary trait: the cause of death of Cheever's paternal grandfather was recorded as 'alcohol and opium – del. tremens'.

Cheever may have inflated the importance of his parents and his ancestors in a harmless form of snobbery, but he was well aware of the truth and wrote about it unflinchingly in his journals:

> I have turned my eccentric old mother into a woman of wealth and position, and made my father a captain at sea. I have improvised a background for myself – genteel, traditional – and it is generally accepted. But what are the bare facts, if I were to write them? The yellow house, the small north living room with a player piano and, on a card table, a small stage where I made scenery and manipulated puppets . . .
>
> Most of my characters are waited on by maids, but I was usually the one who brought dishes to the table. My parents were not happy, and I was not happy with them.

His brother Fred was seven years older, so that Cheever was left fairly much to his own devices in childhood. An attack of tuberculosis confined him to the house for much of the time and he developed a love of reading and inventing plays for his puppet theatre. At school he would be allowed to entertain the other children by telling them stories after their lessons.

Cheever had little interest in schooling. Many writers have had indifferent school careers and a fairly dismal home life; perhaps imagination, like the mushroom, needs a dark, neglected area to grow in. The figures of his father and mother loom large in his work and the marital rows and alcoholism that Cheever witnessed in his childhood were repeated in his own later life and reappeared in a story, 'The Jewels of the Cabots', written when he was well over sixty years old. The story rehearses the atmosphere of his childhood, the parental bickering, and the sense of loss and degradation. The choice of the name, the Cabots, is a potent one. As John Collins Bossidy's toast goes:

> And this is good old Boston,
> The home of the bean and the cod.
> Where the Lowells talk only to Cabots
> And the Cabots talk only to God.

The point of Cheever's story is that his Cabots are the wrong Cabots, 'as there are the wrong Lowells, the wrong Hallowells, the wrong Eliots, Cheevers . . . ' That is, those families insufficiently well connected to their ancestral houses; distant cousins busy failing while the great families endure in riches and position. The *right* families sent their children to the best schools and then on to Princeton or Harvard. In the wrong Cheever family things were going badly.

In 1926 his father lost his job at the age of sixty and never worked again. To make ends meet his mother opened a gift shop. The latent snob in Cheever hated what he saw as a further lowering of the family's social status. He retreated into himself and his already undistinguished school record worsened. He must be one of the few major twentieth century American writers who did not graduate from high school – in 1930 he was expelled, 'for smoking' he said, though it seems a thin excuse. Whatever the reason for leaving, what seemed a disaster at the time was the making of him. He immediately wrote a story, entitled 'The Expelled', about the experience and sold it to *The New Republic*. He was to be a writer from now on, although it was some time before this early acceptance was followed by any further success. For the next few years he took odd jobs, living at home, then rooming with his brother in Boston. In 1934 he moved to New York, encouraged by the poet E.E. Cummings. His short stories were appearing in little magazines and through the influence of the critic Malcolm Cowley, who remained a life-long friend, he was able to stay at Yaddo, the writers' and artists' colony at Saratoga Springs. He was already drinking heavily: a friend who met him at Yaddo told of 'the gin bottles stored outside his door for the maids to dispose of'.

III

Cheever drank heavily from his late teens and continued to do so for nearly fifty more years. The question, as always, is why was Cheever drinking so much so young? Not just socially, but privately, and, presumably, while writing. The attempt to concoct theoretical psychological explanations for the behaviour of others, even of one who exposed so much of himself as Cheever did, is likely to be both impertinent and inaccurate. But it is clear that Cheever was all of his life a haunted man, troubled by feelings of duality and bisexuality. Troubling memories of family, particularly of his father and brother, surface again and again in his fiction and his journals. Indeed, talk of the abortion his father had wanted plays a crucial role in Cheever's last novel, *Falconer*, published in 1975. His brother Fred – who was also an alcoholic – looms even larger in life and work. In 1978, after Fred had died, Cheever wrote:

I have experienced the force of the past in my own life; the profound love of my brother. That I would turn away from this and take lovers and delight in them and marry and raise splendid children would, it seems, in no way diminish the fact that my own true love was my brother.

Stephen Donaldson in his biography of Cheever speculates as to whether there was a physical sexual relation between the brothers, particularly when they roomed together as young men in Boston. It may be so – such relationships between an older and a younger brother are far more common than most people will admit. It takes very little to tilt a life one way or the other and what seems for one partner in a sexual act to have been of enormous and traumatic importance may have been regarded as trivial and quickly forgotten by the other. But the result of such confusing relationships in the younger participant is sometimes followed by an early reliance on alcohol or drugs, and difficulty in later sexual relationships.

IV

Cheever in the 1930s in New York was a handsome, charming young man who wrote, who openly had affairs with women, and, secretively, casual sexual relations with men. He existed on $10 a week that his brother Fred sent him, and on reviewing and writing synopses of popular novels for MGM. In a letter in 1938 he listed his modest ambitions as 'a house, a wife, a bottle of whiskey and a chance to work'. He had sold his first stories to *The New Yorker* in 1935 and was to sell more than a hundred stories to that magazine in the next forty years. It may have been a struggle but as he wrote later, in those days 'there were at least fifteen magazines extremely anxious to find serious fiction'. Some, particularly the *Saturday Evening Post,* paid extremely well, most paid on acceptance, and *The New Yorker* gave him their top fiction rate. He was just able to get by financially. He had work and drink, and in 1939 he met Mary Winternitz, the beautiful and bright daughter of a rich and ferociously intellectual New England family. She became his wife in 1941. In a letter written soon after their marriage, he said that 'we've slipped out of the heavy drinking set'. America was now at war and in May 1942, Cheever was drafted into the army. He underwent thirteen weeks' basic training and wrote to Mary, 'for the first time in what must be nearly fifteen years there is nothing but a little 3.2 beer coursing through these old veins'.

His first book of stories, *The Way Some People Live*, was published in 1943, and for his writing skills he was transferred to the Signal Corps to work on military leaflets and short films. He was lucky: of the infantry regiment he left behind, more than half were killed or wounded at Utah Beach on D-Day. In the latter part of his service Cheever was allowed to live and work at home in New York and in the literary world of the city he was a minor but well known and popular figure: 'the brightest person in the room until ten o'clock, when he fell over drunk'.

Many of the stories in his first book were little more than sketches that had appeared in *The New Yorker* and some reviewers pointed out what they saw as the limitations of *The New Yorker* style: urbanity, wit, and a fundamentally middle-brow approach to relatively safe subject matter. It was how most critics continued to see Cheever and the fact that his work appeared throughout his life in that magazine did him no favours with the critical establishment. They ignored the obvious development in his work from the end of the war, when it took on a much darker and subversive view of his subject matter – the men and women of uptown New York and its wealthy and conservative suburbs. Cheever was irked at the thought of being seen as a limited writer of short stories for a particular middle-class audience. He decided he must try his hand at a novel.

The problem of the short story versus the novel is one that has been largely created by publishers. They rarely regard the short story as the discrete art form it is, but merely as a series of warm-up exercises for 'the novel'. A short collection by a young writer is often published only as a sort of promissory note against the larger work that is expected to follow. In America in particular, it was – and is – a male size problem. But 'mine is bigger than yours' applied to the latest brick-thick novel can lead to diminishing artistic returns. The more commercial a novel is, the more likely it will be read; the more 'literary', the more likely it will be simply a huge, swirling black hole into which no one advances very far, except for some intrepid academic who is never seen again. Has anyone ever actually read all, or even much, of *Letters* by John Barth, for instance? Well, whatever the reason, from ambition, or the need to obtain a large advance, Cheever pressed on with his novel.

In 1951, the Cheever family moved out to the suburbs at Scarborough, near Westchester, the archetypal suburb to and from which the New Yorker commuted. From the seemingly unpromising material of suburbia Cheever was to make his greatest work.

V

From Cheever's viewpoint, in his new, suburban house, the situation did not look good. He was a professional writer, but was nearly forty. In twenty years he had published over one hundred short stories but just one book, which he disowned as immature work. He had failed to write a novel after several attempts and was dissatisfied with what he called his 'confined talents' in comparison with novel-writing contemporaries such as Norman Mailer and Saul Bellow. His income was low, almost entirely dependent on how many stories he could write for *The New Yorker*, and he was drinking steadily.

His letters to friends at this time are charming, funny, and beautifully written. They are concerned with his growing children, dogs, the sale of stories, the keenly perceived beauty of the countryside – but a darker note is struck in a letter of 1952 to his editor at *The New Yorker*, William Maxwell, where a passage on 'the subtlety of the landscape' suddenly lurches into 'the pitiful ruins of the town of Cheever' and 'the view from the terrace, which is mostly the country of chagrin'. The whole letter is mordantly witty and composed but the note of sadness registered turns to despair in the journals Cheever was keeping at the time.

The Journals of John Cheever, as edited for publication by Robert Gottlieb, begin in 1948, and continue until Cheever's final illness in 1982. They must count, with the great collected *Stories* of 1978, as the most abiding of Cheever's writings. They are the record also of 'the instability that conquers me'. There are passages of great beauty showing his love for his wife and children, details of his many affairs with men and women, vivid descriptions of scenery and people encountered, snatches of overheard conversation in buses or bars, dreams, the surreality of the everyday in 'a window full of crucifixes made out of plastic', self-pity and an old-fashioned stoicism and courage. Writing about himself in the first person, he will suddenly continue in the third person as if describing the protagonist in a story, or transforming his life into story. Above all, dominating his everyday existence is the narrative of the chronic alcoholism that at first fired him up physically and perhaps inspired his work and then progressed until it came close to destroying him mentally and physically.

Perhaps to Cheever's relief, their Scarborough neighbours were neither writers nor artists, and there was a lively social life including the Cheevers. Given that most of the men were business or professional commuters and the women busy mothers and housewives, the fun was mostly confined to the weekend. The drinking began at noon on Saturday and continued through meals and conversation, tennis and swimming, until Sunday evening. But if his friends drank as a form of relaxation at the weekend, for Cheever it had become an everyday and, sometimes, an all-day occupation.

The place suited Cheever; the countryside was near and the suburb and its inhabitants inspired a flow of stories. To criticise a writer's

choice of subject matter is obtuse; it is a matter of how he or she deals
with it. Cheever took what was at hand: his work and private journals
reveal himself as a spy reporting on a foreign country; he lives secretly
in his own mind as rootless and ruthless among his settled and
respectable neighbours, as a secret bisexual in a world of seemingly
avowed heterosexuals, and as an anguished alcoholic among happy
social drinkers. The job of writing, he said, was to 'mythologize the
commonplace'. You aren't able to see the mythological terrors and
beauties behind seemingly mundane existence unless you have
experienced them at first hand:

> . . . I think of the violence of the past: an ugly house and exacerbating
> loneliness. How far I have come, I think, but I do not seem to have
> come far at all. I am haunted by some morbid conception of beauty
> cum death for which I am prepared to destroy myself.

His second book, *The Enormous Radio and Other Stories*, published
in 1953, met with mixed reviews, but contained some marvellous
stories. He was producing stories at a great rate now. He seems to
have been able to produce a story in almost perfect form in first draft
within a few days. This may have been deceptive; Cheever was never
one to keep drafts. In general he disliked keeping anything about
him, letters and any other pieces of paper that he judged not to be
immediately necessary were consigned to the furnace. Drinking
could still be a spur, as he said in a letter in 1953, '. . . on Wednesday
I stayed up late, drank a pint of bourbon and worked like a streak on
Thursday'. It was also a reward, and a source of amusement; on a visit
to Yaddo, he reports in a letter that at about five in the afternoon,
after working for a few hours and then skiing, he retires 'to my room,
hide in my closet, pour whisky into a tooth-brush glass and toss it off,
knocking my head against the coat-hangers, I do this several times
and go to the dinner table fairly tipsy'. There are many references
from now on in his journal to drinking. To go out hiking with a

friend necessitated the taking along of a pint of bourbon. A Thermos of iced gin accompanied a trip to the beach with his family. His way of editing his first published novel, *The Wapshot Chronicle*, for publication was to drink 'a good deal of whiskey, trying to relax'. And, ominously, drinking had slipped back from the late afternoon, through a self-imposed barrier of noon, and into the morning: 'Took a slug of whiskey at eleven. Two straightforward martinis at noon.'

With the relentless increase in drinking came the inevitable waking 'in despair at 3 am' and self-disgust; he was 'a small and dirty fraud, a deserved outcast, a spiritual and sexual impostor'.

Whatever he thought of himself, *The Wapshot Chronicle* was published to great acclaim in 1957. It won the National Book Award the following year and Cheever was well on his way to becoming, at forty-six, an established and well-known writer. Most reviews were highly favourable, though again some left-wing critics were angry at the studiedly apolitical Cheever for taking the middle-class suburb as his setting: one of these armchair revolutionaries accused him of being 'a toothless Thurber'.

To celebrate the success of his novel, Cheever took Mary and the children off to Italy for ten months. He didn't do much work there, but the long break restored his spirits and confidence. Despite writing that 'the sea is a deep purple and gin is a wonderful curative', he seems to have drunk less in Italy than had become normal for him. But the return to Scarborough and to work plunged him almost immediately into the old sense of despair. He was now working on his second novel, *The Wapshot Scandal*, and it was not going well. 'I am a solitary drunk,' he wrote in his journal. ' . . . I don't really get to work until late afternoon. At four . . . I stir up a Martini . . . After half a glass of gin I decide I must get a divorce . . . The gin flows freely until supper . . . after supper the whiskey.'

Mary, now with a new young child, their third, Federico, born on the Italian trip, was in no mood for conversation with her sozzled husband; she showed her disapproval by silence and removing herself from the room or sleeping apart. Yet a few days after writing about their fractured marriage Cheever could write that 'I am most deeply and continuously involved in the love of my wife and children'. Indeed, he was, when not so drunk that they wished for nothing but to avoid him. Life continued: Cheever worked, they entertained their friends, and every Sunday they went to church. This was not a complaisant and conventional surrender on Cheever's part to the suburban conservatism of the late 1950s. Whatever his exact religious beliefs, a sense of unattained and perhaps unattainable spiritual grace is present in his works. It is what animates and keeps hope alive in the most hopeless of his creations.

Outwardly, he was still a handsome, attractive, amusing neighbour; a writer with nothing of the bohemian about him. His neat hair was cut once a week, he dressed in conventional clothes, had impeccable manners, and spoke with a patrician New England accent. He had a beautiful wife, three charming children, and a beloved dog. In 1961 they moved to a larger house in Ossining, a village of Westchester County, thirty miles north of New York. To the outsider, his life must have seemed blessed.

VI

By the early 1960s a new series of words begin to appear in the journals whenever Cheever is talking about his drinking: 'battle', 'struggle', 'a four round booze fight'. He acknowledges that he is drinking too much, but admits he has no wish to stop. Yet the late 1950s and early 1960s were the years of his busiest productivity and his greatest work, including that superbly haunting odyssey of lost youth and embittered middle-age, 'The Swimmer', and his second novel, *The Wapshot Scandal*, a dark book all too redolent of the hangovers that must have accompanied its composition. He quarrelled with *The New Yorker* over money, although he had other disputes over editing policies. William Maxwell wrote in a letter to Sylvia

Townsend Warner that the magazine had had to cut 'this beautiful sentence' from a Cheever story: 'With love in his heart and lust in his trousers, he moved across the lawn.'

And there was plenty of lust in Cheever's life at this time. His wife, Mary, may have shut him out of the marital bed and the drink was causing occasional spells of impotence, but he had several casual sexual encounters with men and when Hollywood expressed interest in the Wapshot books he began the first stages of a long-lasting affair with the actress Hope Lange. The mere thought of being labelled as a homosexual disgusted and terrified him. There is a description in the journals of seeing two obvious 'queers' in a city street that is shot through with disapproval and loathing, and to a Russian woman friend he wrote that 'I would like to live in a world in which there are no homosexuals'.

Over these years he consulted psychiatrists about his problems with alcohol and sex: 'I drink Scotch at ten, two martinis before lunch, and go off to the shrink.' The shrinks did not help much. He did not let them. What he wanted to do was hold forth to them in a witty and charming manner about a few little local difficulties. As we have seen with Charles Jackson and Malcolm Lowry, Cheever did not need anyone to tell him what was wrong with him.

Attempts to stop drinking were extremely short lived. One anguished journal entry reads: 'Fend, fend, fend off the gin with the *New York Times Magazine* section. My resolve collapses at eleven.' Shaking with drink and cold he kneels in church and wishes for happiness for his children. In her memoir, *Home Before Dark,* Susan Cheever writes of her father at this period:

> . . . my parents would have dinner together at the long table . . . as they always had, but they would rarely get through the meal without a fight. She would leave the table in tears, or he would get up in a cold, self-righteous rage.
>
> His drinking had begun to have remarkable physical effects.

His speech was slurred and his step was unsteady. Often after he left the table we would hear him stamp and stumble up the stairs and then there would be a series of crashes and thuds as he tried to get down the narrow hall and up the two steps into the bedroom.

Feeling lonely and beleaguered by the demons in his life, Cheever was finding it increasingly hard to write and filled the day with drink or displacement activities such as wood-chopping or long walks; anything to try to evade the image of the bourbon or gin bottle waiting for him in the pantry.

His third novel, *Bullet Park*, was published in 1969. The reviews were mostly polite, although in a bad echo of the reception of his very first book, the *New York Times* called it 'a collection of sketches'. Other critics pointed to a growing coarseness and use of violence in his work, as if he were responding to accusations of gentility by trying to rough up his work. In two interviews given that year, Cheever sounds alternately defensive and aggressive. To Leslie Aldridge of *New York* magazine, he said, 'I chain smoke, I chain drink. I chain everything else . . . I love to drink.' In a long interview in *The Paris Review*, published in 1976 but conducted earlier, he sounded drunk. When the interviewer, Annette Grant, asked him about the 'psychological shock' of finishing a novel, he responded with, 'To diminish shock I throw high dice, get sauced, go to Egypt, screw.' This is reminiscent not so much of the highly sensitive writer John Cheever as the footballer George Best with his 'I screw. I like to screw' in a famous televised drunken interview with Michael Parkinson. Cheever went one better than Best, concluding his interview by stepping out of his clothes and jumping naked into a pond. But he did talk some sense in between, nailing the concept of characters as somehow taking on 'identities of their own' and running out of control as 'contemptible' and as implying 'that the writer is a fool with no knowledge or mastery of his craft. This is absurd.'

In his own exercise of his craft, his working day had shrunk to little more than the time between breakfast and the first drink at ten in the morning. He described himself:

> I am sitting naked in the yellow chair in the dining room. In my hand there is a large crystal glass filled to the brim with honey-coloured whiskey.

Perhaps to try and put some order into his life, Cheever began to teach a creative writing course at Sing Sing Prison, situated near the river front at Ossining. Given Cheever's growing preoccupation with the corruption and violence that was hidden, but not far, below the surface of the society he saw about him, it must have seemed horribly apt for this place holding murderers and other outcasts to be set beside his respectable suburban village.

Cheever enjoyed the writing course; a bunch of prisoners were 'about as straight-looking a group of men as I've ever seen', although he supposed they must have been murderers or drug-pushers.

The drinking continued. He admitted to his journal that it had become a constant obsession and that he could think of 'nothing but the taste of whiskey'. His hands shook so much in the mornings that a drink was the only thing that would still them. In a letter to a friend met on a Russian trip that he had enjoyed, he made the first frank admission of bisexuality to appear in the letters, saying that he was 'tired of drinking scotch for breakfast . . . tired of making love in motels to men and women I'll never see again.' His friends thought that he was almost deliberately setting out to drink himself to death. He was given vitamin B12 injections, which made him feel better for a while. He visited his local chapter of Alcoholics Anonymous. He managed to stay off the booze for some mornings, but soon he was back to 'vodka for breakfast'.

The inevitable crash to which all this was leading came in the spring of 1973. He had been treated for an irregular heartbeat and

collapsed with what he later called a heart attack. As Stephen
Donaldson points out this was not strictly medically true; what felled
Cheever was 'a pulmonary edema brought on by drink'. Whatever
the actual condition, he was in hospital and unable to drink. A
drinker can, as he had, go for forty years drinking heavily every day,
but then, deprived of alcohol for a period of only 24 or 48 hours, the
whole physical and mental edifice can crumble terrifyingly quickly.

As his daughter Susan Cheever wrote in her memoir of her father,
Home Before Dark, 'on the third day he began to hallucinate'. He
imagined that he was in a Russian prison camp and struggled to get
free of the electrodes and drips attached to him. 'We took turns
holding him down.'

For a while after this awful experience he was a chastened man.
He knew that he had escaped death. His son Ben thought that he
had stopped drinking, but the other children, Susan and Fred,
noticed that he was back on a couple of drinks a day, claiming that
this was what his doctor allowed. Then the bottles of whisky once
again began to appear and be rapidly emptied.

In the autumn of 1973 he went to Iowa to teach for a semester on
the university's famous creative writing course and found himself
teamed up with Raymond Carver, at that time also a huge drinker.
The revived, collegiate drinking gave Cheever a new energy. He
claimed to have had affairs with a number of women, and he certainly
had a longer lasting affair with a male student. He must have felt that
the drink might well kill him at any moment and so to hell with it;
he was a drinker, and would go out a drinker. He returned home to
work on his new novel, *Falconer,* based in part on his experiences at
Sing Sing. Having to work brought more attempts to give up drink;
they all failed within days. In his notes to the *Letters,* his son Ben
gives a picture of his drunken father at a Thanksgiving dinner:

. . . why does the man at the table have an open wound on his
forehead? Why is his face swollen? He's trying to eat a forkful of

peas. His hand is shaking so violently that the peas fall off the fork
before he gets it to his mouth.

The answers to the questions are plainly given in his daughter Susan's
memoir. His forehead is gashed by one of the many falls he has taken
as he barges drunkenly about the house. His face is swollen because
of the effect of alcohol on the blood vessels beneath the skin and the
layers of fat deposited by unused calories. His hands are shaking
because of the damage to his nervous system that forty years of
drinking spirits in large quantities has caused.

His marriage was now completely dead – or so he thought. Mary
had announced that she wanted a divorce. He took another teaching
job, this time at Boston. He went there at the age of sixty-two and
embarked on the final course of turning a highly civilised writer into
a drunken bum sitting on a park bench.

Paradoxically, among the motives that cause the drinker to reject
abstinence is fear. Fear of giving up and standing naked in one's
personality can be even stronger than the fear of illness and death. In
a letter at this time he wrote, 'Death is – like drink – sometimes an
irresistible temptation.' He was lonely, always at least half-drunk,
living as he said to a student, on 'oranges and hamburgers'. His
apartment and his clothes were filthy, he was incontinent; it was a
very low ebb. Now his brother Fred stepped in. Fred was at this time
temporarily sober and concerned enough about John to book him
into a clinic.

Withdrawal from alcohol brought on another attack of delirium
tremens; when he was well enough he entered the Smithers Alcoholism
Center in New York. He stayed for twenty-eight days, treated on the
Center's standard de-toxification course. He did not care for the group
therapy in which he was required to admit his addiction and the reasons for it. His letters from what he called the 'dry-out mansion' are
weary sounding, sarcastic and a little resentful, but clear-headed.
He was discharged in May 1975 and never took another drink.

VII

'I was sprung from the alcoholic-rehabilitation clinic yesterday,' he wrote in his journal. 'To go from continuous drunkenness to total sobriety is a violent wrench . . . I seem this morning to have lost twenty pounds and perhaps twenty-five years.' The immediate feeling of euphoria and the returning keenness of his responses to the outside world lasted for some weeks. He felt, and was literally, a different man. His daughter Susan wrote that:

It wasn't just that he didn't drink anymore. The difference in the way he talked and acted was so dramatic that the most astonishing thing for me was the realization of how much he must have changed during the fifteen years his drinking affected him . . . It was like having my old father back, a man whose humour and tenderness I dimly remembered from my childhood.

Susan Cheever inadvertently exposes the confusion in the disease theory of alcoholism when she says 'I know now that alcoholism is a disease, not a failure of will'. There is no doubt that it is an addiction and that it is almost impossible for alcoholics to give up and then to try to drink in moderate amounts without rapidly accelerating their intake, but there is always an element of will in addiction, the willingness to continue, rather than to stop. And a colossal exercise of will is precisely what enabled her father to stop drinking completely.

He went back to work on his novel *Falconer*, itself 'a violent wrench' from his earlier writing. It proceeded well. After an earlier dismissal of Alcoholics Anonymous as a 'bunch of Christers', he attended their meetings regularly. He had always been a great social drinker, but an even greater solitary one, and AA gave his life a new social dimension. He felt younger, looked younger, and his once powerful sexual drive returned. The removal of drink now released what it had perhaps been taken to repress – his bisexuality. As for his enduring marriage, he wrote in his journal, 'I have no wife', meaning presumably that they had slept apart for many years. The love and sexual gratification to be had from men was now his prime desire. 'Lunching with friends who talked about their tedious careers in lechery, I thought: I am gay, I am gay. I am at last free of all this.' Typically, he added that this feeling 'did not last for long'. He had imagined living with a man, but 'how one would long for a woman, even a shrew'. He had regained his love of the outdoors and it was while skiing that he met the man who was to become his lover until his death.

He was sixty-five years old in 1977 when *Falconer* was published. It had been begun in the depths of alcoholic despair and completed after Cheever had become sober and rejuvenated. The book at the time appeared as a major departure in Cheever's work but now, looking back with our knowledge of the author's life, we can see how apt a conclusion to his work it was. Apart from flashbacks, the action of the novel takes place entirely inside the prison that bears the name Falconer. Ezekiel Farragut is doing life for the murder of his brother. He is a middle-class college professor, unhappily married to a promiscuous wife. He is also a heroin addict, surviving on methadone in prison. He witnesses horrific violence and enjoys male erotic tenderness. He suffers periods of madness and is pacified by hard-earned calm. Sometimes it reads like a highly personal nightmare of Cheever's; drug addiction is substituted for alcoholism, but images of enclosure and imprisonment by family and social constraints had always been present in his work, and the figure of the murdered brother had been present in earlier stories. Farragut finds release from his drug addiction and physically escapes from the prison at the end of the novel by hiding in the body bag of another convict (as did Edmond Dantès in *The Count of Monte Cristo*). But the immense fortune that this particular hero, Farragut, gains is simply to be able to walk freely in the world again; the final words of the novel are: 'Rejoice, he thought, rejoice.'

In the following year the monumental *The Stories of John Cheever* was published and he was at last seen as what he had been for many

156

years, one of the finest American writers of the second half of the twentieth century.

During the final years of his life his marriage flowered into close affection again. He missed drinking, but remained sober. Only one new book came, the novella *Oh, What a Paradise It Seems*. He was fit until the last two years of his life when he suffered from cancer of the kidney, and he met the pain and terror of illness with great courage. He died in 1982.

John Cheever was a mass of contradictions: he was a suburbanite who could have been mistaken for a banker or lawyer, and a wildly imaginative and poetic writer; he was a coarse and aggressive drunk, and a charming, gentle and humorous father and husband; he had a horror of effeminacy and 'queers', and was an active lover of men for most of his life. A passage in his journals from 1978 summed up his life thus:

When I was a young man, I woke one morning in the unclean bedsheets of squalid furnished rooms, poor and hungry and alone, and thought that some morning I would wake in my own house, holding in my arms a fragrant bride and hearing from the broad lawn beyond my window the voices of my beloved children. And so I did ... And so I wake this morning. I hear again the roar of the brook. I sleep alone these days, having been exiled from my own bed, closet and washbasin by a troubled wife ... But my children are comely and loving and self-possessed and walking over those parts of the world that interest them; and my daughter once kissed me and said, 'You can't win them all, Daddy.' And so I can't.

Chapter 8

'A pint of plain is your only man'

Flann O'Brien (1911–1966)

I

HE SITS on a stool at the bar of McDaid's pub, a cigarette between the first two yellowed fingers of his right hand, both hands cradling a glass of Irish whiskey. He is wearing a dark overcoat that reaches almost to the floor and a black wide-brimmed hat. The only other drinker in the bar stands perhaps a foot apart from him, a tall, bespectacled man who leans forward at a slight angle like a heron. Neither man speaks. They have known each other for years. They might be called friends but for the fact that they are quite frequently, in public and private, scornful of each other. The man standing is Patrick Kavanagh, poet; the man on the stool is Brian O'Nolan, civil servant, novelist, and regular satirical columnist for the *Irish Times*. They are drinking the afternoon away.

II

This is a sample picture of many days, indeed most days, in the adult life of O'Nolan. The pubs and the companions may have varied: the 'Plain Men' of Ireland in the Scotch House, the journalists and poets in the Palace Bar and the Pearl; the racing and rugby crowd at the Dolphin, the writers in McDaid's, but in all of them he was known as 'Myles', from the name with which he signed his column in the *Irish Times*, Myles na Gopaleen. He had also been known, at various times and places, as Flann O'Brien, Lir O'Connor, John James Doe, George Knowall, Brother Barnabus, The O'Blather, and even, it was rumoured, Stephen Blakesley, author of several in a long running series of pulp paperbacks featuring the detective Sexton Blake.

The original of them all, Brian O'Nolan was born on the fifth of October 1911 in the town of Strabane, Co. Tyrone, in what was to become Northern Ireland. The family was relatively prosperous, middle-class, Catholic and nationalist – the father allowed only Irish to be spoken in the home. The mother was greatly loved by her children and one of the few signs of outward emotion that O'Nolan ever showed was in his distress at her death in 1956. His father was an aloof and distant figure, often absent from home on his business as a customs officer collecting revenues from whiskey distilleries. In view of the nature of his work it was fortunate that he was a strict teetotaller.

As there was no suitable Roman Catholic school nearby, the children were educated at home. That is, they were taught to read, write and to exercise their imaginations by making up plays for a toy theatre, learning musical instruments (in O'Nolan's case, the violin), drawing and generally having an amiably relaxed childhood under the care of their mother. English was picked up by reading comics and from other children. Their father attempted a rather more formal sort of education, even sending letters of instruction when he was away. The results were of little practical value, but they may have suggested the ludicrous correspondence course in tightrope walking described in *The Hard Life* many years later.

This all came to a bitter and abrupt end when the family moved to Dublin. O'Nolan was sent to the local school run by the Christian Brothers. This religious order of men sworn to poverty and celibacy has had a poor press from those who passed through its ungentle hands. It appears to have recruited men on the basis of the ability to display brute force and ignorance rather than intelligence and a sound knowledge of modern pedagogy. Poorly trained, the Brothers relied on physical intimidation in the classroom, liberal beatings for the most innocuous offences, and the imposition of a huge amount of homework to cram their pupils with a curriculum probably few of the Brothers fully understood themselves. They taught by rote and any pupil foolish enough to show the slightest deviation from what was in the textbook was in for a hiding. Brutality by the staff and bullying by other pupils came as a considerable and lasting shock to O'Nolan, but he absorbed his Latin and English: a great part of the exactitude of his later style and his fondness for parodying pedantic language must have come from his schooldays.

Four miserable and resented years were spent at the mercy of the Christian Brothers and it was not until the family moved out to a large house in Avoca Terrace in the suburb of Blackrock that O'Nolan experienced a more enlightened form of education. Blackrock College was run by the order of Holy Ghost Fathers and modelled on the English public school system. There was an emphasis on literature and the other humanities, although still a strong religious element to the teaching. All of O'Nolan's secondary education to the age of eighteen was conducted by strict, sometimes rabidly so, Catholic teachers. The surprising thing is that he never rebelled against these years of religious indoctrination but remained all his life a practising and believing Catholic. He flourished in the new school and in 1929, at the age of eighteen, passed his examinations with ease and entered University College Dublin to study English and German.

III

A photograph taken at the time shows a good-looking young man, with a slightly pugnacious expression, piercing eyes, and a fine head of black hair. It was not to be too many years before drink began to dismantle his features: in most later pictures a flabby-faced and balding O'Nolan looks as if he is suffering from a vicious hangover.

He soon became a well-known figure in the college. Joining the debating club he established himself as a fierce and witty speaker. The debates were very well attended, but the chamber could only hold about two hundred and the overflow of students milled about in the lobby outside. This body of students was, O'Nolan wrote, 'known as the mob, and I had the honour to be acknowledged as its president'. O'Nolan's preferred position was in the doorway between chamber and lobby, from where he could direct his wit at the 'official' speakers, while entertaining the 'mob' outside.

This position, half-in and half-out, could describe O'Nolan's future lack of any consistent political or moral position. All of his life he ridiculed the intellectual and self-appointed 'intellectuals'; the 'literary' and 'artistic' were castigated for taking their concerns too seriously. He had had little education in the sciences and he seems to have regarded them as foolish nonsense to be parodied in his work by the careful and lengthy setting out of the insane theories of his mad scientist and philosopher, de Selby. It seemed that all overly 'intellectual' activity was to be viewed as fundamentally pretentious and undeserving of applause. As Kingsley Amis did later, O'Nolan saw no reason why he should join in what he regarded as the conspiracy of modernists to elevate the irrational above normal and reasonable behaviour and its exact and realistic description. That his work has been championed by post-modernist critics would have probably drawn forth a few well-chosen and obscene epithets.

Social life centred around the male life of the pub and amusement was provided by the company of a few like-minded friends, whose conversation, facetious and sardonic, is well represented in his first novel, *At Swim-Two-Birds*. His best friend of the time, Niall Sheridan, is transparently disguised as 'Brinsley' in the book, and although the student-narrator and Brinsley go off on periodic nocturnal hunts for girls there is no success in that direction in the novel; nor was there, it seems, in life. There were young women students at University College, but O'Nolan took no apparent interest in them and in the Ireland of the 1930s respectable young women were attainable only through the complex rites of courtship and marriage. O'Nolan took the traditional route by which celibacy may be made more tolerable – drink.

He spent a great deal of time in the public houses of Dublin. His student life came to an end with his graduation in 1932, but he continued to see the same friends in the same places. The one trip he made outside Ireland was a slightly mysterious journey to Germany in 1933. This was undertaken, presumably, as part of his German studies, although there is no record of him at the University of Cologne where he claimed to be studying. It was an extremely unfortunate time to visit the country: the Nazis had just come to power and O'Nolan claimed later, in a 1943 interview with *Time* magazine, that he had been thrown out of a beer hall for making uncomplimentary remarks about Hitler. He also said that he had married an eighteen-year-old girl called Clara Ungerland, the 'violin-playing daughter of a Cologne basket weaver'. She died a month after their wedding. Again, no record survives of this marriage. It was more likely that the whole affair was an early example of the wilful confabulation of his life by O'Nolan that has bedevilled biographers and scholars ever since.

Upon his return he published a little local journalism and then, with friends, launched a satirical magazine called *Blather*. It failed to establish much of a readership and closed after only a few months. In July 1935, O'Nolan joined the Irish civil service as an assistant to the Minister for Local Government.

IV

Outwardly, apart from heavy drinking sessions, his life appeared conventional enough: a junior civil servant beginning a safe, life-long career, unbothered by women, and living at home. But what he was doing at home, in a back bedroom of the house in Avoca Terrace, was a great deal more extraordinary. It was here that he wrote his two best novels – *At Swim-Two-Birds* and *The Third Policeman* – before the age of thirty. In the next three years, up to 1938, O'Nolan constructed the most exquisitely funny series of Chinese boxes in which his student narrator is writing a novel about one Dermot Trellis, landlord of the Red Swan Hotel, who is also writing a novel, with advice from William Tracy, a writer of Westerns, whose cowboy characters periodically escape from his pages to rustle cattle and hold up the Dublin trams; all three narrators are aided and annoyed by characters from Irish mythology and escape into and interfere with each others' worlds. Trellis's characters even conspire, while he sleeps, to put him on trial for all the terrible experiences he has made them endure.

The customary business of the novel, the delineation of emotion, of the social world, love and hate, guilt and redemption, are not to be found here except in a satirised form. There is no sex – all women are seen only in parodied contexts taken from art or literature, and there are no normal sexual relations. The only approach to realism is in the early scenes of student life and these are mainly concerned with discussions on literature interspersed with or accompanied by drunkenness.

There is no normal family life in any of O'Nolan's work: no father figures, but plenty of comic uncles. In fact, his father had died suddenly in 1937, leaving O'Nolan as the breadwinner for his mother and younger siblings. The death of his father affected O'Nolan deeply and may account for the black ending of *At Swim-Two-Birds* and the darkness that pervades *The Third Policeman*. The narrator of *At Swim-Two-Birds* lives with his Polonius-like uncle, who regards his nephew as an idle and drunken wastrel who spends altogether too much time in bed. The narrator's first experience of drinking results in 'leaving a gallon of half-digested porter on the floor of a public-house in Parnell Street' after which he puts himself 'with considerable difficulty into bed, where I remained for three days on the pretence of a chill.' He secretes his vomit-stained suit beneath the mattress. When his friend Brinsley calls round to see him, he describes the peculiar sensations he felt on drinking: 'I was talking to the Shader, I said, talking about

God and one thing another, and suddenly I felt something inside me like a man trying to get out of my stomach.' This description of the sensation of suddenly needing to vomit tells us that we are in the hands of a magnificent comic writer. A little later, drunkenly making his way through the streets with Kelly (the Shader) and Brinsley:

> . . . a small man in black fell in with us and tapping me often about the chest, talked to me earnestly on the subject of Rousseau, a member of the French nation. He was animated, his pale features striking in the starlight and voice going up and falling in the lilt of his argumentum. I did not understand his talk and was personally unacquainted with him. But Kelly was taking in all he said, for he stood near him, his taller head inclined in an attitude of close attention. Kelly then made a low noise and opened his mouth and covered the small man from shoulder to knee with a coating of unpleasant buff-coloured puke.

The writing throughout employs beautifully precise language; the mock-pedantic style is sustained throughout, rising to a sort of surreal poetry at the end of the book.

For all its brilliance and originality, *At Swim-Two-Birds* is the ultimate student novel. It is the novel all (male) students think they could write, would love to write, but never do. The reason why most fiction by very young men fails is that they have nothing to write about, no 'stuff', no significant adult life. Their childhood is too near for them to see it in any perspective; they have had few emotional experiences, they are full of their discovery of an independent physical world and the excitements of that are more effectively realised as lyric poetry than in any extended work. O'Nolan avoided the problem of the lack of real-life experience by never bothering with it. His fiction and journalism is set alight by verbal ignition, the fuel is literature and so his first novel was formed out of his reading. The book is a wonderful bag of tricks, a treatise on how – and how not – to write a novel.

The male students of the novel are not that different from succeeding generations; they are boozy, addicted to parody and ridicule of the pretentious. O'Nolan, despite his marriage when he was thirty-five, remained more or less like this all of his life. His few longer works are in the form of immensely extended jokes. *At Swim-Two-Birds* is a novel best read young and given to like-minded friends; as Dylan Thomas said, it is ' . . . just the book to give your sister if she's a loud, dirty, boozy girl.'

It would also be of great use – with its interlocking narratives and play on language and multiple references to modernist literature and mythology – on creative writing courses. To be recommended particularly to some of those poor students who emerge from university writing courses more puzzled than ever. A dose of O'Brien would do them a power of good.

V

In 1938, O'Nolan despatched the typescript of his first novel to the London literary agent A.M. Heath. The agent sent it, after one rejection, to the publisher Longmans. It was a piece of luck that Graham Greene was a reader for Longmans and that he recommended it so highly. It was published in the spring of 1939.

The reviews were mixed. Most remarked on its cleverness and humour, all unflatteringly compared him with Joyce. These repeated references to Joyce were inevitable and resented by O'Nolan. Joyce was at the same time a tutelary god to younger Irish writers and a resented and envied figure. Most of the Irish writers who stayed at home had harsh words to say about Joyce, who had escaped early and never returned to live in the country. O'Nolan made sure a copy reached the great man, delivered by hand by a friend to Joyce in Paris. Joyce responded enthusiastically: 'That's a real writer, with a true comic spirit. A really funny book.' But this did not lessen O'Nolan's growing antipathy to Joyce. In years to come, he seems to have resented any praise for the book in any form and from anyone, describing it dismissively as 'juvenilia'. He was now working on *The Third Policeman* and had great hopes for it. He sent it to Longmans. They rejected it. No doubt if his first book had been a commercial success Longmans would have regarded its successor more kindly, but *At Swim-Two-Birds* had sold only 244 copies and the remaining books were destroyed in an air raid. It was not, of course, a good time, in a London that was being heavily bombed in the second year of war, to launch a novel of any sort, but the rejection of his second novel seemed to kill something in O'Nolan. He pretended the manuscript had been lost – in fact it sat in a drawer for a further thirty years and was only finally published in 1967, after his death. It was then immediately hailed as 'hilarious' and a 'comic masterpiece'. I have also seen it described as 'a real delight'. Indeed it is, full of wonderfully convoluted absurdities and dour humour, but it can be read as comic only once – that is, until the reader realises its true nature as a pitiless description of eternity and Hell.

The fact that *The Third Policeman* was not published until after O'Nolan's death has made it look like a great last work of his maturity, a summation of his career. But it was the companion novel to *At Swim-Two-Birds* – the penultimate page of which mentions the peculiarities of bicycles and their owners, to be elevated into a major theme in the anti-world of *The Third Policeman*. After the publication in 1941 of his parody *An Beal Bocht* (written in Irish and translated as *The Poor Mouth*), O'Nolan published no more novels for a further twenty years.

VI

With the packing away of his rejected novel in a drawer, the profoundly disappointed O'Nolan cast off the Flann O'Brien cloak and put on another, that of Myles na Gopaleen, daily columnist of the *Irish Times*. At first the column was written entirely in Irish, then in English on alternate days. Eventually, apart from occasional reversions to Irish (and Latin) it appeared in English only. Its mixture of fierce satire, literary parody, deflation of pomposity, dissection of bores, catechisms of clichés, shamelessly laboured-for puns, and descriptions of absurd inventions was immediately popular.

The column was not unprecedented; the tradition of ridiculing 'all the false tastes in learning' went back to Swift and Pope, and to Swift's use of parody and mock-pedantry. It had echoes in the sardonic journalism of Heinrich Heine, of Dickens and other boisterous Victorians, and the 'By The Way' columns of Beachcomber (J.B. Morton) in the *Daily Express* in the 1930s. Beachcomber's creations, Captain Foulenough, Mr Thake, Mr Justice Cocklecarrot and the insipid poet Roland Milk are antecedents of Myles's 'The Brother', blackmailing ventriloquists, the Court of Voluntary Jurisdiction, and the poet Lyndsay Prune. Beachcomber's mad inventor Dr Strabismus of Utrecht would be a worthy director of the Myles na Gopaleen Research Bureau. Later, the tradition was continued in the Peter Simple column in the *Daily Telegraph* and in more diffused form by the magazine *Private Eye* and the companies of *Beyond the Fringe* and *Monty Python's Flying Circus*.

The money made from journalism was an essential supplement towards O'Nolan's support of his mother and brothers and sisters. O'Nolan often expressed his desire to write a bestseller and there was little regard for literature as 'art' in his make-up. He had accepted his family responsibilities and rejected the bohemian flight to England or Paris or New York. And now Europe was at war and Ireland was in a peculiar position. The republic had declared itself neutral ('Neutral against whom?' was the Dublin joke) but in those war years the world of literary reputation and feud was inflated by isolation. There is barely a mention of the war in O'Nolan's columns. He was a journalist who had once published a novel in London; a novel he deprecated as apprentice work. Now he was living the opposite of the rootless cosmopolitan life that Joyce had chosen, that of the artist devoted to one great work. O'Nolan was a civil servant, a jobbing journalist, still, in his early thirties, living at home. It is not really surprising that he spent much of his time in the pubs.

The name O'Nolan gave to his *Irish Times* column, 'Cruiskeen Lawn' is Irish for 'The little brimming jug'. The pseudonym Myles na Gopaleen can be translated as 'Myles of the Little Ponies'. Not a reference to horse racing, but to the little ponies O'Nolan drank – a pony being a measure a little under half a pint, the measure of the many bottles of Bass No.1 Barley Wine he drank until his face turned black and his doctor warned him off. All of his friends were heavy drinkers, a good few of them alcoholics. Drinking took up all of the slack time that was not used for work or sleep and the references to drink in the column itself are many and often wildly funny.

There is the wonderful invention 'Trink'. This is a product of the Myles na Gopaleen Research Bureau: ink that when printed on paper gives off an alcoholic vapour for several days. Unfortunately the invention takes quite a time to perfect because those working on it become hopelessly drunk. Gas masks are issued to the printers and enough of the ink is manufactured to try it out first on public posters, before proceeding to printing the *Irish Times* in the stuff, with the promise that intoxication will ensue, 'mild or acute, according to how much reading is done'. A further development by the Research Bureau is of alcoholic ice cream, with units measured in wafers and cornets. To get over the problem of pub closing times, the Bureau comes up with the idea of emergency trousers which can hold four bottles of stout in each leg, or being lined with stout-proof material and can be filled so that men can 'saunter home on their puffy, tubular and intoxicating legs'. A novel and alarming alcoholic drink is invented that results in instant nausea and intense headaches when consumed in the evening, but on awaking in the morning a feeling of great euphoria and health, a 'hang-under', pervades the drinker's body. For what Myles calls the 'drinking man', who cannot get hold of this reverse alcohol, there is the prospect of a revision of the licensing hours to between two and five in the morning; arising, 'the perished pint lover draws dressing gowns and coats over his shivering body and passes out gingerly to the stairs'. When he gets to the pub he is met with the view of a 'row of dishevelled and shivering customers, drawn of face, quaking with the cold. Into their unlaced shoes is draped, concertina-wise, pyjama in all its striped variety.'

O'Nolan continued to work in the Ministry of Local Government. He was well-regarded in the office, but some days had finished his work by eleven in the morning. He would leave his overcoat on the office door hook as a token of his presence and be off to the pub, usually the large and busy Scotch House where he could drink without being noticed, listening to the bar chat of other customers and gleaning priceless material for the ludicrous tales of The Brother and other bores who appear in 'Cruiskeen Lawn'. He was such a retiring figure that even when he went along to the Palace Bar, frequented by fellow writers Patrick Kavanagh and Brendan Behan, he rarely joined in the general conversation. He used many bars during the course of the day and evening. The last to be visited at night might be O'Rourke's, followed by further drink after closing time at the homes of friends.

Drink was the element in which he and his friends swam: in an Ireland that even after the war was oppressive and repressed, at the same time puritanical and Catholic, more akin in some respects to Franco's Spain or Salazar's Portugal than to any other Western European country, the pub was a licensed and necessary relief.

To his friends O'Nolan was a kind and humane man, as Denis Donoghue wrote, 'Myles was a genial man, a wag, a humorist, himself a comic humour', but he was contemptuous of liberal thought in political and social matters. To him, the world was run by fools and any attempt to better it would most probably result in it being run by even greater fools. Over the years his column became increasingly bitter and taken over by too many indignant rants about minor bureaucratic mistakes. He was now known to all as 'Myles' – Brian O'Nuallain (he used the Irish form at work) retreated to the office.

It was the opinion of some – and comforting to the many lesser would-be writers in those pubs – that Myles had written one brilliant work as a young man and then run out of creative steam. The thought must have occurred to O'Nolan also that he was frittering his life away by writing amusing nonsense instead of novels. But it was unlikely that they would have been written anyway; he was sometimes so drunk that he could not type his columns, although he was able to dictate them faultlessly to a more sober amanuensis.

In 1948, O'Nolan, to the general surprise of his friends, announced that he had married. None of his friends was invited to the wedding ceremony. Evelyn O'Donnell was employed at the Custom House and was evidently very fond of her new husband and certainly provided him with a measure of comfort and solidity in his life. He moved out of Avoca Terrace at last and set up home with Evelyn in a small house in Blackrock. Marriage changed his way of life very little, however; he drank as much as ever, and that was a great deal.

VII

The early 1950s were a period of rapidly accelerating deterioration for O'Nolan. The re-issuing of *At Swim-Two-Birds* by a publisher in New York seems to have depressed rather than elated him, particularly when sales turned out to be poor. Bertie Smyllie, editor of the *Irish Times* and yet another McDaid's alcoholic, began to find increasing fault with the author of the Cruiskeen Lawn column. More seriously, so did his employers at the Ministry. O'Nolan, as a civil servant, was not supposed to become involved in factional politics, but his column was seen as now satirising politicians and city officials to an unpardonable degree. This, together with his frequent drunkenness and absence from the office gave his many enemies their chance and in 1953 he was forced to resign on the grounds of ill-health. Only by the intervention of his boss in the Ministry was his small pension saved. Freed from the last obligations of regular work, O'Nolan now devoted his days to drinking. He continued with Cruiskeen Lawn, sometimes writing as many as six columns a week – these were done either early in the morning, in the brief gap between the waning of his hangover and opening time, or en bloc on Sunday afternoon, the one almost sober spell of the week, and delivered on Sunday evening.

A neighbour remembered seeing him stepping out in the early morning 'with the martinet step of the habitual drinker' to get to the nearest pub by opening time. From there he would go into the city for further drinking business. His friend and biographer Anthony Cronin in his memoir *Dead as Doornails* gave an analysis of O'Nolan the drinker at this time:

> [He] drank through the forenoon and early afternoon. Like many thoroughgoing alcoholics he had an early bedtime and because of sleeplessness . . . a very early rising. He was no stranger to the market pubs, which open at seven o'clock . . . he was, I think, a true alcoholic . . . meticulous and methodical. He seldom drank anything but Irish whiskey. Drink and the monologue which was his idea of conversation sufficed him.

O'Nolan had often had enough by the afternoon and would be seen home by a friend. Evelyn seems to have accepted this as the normal order of events for her husband. If he was too far gone he would go straight to bed; that was it for the day. Whatever else went on his home life in the evening or night was barred to any but his immediate family.

By the mid-1950s, he spent a good deal of time in bed, like his character Dermot Trellis. He ate little, smoked heavily, and drank enormously. For most of the time, even in the pub, he appeared bad-tempered and depressed. It was at this time, in 1954, on the fiftieth anniversary of Joyce's Bloomsday that the notorious celebratory brougham ride around the landmarks of *Ulysses* took place. Those taking part were O'Nolan, John Ryan, Con Leventhal, Patrick

Kavanagh and Anthony Cronin. The odyssey began with drinks close to the Martello tower in which the novel opens. Their progress – or lack of it – was recorded on film by Ryan and O'Nolan cuts a sorry, cross-looking figure. The horse-drawn carriages made frequent stops on their way and at one pub the landlord mistook them for a funeral party. John Ryan set out the scene in his book, *Remembering How We Stood*:

'Nobody too close, I trust?' he queried hopefully.

'Just a friend,' replied Myles quietly, 'fellow by the name of Joyce – James Joyce . . . ' meanwhile ordering another hurler of malt.

'James Joyce . . . ' murmured the publican thoughtfully, setting the glass on the counter. 'Not the plastering contractor from Wolfe Tone Square?'

'Naaahh . . . ' grunted Myles impatiently, 'the writer.'

'Ah! the sign writer,' cried the publican cheerfully, glad and relieved to have got to the bottom of this mystery so quickly, 'little Jimmy Joyce from Newton Park Avenue, the sign writer, sure wasn't he only sitting on that stool there on Wednesday last week – wait, no, I'm a liar, it was on Tuesday.'

This ignorance of the great writer in his home city would have gladdened O'Nolan. His own reputation had long been obscured by the endless comparisons with Joyce. What reputation he had left as a serious writer, that is. It was at a pretty low ebb and O'Nolan was in slow alcoholic decline when a publisher in London contacted him in 1959.

VIII

It is from the 1960 re-publication of *At Swim-Two-Birds* in London that O'Nolan's present fame and reputation date. A crowd of eminent writers, including Anthony Burgess and V.S. Pritchett, greeted the book with huge praise. However glad this may have made him secretly, O'Nolan continued to describe it as a piece of mere 'juvenilia'. But it did give him the confidence to write – or perhaps resurrect in earlier draft form – another novel, *The Hard Life*. He hoped it would be labelled as irreligious and so become a great success as a banned book. But, as ever, there was no sex in the book and, despite the naming of a priest as Father Fahrt, the basic idea of its hero Mr Collopy lobbying the Holy Father to support the erection of a decent number of public lavatories for women in Dublin did not sufficiently enrage the censors. Neither the reissue of the old novel nor the publication of a new one made him much money. His column in the *Irish Times* was appearing less frequently now and the work he solicited from provincial papers (as 'George Knowall' and others) was poorly paid. The O'Nolans had moved further out to a bungalow in the suburbs and O'Nolan for a time used the local pubs. In a letter to the landlord of one, after the man had barred him for allegedly stealing a bottle of whiskey, O'Nolan wrote: 'I know nothing about the bottle of whiskey . . . It is quite true that I am capable of drinking the contents of a bottle of whiskey, but not the bottle itself. There is no empty bottle in my house.'

In a bid to increase his income, O'Nolan wrote several plays for the Irish television service; he even scripted an unsolicited television commercial for Guinness. It was never used. His next novel, the last published in his lifetime, was published in 1964. *The Dalkey Archive* is sporadically amusing, but it is an obvious throwback to *At Swim-Two-Birds* and some scenes read like inferior rejected passages from that first novel. Other elements, particularly the musing of the philosopher de Selby, are virtually plagiarised from the still hidden-away *The Third Policeman*. His friend Cronin thought it 'old stuff rehashed' and a 'dull and inferior work'. O'Nolan himself apologised to his English publisher for this 'farrago of miswriting, slop, mistypes, repetition . . . '

He was unwelcoming to the fame that was now pressing upon him. A television interview was arranged for 8.30 one morning as this was reckoned to be the only time of day to catch the writer sober. But O'Nolan had a bottle hidden ready for emergencies and he retired to the lavatory and drank it all while the camera crew waited for him. The interview that followed was not broadcast.

By now the drinking was affecting more than his writing. Aside from the usual trials of a drinker's life – the falls, hangovers, endless 'colds' and gastric upsets, he was now taken off to hospital suffering from uraemia, a condition of the kidneys that can be serious enough to result in death. Shortly after his release, he fell and broke a leg. He took to his bed. At last his wife prevailed upon him to seek help with his drinking. He could not afford a private drying-out clinic and entered a public mental hospital, Grangegorman. It was obvious that he was trying to master his physiological addiction to alcohol but on leaving Grangegorman it rapidly crept back to its old levels.

He began a new novel, with the unpromising title of *Slattery's Sago Saga*. It was again a series of extended jokes, stuck in his student days of the 1930s, the novel as a parody of itself, perhaps as a self-protective reflex against criticism or 'serious' attention.

In 1965 he became ill with cancer of the nasal passages and mouth. He continued to drink in his hospital bed; there was little point in trying to give up now. When a journalist, Michael Wale, came to see him, O'Nolan talked about drink and said that each of us has a choice, 'between drinking and being bored to death'.

He died on the first of April 1966. A month before his death he wrote of 'the awful human condition' and 'that tiny periods of temporary release from intolerable suffering is the most that any individual has the right to expect'.

For him the 'temporary release' had been given by drink and writing; no one but he could know what form his 'intolerable suffering' took. His masterpiece, *The Third Policeman*, appeared only after his death.

Chapter 9

'Writing is an agony mitigated by drink'

Anthony Burgess (1917–1993)

I

WHEN NABBY ADAMS wakes up in the morning, every morning, the first thing that he wants, the one thing he must have, is a drink. After yet another night on the booze he reaches for his one remaining bottle of Tiger beer. He craves 'the hymeneal gouging-off of the bottle-top, the kiss of the brown yeasty flow, the euphoria far beyond the release of detumescence'.

Kingsley Amis would probably have objected to this language as possessing too much of what he called 'wow' and 'interference' for plain description, and as being unlikely to have occurred in such a form to a police inspector in the Malaya of the 1950s. But Adams is a character in a novel by Anthony Burgess, *Time for a Tiger*, published in 1956, and what he feels for drink may well have been what his creator also felt, and Burgess was certainly never one to stint himself or his characters in matters of drink or language.

II

Burgess's life falls into two halves, two separate identities. He was born in 1917 and christened as John Burgess Wilson (Burgess was his mother's maiden name), and Wilson is what he remained for nearly forty years. He adopted the pseudonym of Anthony Burgess with the publication of his first novel.

Despite the grand manner of his later years and a preposterous family tree he designed for himself, which suggested descent from an illegitimate son of Bonnie Prince Charlie, it is fairly clear that the Wilsons were pretty low down the social scale, in what used to be called the 'upper working class': Burgess's father was described variously as a pub piano player, a publican, and a tobacconist. A photograph of him shows a merry looking man, a bit of a card, a cigarette stuck jauntily between his lips, a beer paunch pushing out his buttoned waistcoat. Burgess said in his autobiography, *Little Wilson and Big God*, that his mother was 'a dancer and singer . . . pleonastically named the Beautiful Belle Burgess'. She died in the post-Great War influenza epidemic when her son was only two years old. His father married again in 1922 and Burgess loathed his stepmother; according to him, she was illiterate, slovenly, unclean, and boozy. Both father and stepmother were very fond of draught Bass ale and his father was a heavy enough drinker to be barred from his favourite pub. It must have been seen as a good move, combining business with pleasure, to take over the management of the Golden Eagle pub in Manchester.

There cannot have been many other famous English writers who spent their formative years living above a pub, particularly in what looks from photographs to have been a fairly rough one. The Golden Eagle was situated on a street corner and had a tiled exterior and the usual divided array of public bar, saloon bar, Gents Only and Ladies' snugs, and an outdoor counter from where jugs of beer could be filled and taken home. As a small boy, Burgess went to bed at night hearing the muffled cacophony of voices and three pianos that 'thumped and tinkled simultaneously, like something by Charles Ives'.

Until recent years, when many pubs have shut or been converted into something else, such pubs were common on nearly every street corner of both the working class and commercial areas of cities; it was not uncommon for an inner city crossroads to have one on each corner. They were not places to which the middle class went, except perhaps in London, where, in such sub-bohemian areas as Soho and Fitzrovia, they were frequented by writers and artists and their hangers-on. These street-corner pubs were loud and jovial, and, in among all the polymathic, polyglottic show-off of learning in his writing, there is also a public bar lack of respectability and a knock-about rambunctiousness in Burgess's life and work that is very heartening.

Burgess went to school and to university in Manchester, but perhaps his real education came from the very wide reading he undertook on his own initiative from an early age. Burgess was one of those fortunate children who lived in the golden age of the public library, when these buildings were stuffed with real and substantially nourishing books, unlike the pitifully half empty shelves of the modern library with their skimpy arrays of true crime, celebrity novels and autobiographies, and works offering help with problems of 'Mind, Body, and Spirit'. Burgess would have dwelt long and scathingly on the philosophical implications of that particular sign above the shelves.

He was a child prodigy in more ways than one; his sexual life began very early, as a nine year old, sharing a bed with an Irish serving girl who, as Burgess wrote, 'not only showed me her breasts, but insisted that I play with them'. While he was still in the sixth form at grammar school, he had his first serious if brief affair with a much older woman, a widow. But for most of his youth he was sexually frustrated, like almost every other adolescent or young unmarried man of his time. 'The alternative,' he wrote later, 'very Irish, was to pretend that sex did not exist and to drink.'

Burgess worked as a pub pianist at the age of eighteen, presumably accompanied by the obligatory glass of beer or whisky, and a cigarette burning on the top of the instrument. By the time he went to Manchester University in 1937, he was regularly crawling the pubs and getting drunk. He also now had a girlfriend, a fellow student, Llewela Jones, who called herself Lynne. His father died in 1938 and until August 1939 he lived with his stepmother. In view of the loathing he expressed later this must have been an awful experience, with the weekly doling out of his allowance of a few shillings. But Lynne solved his sexual problems for the time being. They went on a walking tour of France, Belgium, and Germany in August 1939 and only just managed to get back to England before the outbreak of war.

Burgess graduated in 1940 with a Bachelor of Arts degree in English. In October 1940 he was called up into the army. His early army days after initial training were, by his own account, full of sexual and alcoholic adventures. He continued to correspond with Lynne and to see her on leave, and in January 1942 they married. By now promoted to sergeant, he was transferred to the Army Educational Corps.

Up to this point, Burgess had done only a little student writing. He saw himself as a musician, with a future career as a serious composer. The only people he knew in the arts were provincial amateurs like himself, but in 1943 Lynne moved to work at the Board of Trade in London and when Burgess came home on leave they went together to the pubs of Soho and Fitzrovia. It was here that he first met 'real' writers like Julian Maclaren-Ross and Dylan Thomas. There is little doubt that Lynne was already being unfaithful to her husband. She had always had a freewheeling and casual attitude to physical sex and Burgess claimed that while he was away serving in Gibraltar, she had a fling with Dylan Thomas.

He had a relaxed attitude to this. 'To go to bed with Dylan was to offer little more than maternal comfort . . . all he really wanted was female warmth and a protective cuddle.' This, and other comments about Thomas's sexual activities, seem to owe a little too much to similar remarks in Constantine Fitzgibbon's biography of Thomas published in 1965. Andrew Biswell says in his later biography of Thomas that Burgess gained knowledge of Thomas's masturbatory activities from Lynne. Well, I think most people, certainly most men, would agree that this is unlikely, this not being the sort of thing a chap usually passes on to his girlfriend. And, after all, many people had a drink with Dylan Thomas in the Soho pubs and even more claimed to have done so; only Burgess was alone with the poet sometime in 1945, and saw him drinking pints of orange squash in the bar on Richmond upon Thames station (it had been lime juice in an earlier account). However well, or little, Burgess really knew Thomas is impossible to say now, but Burgess never wavered in his admiration for Thomas as 'the greatest lyric poet of the twentieth century'.

III

Burgess was still serving in Gibraltar at the end of the war, when Lynne was badly beaten by a gang of American GIs or deserters in London. The only source for details of this appalling happening is Burgess himself, and like most events in his life it changed in various tellings and retellings, although it is obvious that something horribly traumatic occurred. Burgess himself was a pacific and gentle man, but physical violence is present in much of his work, reaching sickening levels in *A Clockwork Orange*. One result of the attack was that Lynne, who had always loved pub life and drinking, now began to drink continuously and heavily. When Burgess was finally demobbed and arrived back in England, it was not to a particularly happy reunion between husband and wife. There were sexual problems, alcohol – and the necessity of earning a living.

Burgess still regarded himself as primarily marked out to be a composer, but his academic training was in English and in June 1950, after taking a couple of lesser teaching posts, he obtained a post as English Master at Banbury Grammar School. Although regarded as quite strongly eccentric and unworldly, he was a good teacher and popular with his pupils. His neighbours saw the couple as bohemians: 'their garden was filled with empty bottles'. Perhaps because he had become engaged with literature on a daily professional basis, and perhaps because of Lynne's intense dislike of his music, it was now that Burgess began to write seriously – not music, but prose and verse. Writing is, after all, an occupation that causes little noise or disturbance

– unless one insists on reading the stuff aloud – and, as its processes are little understood and held in some awe by non-practitioners, it can afford a convenient refuge from wives, children, and others. Two short novels, *A Vision of Battlements* and *The Eve of Saint Venus* were written in the early 1950s, but were rejected by publishers and not published until Burgess had established a reputation years later. He was earning no extra money from writing and his meagre salary seems to have been spent mainly on cigarettes and alcohol. He smoked eighty cigarettes a day and both Burgesses drank every night and got well and truly drunk each weekend. By his own account it was weekend drunkenness that brought about his escape from this life. He had started to send off applications for other jobs and thought he had been granted an interview by the Colonial Office for a job in the island of Sark. When he attended the appointment board the job offered was that of an Education Officer in Malaya. The story, as told by Burgess, is funny and possibly even true. As it was, the salary offered was far more (and tax-free) than he could ever earn as a teacher in England. On the fifth of August 1954, he and Lynne sailed from Southampton.

IV

It was in Malaya that John Wilson, teacher, became Anthony Burgess, writer. Grey England fell away from him and the alien and sometimes bizarre mixture of cultures he was exposed to resulted in the first novel of what is now called *The Malayan Trilogy*. Burgess felt that he was always an outsider in any world in which he happened to find himself and in these three early novels he inhabits the minds of Chinese, British and Indians with complete ease, as if he could exist far more freely in an exotically fictional world than the real one.

The Burgesses were able to afford a comfortable house and three servants, but they largely rejected the expatriate community, preferring to drink with local policemen and traders. Lynne was by this time subsisting almost entirely on gin; Burgess supplemented this with bottled beer and a local and lethal version of poteen, of which he had his character Nabby Adams say, 'The smell of decay was ghastly, but you could always hold your nose. The taste wasn't so good either: burnt brown paper, but, still, it was a drink. Good for you, too. If it wasn't for the smell and taste it would be a damn good drink.'

Burgess learned Malay, partly from a Malayan mistress (Lynne had embarked on a series of adulterous affairs conducted with Burgess's knowledge if not wholehearted consent). And in among all the drinking and lovemaking and work Burgess wrote his first novel. *Time for a Tiger* was finished in 1955 and was published by Heinemann the following year. Colonial Office regulations would not permit serving officers to use their own names for non-official publications so John Wilson chose his mother's surname, Burgess, and, at Lynne's suggestion, Anthony. The next two Malayan novels, *The Enemy in the Blanket* and *Beds in the East* were published in 1958 and 1959 respectively. However, before the last of these came out, the Burgesses had returned to England in typically chaotic and confused Burgessian style.

V

The story Burgess used to love to tell on the television chat shows on which he frequently appeared in the 1970s and 80s ran something like this (as in many Burgess reminiscences there are variants). His contract with the Colonial Office came to an end and he and his wife returned to England. For a time they lived in a suburb of Leicester and spent much of their time in a pub called The Black Horse while Burgess wrote after jobs. He got another teaching post in Brunei and they returned East in January 1958. In September 1959 he collapsed while teaching, and lay perfectly conscious but refusing to move, until stretchered off to hospital. He was examined and sent back to England for further tests. In London he was informed that he had an inoperable brain tumour and was given a year to live. On hearing this he, with great fortitude, set out to write four novels in this last year, in order to provide Lynne with some income after his imminent demise. But the brain tumour, if it ever existed, somehow disappeared with no further ill effect. Well, the biographies of Roger Lewis and Andrew Biswell attempt to pick the bones of truth out of this; one thing certainly is correct though, Burgess did write five (as it turned out) novels in a very short time indeed and for the rest of his life was an incredibly prolific professional writer.

Not surprisingly these early novels take their material from what had been Burgess's life to date, and as that had been composed mostly of drinking, fornication, adultery, the Far East, and teaching, that is what they are about. The Malayan novels had been generally well received as portraits of life in a waning imperial outpost; the next two, *The Doctor is Sick* and *The Right to an Answer*, are the stories of outsiders adrift in a contemporary England they find generally antipathetic. The defining actions of both books take place largely in pubs or other drinking places.

For Burgess, in his novels, and sometimes in his life, pubs are stages where action of an extraordinary kind, ranging from the ebullient to the mad, takes place. Many of the characters in these bars are far from happy or wholly sane in the first place and alcohol simply exacerbates the dramatic humours of their characters. The pub is where matters are brought to a head. The regulars swim in alcohol, occasionally gawping out of their tank, but otherwise largely ignoring the strange interlopers who are using part of the space for their own private dramas and public fireworks.

VI

The pub in *The Right to an Answer* is called the Black Swan, or the Dirty Duck by the locals. It is placed somewhere on the edge of a city in the East Midlands and the pub and locale are obviously taken from the Leicester suburb where the Burgesses had lived a couple of years earlier. The first person narrator of the book is J.W. Denham (nothing much is accidental in a Burgess novel, so the choice of initials is probably quite deliberate). Denham is a businessman, based in the Far East, and he has returned to the Midlands to visit his ailing father. He does not like England; he drinks a lot; he has no wife. The story is basically a black farce, involving adultery and a murder late in the book, but what makes the novel chiefly of interest is that most of it takes place in the pub, or at a drinking club in the nearby city.

Anyone who knew the world of pubs in the England of the late 1950s and early 1960s will nod their head in agreement with Denham's contention that 'England is perhaps the most mysterious country in the world.' And nothing would seem more mysterious to a later generation than the village or small town or suburban pub of fifty years ago – the 'local'. The pub in *The Right to an Answer* is one of those; there were many thousands and they differed considerably from the large anonymous pubs of the industrial city or the socially mixed or socially stratified pubs of London.

In 1959, the year in which Burgess's novel was published, a local pub would, typically, be leased from a brewery, or perhaps even be owned outright by its landlord – in either case there was far more local autonomy than at the present day when almost every pub or bar is run by a manager kept on a very tight commercial rein. Fifty years ago licensing hours were shorter and stricter, but the pub was run as an individual, and often highly individualistic, fiefdom. The customers were mostly male, though wives were permitted and might even be welcomed at weekends. Older customers, always men, had their specific seats in the corners of the public or saloon bar; many of these old men, especially those in small towns and villages, had only been out of the country once in their lives and that was to see service in the First World War. Their duty done, they had returned and never stirred since. Men still only in their late thirties had served in the Second World War and most of the younger men had done National Service in the army. The 'teenager' did not really yet exist as a separate cultural object. A male was either a boy or a man; that is, a sexless boy and a heterosexual man: dissenting others ran off to London. Every man had a job: in a factory, on the farm, as a small tradesman, more rarely in a commercial office; some of the more raffish small businessmen would drink in the saloon bar, otherwise the respectable middle-class was absent. And every man had short hair or was unselfconsciously balding. All, especially in the evening, wore jacket, shirt and tie. Drinking was usually moderate, except on the occasions (we shall come to them in Burgess's fiction) when the landlord allowed special licence to his customers. For they were *his* customers. The laws governing public houses have always allowed the publican discretion in whom he admits and how his guests should comport themselves. In a way that the French café or American bar never knew, the pub was also the dwelling place of its landlord and his wife and the drinking areas were in a subtle sense an extension of their home. (For some odd reason pub-keepers' children were a rarity, and if they existed were rarely seen.) The living quarters were upstairs and no stranger or customer was ever permitted to view them; the door marked *Private* was like the *eikonostasis* of a Greek church, hiding the holy secrets of the landlord's life, from behind which he would emerge to perform his oddly priest-like duties of serving liquor and sandwiches, hearing confessions, granting absolution to those who had overstepped the mark the night before, hosting parties for weddings, christenings and funerals, and, in the last resort, expelling persistent miscreants into the night and excluding them permanently from his little paradise. Burgess relished what he saw as the sacerdotal nature of the pub landlord; indeed in Ireland barmen used to be known as 'curates'.

Below the landlord's family quarters, the bars were furnished domestically with tables and armchairs, ornaments, and prints on the wall; sometimes even a large and dingy oil painting that had found its way mysteriously into the landlord's family years ago. One I saw in the back bar of a Birmingham inner-city pub in the early 1960s was huge and ornately framed. It was possibly seventeenth century, looked Italian, and, beneath the dark varnish of half a century of cigarette smoke, large and animated figures could be seen enacting its surprising subject of 'The Rape of the Sabine Women'.

Rooms in the local pub were differentiated by class. The saloon bar, or 'lounge' as larger and more modern pubs pretentiously called it, was the room where working clothes were not permitted and where the slightly more socially elevated of the community met. And met is the word, for most of the customers knew each other on first-name terms and any stranger was regarded with interest of various kinds: suspicion, disdain, or dislike. It was one of the properties of a landlord that he could at once assess the social and economic status of any stranger entering his pub. A hearty 'Yes sir, and what will you have?' combined a welcome with a hint of a warning shot if there was the smallest doubt about the stranger's eligibility to join the club, however temporary his stay might be. The other main bar was the public, of a rougher character in terms of both furnishing and drinkers; it was a little rowdier, but still within the limits set by the landlord. By present standards, the local was a place of limitation not excess.

Except in the roughest pub, swearing ('language', as the publican's wife would have called it) was restricted to 'bloody' and perhaps, exceptionally, 'bugger'. This latter word, by some English idiosyncrasy, was reckoned to be considerably more innocent than 'fuck' – perhaps because the act of buggery was regarded as an act so outlandish that it had long before severed any connection with the swear word. Indeed, it could be used as an expression of affection between males, as in 'You old bugger', whereas fucking was an indelicate activity rumoured to take place between, generally, married couples and to make any direct mention of it was to break a powerful domestic taboo. Plenty of men may have sworn obscenely in the Forces or on the factory floor, but they were not expected to import the words back into 'company', especially when women were present. The four-letter words 'shit' and 'fuck' were only really prevalent and fashionable among 'educated' people (see the letters of Amis and Larkin, *passim*).

Conversation was general, mainly concerned with sport, that is, football in the winter and cricket in the summer, and racing all year; local gossip and mentionable scandal; dogs might be discussed, but

not cats; the peculiarities of foreigners aired, but little foreign news –
what was definitely not allowed was any controversial discussion. 'No
religion or politics, please!' was the strong adjuration. These were
matters that led to heated conversation and that, plus alcohol, led to
fighting. Any fighting had to take place outside.

Surprisingly, given the purpose of the pub and the need for the
publican to make a living from the amount of drink sold, there were
commonly and firmly understood limits on the amount of drink that
could be taken by a customer. Of course, capacity differs, but to be out
of control was not acceptable and repeated drunkenness would lead to
'getting your ticket', for either a defined space of time, until you came
to your senses, or for ever, if your drunkenness was chronic and a persistent nuisance to others. As it still is in most of Europe, drunkenness
was looked on as unmanly and a sign of weakness. The pub was a place
to go and have a drink, or drinks, not a place in which to get drunk.

This was a typical village pub in the late 1950s and Burgess's Black
Swan in *The Right to an Answer* is a perfect description of one such place.
Given that pubs were conservative institutions (and publicans a notori-
ously illiberal group) where change was not welcome and ritual and
custom were all important, it follows that any disruption must come
from outsiders. In Kingsley Amis's writings the pub is generally a place
of what could be called 'willed stasis'; a refuge from the barmy doings of
women and the young and others that Amis sees as deranged members
of society. But pubs in Anthony Burgess's novels are places to which
strangers come, creating mystery and danger, generating chaos and near
surrealist happenings, and turning the pub into a comic inferno.

The landlord of the Black Swan is Ted Arden. Arden was the
maiden name of Shakespeare's mother, and Ted has 'the early baldness,
the big-lidded eyes of the best-known Shakespeare portrait'. Ted also
has a wife, who is a cut above him socially, as landlord's wives often
are, at least in fiction. Ted brings life to his pub; in his absence it
reverts to being 'a tavern for dreary drinkers with loud mouths'. This
is a common effect – I remember a Derbyshire pub I used to drink in

in the 1960s: I was surprised and disconcerted to find what a poky, small and dreary place it appeared when the tenants, Big Jack and even bigger Annie, were on their annual two-week holiday – it was they who provided the energy and warmth that vitalised the pub.

The climax of each week at the Black Swan is Saturday night. Denham, newly home from the East, visits the pub with his father, who is a respected regular. This gets over the awkward point of an outsider introducing himself into the usual Saturday night crowd, and Denham's wallet full of fivers attracts much friendly interest from Ted. Denham is admitted to a very select company; he is asked to stay on after the pub closes that night.

> When I started to leave, Ted Arden put his arm round me and whispered, 'No need just yet if you don't want to. Ave a little arf with me and the missis. Just wait till these buggers is gone.'
>
> This, I knew instinctively, was a very high honour.

Denham has been spared on this occasion: 'Ted was giving me the grace of his will, holding back death – which is closing time – making a lordly grant of extra life.'

And, after a couple of extra hours of being allowed to buy illegal extra 'little arves' for Ted and his missis and a few cronies, Denham totters home and wakes to a grey English Sunday.

Denham drinks continually each day in the week. He looks forward to the first drink of the day as early as possible and as the real and natural opening to a day. He drinks brandy and beer at lunchtime on Monday and when the pub shuts at 2.30pm, he dreads the three-hour gap until re-opening time. When the lunchtime pub door closes behind him 'the afternoon gaped wide; that mouth that had to be stopped with something'. Luckily a local would-be poet introduces him to an afternoon club of unspeakable dreariness, but with alcohol available.

This is provincial drinking: partly to be done because there is nothing else to do, partly as an armour against boredom. But Denham continues to drink in London and, when he returns to Colombo, on the boat out:

> Drinking a gimlet [a gin and lime] before lunch, I thought nostalgically of barmen on other ships of the eastern run: fat Bill Page, who drank two cases of stout every morning; Dicky Carstairs, who always fell out of the launch at Aden; Bob Something-or-other, who strangled a man in Port Said after brandy and black beer.

On this trip out, all the passengers are drunk by the time they reach Port Said.

VII

The Right to an Answer is only a minor novel in the huge Burgess canon, but it does exemplify better than any other his attitude to drink and drinking places. But from all accounts hardly any of his fictional characters, even the most drunken, drinks as much as Burgess was putting back at the time. How he found time or mental energy for his huge round of reviewing (he calculated that he wrote 350 reviews in two years for the *Yorkshire Post* alone), the novels, the general journalism, the broadcasts, the trips to London is a mystery. He had the support of his wife Lynne in proof reading and sorting out his general affairs, but only when she was sober, which was not very often by this time.

Both were in bad health, mentally and physically, and Lynne attempted suicide more than once in the 1960s. If Lynne was a full-blown alcoholic, Burgess could not have been far behind. Andrew Biswell, in his biography of Burgess, says that they 'would get through a couple of bottles of wine over dinner, and a dozen bottles of Gordon's Gin were delivered to the house every week'. In addition, Burgess was drinking beer and whisky in the pub and, presumably, while Burgess was working his eight-hour daily stint at his desk, Lynne was quietly putting the gin away. The excesses of this life needed the occasional pick-me-up and Biswell quotes Burgess's prescription, which he named Hangman's Blood:

> Into a pint beer glass doubles of the following are poured: gin, whisky, rum, port, and brandy. A small bottle of stout is added and the whole topped up with champagne or champagne-surrogate. It tastes very smooth, induces a somewhat metaphysical elation, and rarely leaves a hangover.

Lynne was warned that if she continued to drink at the rate she did she would die. Liver disease and a haemorrhage duly killed her in 1968. Burgess was devastated, but it could hardly be said the marriage was a conventionally happy one; he had been engaged in an affair for the past four years and remarried within a year of Lynne's death.

VIII

In the twelve years since his debut in 1956, Burgess had been incredibly prolific, publishing seventeen novels, all of which are at the least entertaining. Some were more than that: the Malayan trilogy remains in print, as does his most famous, and notorious, book, *A Clockwork Orange*. The next twenty-five years produced only a half dozen full-length novels, and of those only *Earthly Powers* remains in print. His huge productivity continued, but in many, perhaps too many, directions, producing a blizzard of lectures, reviews, articles, introductions to the books of other writers, film scripts, translations, stage adaptations, television series (including *Jesus of Nazareth*), critical works, musical compositions, opera libretti – anything, it seemed, which offered him a commission and money. He found time to teach at Princeton. Some of his choices are puzzling. Why in 1973, at the age of fifty-six, did he take up a post as Visiting Professor of English Literature and Creative Writing at City College, New York? It turned out to be a gruelling and embittering experience. Burgess had enjoyed his days in grammar schools in England and was a naturally good teacher. But the college had instituted a system of open access to students who needed no entrance qualifications. The result was a large number of poor and disaffected students, unimpressed by (and astonishingly rude and cruel to) this strange middle-aged man attempting to enthuse them with his love of literature. Joseph Heller, a fellow guest lecturer, who did not have the same patience with loutish students, called Burgess 'one of the most modest, the kindest people you'd ever meet'. But even Burgess had had enough after a year. After all, he hardly needed the money. In 1974 he retreated to tax-free, student-free Monaco.

The article on Burgess by Michael Ratcliffe in the *Oxford Dictionary of National Biography* says of this period that his work 'became more disciplined, more adventurous, and more European'. This begs the question of what is meant by 'European'? Others would say, and did, that it grew more wayward and pretentious and lost a lot of its vitality. He certainly lost touch with English literary life at this time, and his reputation suffered accordingly. The English, particularly English writers, have always had a rather arms-length relationship with Europe and 'ideas'. Kingsley Amis, for whom Burgess always had the greatest admiration, regarded Burgess's work with scorn. Burgess regularly sent him copies of his own works as they were newly published; Amis did not reciprocate.

Burgess lived most of the time abroad, in Europe. He ceased to be an English novelist and became an international man of letters; this may have made him rich, but it is a moot point whether it made him a better artist. And as his career and fame grew, Burgess became in a way a different man. He still drank, but not excessively for a man of his capacity. The young Burgess, the unknown Burgess, struggling to get free from the cocoon of John Wilson, that man had been replaced by the cigar puffing, endlessly hectoring and lecturing, public Anthony Burgess. Even his physical appearance changed; the whey-faced, hung-over, over-worked Burgess of the 1960s photographs became the florid-faced dissolute Roman Emperor of his later years. He had fashioned a mask for himself and was happy to be firmly hidden behind it. Andrew Biswell's biography devotes only twenty pages to the last twenty years (1973–1993) of Burgess's life and this seems fair; although the late 80s did see the writing of what may turn out to be Burgess's masterpiece, his two volume autobiography, which, although highly unreliable in matters of strict fact, works, especially in the first volume, *Little Wilson and Big God*, as a superb *Bildungsroman*.

IX

Drink played a huge part in Burgess's earlier life and work. But, far from being a debilitating influence, it seems to have energised him. The half dozen or so of his best novels are filled with characters who are half-sozzled most of the time; they also deal with subjects such as the problems of the perplexities and failure of Empire (in the Malayan trilogy), the creative spirit (the Enderby novels), and Middle England (in *The Worm and the Ring* and the *The Right to an Answer*) in ways that still appear fresh and original.

The heavy drinking of the first thirty years of his adult life damaged Burgess physically: still in his early fifties, arteriosclerosis gave him a limp in his right leg that hampered him for the rest of his life; he developed haemorrhoids (which he called the 'writer's curse') and high blood pressure. But as he aged, his drinking assumed more or less reasonable proportions, although he continued to smoke heavily, the massive consumption of cigarettes now replaced by an almost equal number of perhaps even more poisonous small cigars. Like an ancient wheezing steam engine, puffing out clouds of smoke, he continued to work unremittingly, completed his last book *Byrne*, an inventive verse novel, shortly before he finally ground to a halt and died at the age of seventy-six in 1993.

Quite an achievement for the man who invented 'Hangman's Blood'.

Chapter 10

'That's an interesting fridge you have there'

Kingsley Amis (1922–1995)

I

I N 1951, Dylan Thomas visited the University of Swansea to give a reading to the English Society there. Kingsley Amis, then a lecturer at the university, met Thomas for the first and only time. He had already expressed his dislike for Thomas's work and person in letters to Philip Larkin, saying that he 'could end up by WALKING ON HIS FACE and PUNCHING HIS PRIVY PARTS'. Now, after the reading, Amis wrote again to his friend about Thomas. It is interesting to compare this 1951 letter with an article about the Swansea reading that Amis published in the *Spectator* in 1957. In Amis's earlier letter, Thomas was 'half-stewed' (in the article, 'if . . . he had already been drinking for some time he gave no sign of it'). Amis went on gleefully to Larkin, 'In the pub afterwards the more intelligent students sneered at him gently . . . I am glad, because he made a very strong and nasty impression on me' (in the article, 'I have since realised that he was far too good-natured ever to contemplate giving anybody the cold shoulder').

There were quite a few more swipes at Thomas in later letters and Larkin felt compelled to remonstrate with what he considered Amis's callous comments on the poet's death in 1953. But Amis continued to make clear his loathing, and pursued the matter in public. In what looks close to an obsession, he reviewed both posthumously published work of Thomas's and most of the books written about the poet. As late as 1985 he reports to Larkin that he has bought a new collected edition of Thomas, ' . . . I keep peeping at Dylan'. In 1994 he took George Tremlett to task for implying that he had 'spent the past 30 years (i.e. 1958–87) abusing Dylan Thomas in print'. Amis protested rightly that he had been quite busy doing a number of other things, but there is no doubt that it was quite rare for him to let go an opportunity to slate his old enemy, including parodic versions of the poet in *That Uncertain Feeling* (1955) and *The Old Devils* (1985). For the character of Brydan in that novel, Amis wrote to Larkin, asking him to 'knock up' a few lines of sub-Dylan. A bizarre climax to the one-sided Amis–Thomas feud came while he was writing *The Old Devils*, when he accepted a place as a trustee of the Dylan Thomas estate, which was overseen by an old Swansea friend and drinking partner, the solicitor Stuart Thomas.

II

Actually, to the outsider, Amis had quite a lot in common with Thomas (one feels a peculiar pleasure in considering what the response of Amis would have been to *that* statement; not a prospect to be regarded lightly by the faint-hearted). They were both sexually promiscuous, although in very different ways. Where Thomas was an awkward lecher, able to operate only when drunk or nearly so, Amis could appear a relentless and confident seducer. Both writers drank every day; Amis seems to have been able to hold his drink better, whereas Thomas became hopelessly drunk on almost each and every occasion that he drank heavily. Praise of Thomas's comic abilities as a wit and mimic would have been the sort of thing Amis heard constantly during his years as a lecturer in Swansea from admirers of Thomas. It may explain much of the wildly personal antipathy he felt towards Thomas: a comic always hates reports of a rival holding the stage.

Both men were excellent mimics and storytellers. Of course, most of this stuff, delivered verbally and extemporaneously, disappears forever into the walls of pubs, clubs and dining rooms. The only witnesses are usually friends, often with drink taken, and wit and humour depend very much on the willing collusion of an admiring audience. How their monologues and jokes would have appeared to outsiders is another matter, but then outsiders shouldn't eavesdrop.

Both were natural writers; despite the obscurity that, for Amis, marred much of Thomas's work, he did always admire the clear prose of the stories in *Portrait of the Artist as a Young Dog*. So what, for Amis, was wrong with Dylan Thomas? Their one meeting had been, at least in Amis's public account, and in the eyes of other witnesses, an affable enough affair. No, it seems to have been the *idea* of Dylan Thomas, of the mere existence of *a* Dylan Thomas, that so infuriated Amis. He could not grasp that anyone, any normal sentient human being, could actually enjoy and derive any pleasure from the poetry of Dylan Thomas. Anyone professing a liking for poetry such as Thomas's must be a fellow charlatan or a moron. There could be no half measures. Many of Amis's adverse reactions to writers are along these lines; a complete denial of any virtue whatsoever in Dickens, Chaucer, Keats – at least in Amis's private letters, which are presumably his real thoughts. After reading Amis's letters it is wryly amusing to find him telling off Thomas, in a review of the poet's collected letters, for 'quite a few ventings of spite' and seeing 'nothing much in any contemporary'.

Amis's reaction to Dylan Thomas was fairly extreme, even by his standards, but it is difficult now to realise the extraordinary venom reserved for Thomas by academics and critics in the late 1940s and early 50s. Some of the attacks, vicious and ad hominem, on Thomas, even in academic works, went far beyond those meted out to any other poet. Here are some references to Dylan Thomas the man from David Holbrook's *Llarregub Revisited: Dylan Thomas and the State of Modern Poetry* (1962):

> The impotence in the writer goes with the shrinking from adult life
> and its exigencies . . . Unconsciously he desired to return to the
> blissful state of suckling at his mother's breast . . . Thomas was a
> baby man . . . infant sexual exhibitionism . . . Thomas must
> have feared sexual intercourse as a kind of drowning . . .
> necrophiliac . . . a deadening failure to mature . . . lack of moral
> control.

These disgusting speculations are in a work of literary criticism,
produced only a few years after Thomas's death and with his widow
and three children well able to read them. It is interesting to note that
the other poet who comes in for a hammering by the moralising
Holbrook is Kingsley Amis – for writing 'sophisticated dirty jokes'.
The poetry of both Amis and Thomas is compared unfavourably
with the 'folk song' of the 'English rural people, from, say, 1350–
1850'. Well, by all means, you can say what you like, but nowhere
does Holbrook explain how a composite 'unconscious' and 'innocent'
'folk' can compose discrete works of art such as the Border Ballads.
'Anon' was certainly one of the greatest poets, but comprised a large
number of different persons, not a committee.

The first biography of Dylan Thomas, by Constantine Fitzgibbon
in 1967, had not skirted round the thieving, cadging, boorish
behaviour, selfishness, promiscuity and other deplorable character
traits that Amis levelled at Thomas, but Fitzgibbon had been a friend
of Thomas and his book is an intensely affectionate portrait that at
least seeks partially to excuse the faults, considering them paid back
by the charm and humour of the man, and above all, his talent as a
poet. Indeed, others thought this way. In November 1941, Philip
Larkin wrote excitedly to his friend Jim Sutton:

> Dylan Thomas came to the English Club last week. Hell of a fine
> man: little, snubby, hopelessly pissed bloke who made hundreds of
> cracks . . . he read a parody of Spender . . . which had people

rolling on the floor. He kept up this all night – parodies of everyone bar Lawrence – and finally read two of his own poems, which seem very good. If you see this week's Lilliput you will find a very good photo of Dylan T. also.

Larkin's youthful enthusiasm for the poet did not last, at least in the exchange of letters with Amis; he changed his tune after Amis HQ had laid down the line on Thomas. One gets the sense in reading their correspondence that Larkin learned to keep many of his literary tastes quiet from Amis. And although Amis may have admired and envied the early literary success of his friend – two novels, *Jill* and *A Girl in Winter*, were published while Larkin was still in his twenties – he certainly never deferred to him in literary argument. Indeed, it is often Larkin who seems to be trying to keep up with Amis's fierce and aggressive thoughts. The only area in which Amis would gratefully admit criticism and advice from Larkin was in writing the early versions of the novel that became *Lucky Jim*.

III

As friends the two men were exceptionally close, but for many years met only occasionally. Larkin was not a clubbable man: most of his drinking was done at home, after work, listening to records. But Amis had a love of pubs, and later his club, the Garrick. The pub was lit and safe and full, he hoped, of good company. But the Amis pub is not exactly a welcoming place. There is an Amisian ranking code for all those entering a bar: it runs from its lowest, the young and usually repellent male, his intrusion mollified perhaps by the accompanying presence of a young and attractive female, up to the elderly regulars who accept their places vis-à-vis each other, the landlord, and the institution.

In *The Old Devils*, the regulars of the pub, in which they meet most mornings, exhibit many gradations and rankings of age and sexual potency or otherwise, and drinking capacity, and interesting or boringly mundane diseases and illnesses. By the time of publishing this novel in 1985, the pub-going characters Amis seems to admire were the sort of people he would have retreated from in horror in his youth.

But *The Old Devils* is fairly late Amis, with his characters forming a circle to protect themselves from the modern world and all they despise. Amis had already portrayed the sort of pub he liked; it was like the Green Man in his novel *The Green Man* (1969). The narrator, Maurice Allington, is the landlord, and a character – adulterous, putter down of a bottle of whisky a day, and of uncertain temper and decided tastes – very like Amis himself. Allington hates most strangers, white burgundies, and the local vicar. The beers he stocks are rather ordinary, the only good draught one being Bass. But he does have that prince of bottled beers, Worthington White Shield. The wine list is short. The menu is solid English fare. His ideal customers are the locals who 'put back their pints steadily and quietly in the public bar'; the saloon bar is a more uncertain area, being often filled with strangers, some okay, some loathed, especially the sippers of half-pints, which habit, in a male, suggests to Allington a certain timidity in facing up to life.

Pubs like the one in *The Green Man* are disappearing fast; the rural ones are closing, their urban equivalents are being transformed into 'gastro-pubs' offering, in common, microwaved menus of vaguely Mediterranean origin and pretension. In the towns they have been taken over completely by the young, and their surroundings remodelled as large barns with bright, harsh lighting, terrifyingly high ceilings, few or no comfortable seats and a constant barrage of thumping 'music'. They are anti-Amisian places, expressly designed not for conversation or company, but purely for the consumption of alcohol. The older drinker must now presumably drink at home, alone, or with an equally or unequally soaked spouse, and, presumably, drink more and more in his own comfortable domain, and become more and more alcoholised. The destruction of the traditional pub was beginning to happen in Amis's lifetime, but there were still a few pubs, like the George, near his home in Regent's Park Road, in which he and friends felt at home. He always defended himself against the name of 'alcoholic' by protesting that alcoholics were people who drank by themselves, and that he loved the company of other drinkers and talkers; for him the mark of a man was the ability to hold a drink, take insults on the chin, answer back robustly, and, above all, be fun.

The need for company, to be never alone was a constant obsession. Since his childhood, Amis had had a fear of darkness and isolation and, for all its humour, the portrait of Jim Dixon in his first novel *Lucky Jim* (1954) is of an isolated and beleaguered man. Jim lives in his own head; the world, and most of its grotesque inhabitants, is against him, and the two ways of escaping or changing the world or present company for the better are by drink and sex. Drink plays a part in two major episodes in the book; the first when Jim flees the ghastly cultural evening at the Welch house and seeks sanctuary at the village pub. Hilary Rubinstein, Amis's editor at the publisher Gollancz, objected to Jim's consumption on this one evening; his ten pints were reckoned to be impossibly excessive and were toned down to six in the printed version. Jim wakes with one of the worst, and best described, hangovers in English literature:

> The light did him harm, but not as much as looking at things did; he resolved, having done it once, never to move his eyeballs again. A dusty thudding in his head made the scene before him beat like a pulse. His mouth had been used as a latrine by some small creature of the night, and then as its mausoleum. During the night, too, he had somehow been on a cross-country run and then been expertly beaten up by secret police.

This is use of alcohol as a temporary and escapist expedient; it assumes a much larger, life-changing aspect when Jim gets drunk before delivering a lecture on 'Merrie England', actually written by his superior, Professor Welch. This is general nonsense on the theme, promulgated by the followers of the literary critic F.R. Leavis, that there had been some golden age in the past, unspecified in exact date, when people had lived in 'organic communities' and 'made up' folk songs; when everything was much more like 'life' than modern life. Not unnaturally, Jim Dixon, intoxicated, departs from his ludicrous text, delivers an excoriating denial of Welch's vision, and thereby wins a new and better girl, and a new and better job.

IV

Amis's own early drinking habits as a student at Oxford were unexceptionable, the usual beer drinking and occasional excess of more than a few pints. He also lost his virginity; the overture to his tumultuous later sex life. Amis served for three years in the army during the war. He sounds from the accounts of others to have been a pleasant and sensitive young man, not greatly attuned to army service, rather inefficient, devoting what spare time he had to affairs with quite a few young women, and pursuing a rather more serious affair with a married woman. There were drinking bouts, as was to be expected when the prospect of being perhaps killed or mutilated by the enemy was a distinct possibility, but, at this time, sex seems to have been more important to him than drink. Back at Oxford, finishing his studies, and then in Swansea, as a poorly paid academic with a wife and growing family, he drank mostly beer. Unlike many of his fellow academics at that time, he drank with his students in the pubs of Swansea.

Even before their marriage, his first wife, Hilly, had noticed Amis's irritability when faced with the most commonplace of situations and how 'brilliantly selfish' he was. He had a horror of being bored, hence the insistence that works of art, whether novels, poems, jazz records, or pieces of classical music should be immediately engaging or they were simply not worth persevering with. Much the same yardstick was applied to fellow human beings. Drink is an excellent buffer against social boredom; it either creates a barrier against the bore, or gives enough aggressive courage to be rude to the bore and to see him off. When he was forced to put up with someone he regarded as supremely boring, as in the case of Hilly's father, Leonard Bardwell, the man was treated politely enough in person, but then subjected to Amis's rage in grotesque tirades at Bardwell's innocent enough interests in letters to Larkin. Hilly's brothers were in for even worse – they were 'EXCREMENTALLY EVIL'.

In Swansea, in the early 1950s, Amis and his wife entertained at home, particularly when Hilly spent a legacy on a larger house and they for the first time had disposable income. Their parties involved much noise, drunkenness, and incidental sexual fumbling and fornication. Amis continued to be unfaithful whenever he could; in South Walian rugby terms, he tried every attractive woman he could and had a satisfactory conversion rate. These early Swansea years seem to have been the happiest of Amis's life. He was the centre of an admiring circle, happily married and happily unfaithful, although a growing frustration at the difficulties of finding someone to publish his novel nagged at him.

But his life was about to be changed forever. With the publication of *Lucky Jim* in 1954, he became and remained until his death over forty years later a famous writer and public figure.

From the mid-50s on, Amis was very often in London and formed new friendships and found new drinking companions to collude in alcoholic and sexual adventures. In Swansea, he mixed with a middle-class Swansea drinking set, led by the solicitor Stuart Thomas. With critical and popular success and film rights to his first novel sold, the money began to roll in. Money is very welcome to the drinker. You can drink better and more. Lots more.

V

In September 1958, Amis took up a position as Lecturer and Resident Fellow in Creative Writing at Princeton. Because of his fear of flying, the family crossed on the liner *Queen Elizabeth*. The children, Philip, Martin and Sally, settled in well at school. For their parents the next year was one of the wildest of their lives. Kingsley made love to every woman he could and drank like a fish, though now it was martinis and bourbon, not beer and cider. He was able to drink most people under the table; as a friend recalled in Zachary Leader's biography: 'physically he must have been a very tough guy. He could drink a lot and stay up all night.' Certainly, Amis said in a letter to Larkin that he had been 'boozing and fucking harder than any time'. One of the reasons that he resisted the temptation to stay after his contracted year was up was that he felt his own 'creadive wriding' had suffered; he had done hardly any in that American year. Passionate drinker and lover as he was, Amis now regarded himself as a thoroughly professional and dedicated writer.

But, for the rest of his life, the creative work would be done largely in the morning, before the day's entertainment began. Amis once said that 'Whatever part drink may play in the writer's life it must play none in his or her work. The bottle on the desk is all very well in what used to be Fleet Street but not for anything anybody may hope will be read more than a couple of days later.' A laudable enough prescription. How far did he live up to it? Its sentiment is rather belied by a picture of Amis in his study in the early 1970s; the floor is covered with spirit and wine bottles.

If America was not the place to be, then he found it difficult to settle back into life in Swansea. It now bored him; his marriage was in difficulties because of his ceaseless infidelity; a change was needed. He found it in the offer of a fellowship in English at Peterhouse College, Cambridge.

This was not entirely successful; Amis felt slighted by the dons of the English faculty and complained that he got from them 'less than my due as a man of letters', an attitude that came to characterise increasingly Amis's view of his position in modern literature; years later, he felt aggrieved when he thought that Julian Barnes had not treated him with the deference due to 'a senior writer'. The drinking habits at College dinners left him dissatisfied; there was never quite enough wine. In Cambridge, Amis continued his Swansea habit of taking his students, mostly male, to the nearby pub. This earned him the rumoured reputation of being a homosexual. It was at this time, in 1962, that his affair with Elizabeth Jane Howard began. He was forty years old. In 1963 he and Hilly parted, and later divorced. He married Elizabeth Jane Howard in June 1965.

The detail of Amis's life with his two wives has been thoroughly examined in the biographies, and there is no doubt that the first marriage foundered because of Amis's unwillingness to give up other women; the second because of his unwillingness to give up drink. For a time, in the early stages of life with Jane, Amis seems to have considered cutting down drink, but as Leader's biography states, a friend, Mavis Nicholson, warned Jane 'that she was not to believe that Kingsley would not be a heavy drinker'.

VI

In what was another escape from the past, Amis had been steadily moving politically rightwards throughout the late 50s and early 60s. Most of his closest companions in London were hard drinking right-wing journalists and by the mid-1960s the deliberately provocative manner of a Waugh-like reactionary was largely in place. He met with like minds at weekly lunches at Bertorelli's restaurant. They included Robert Conquest, author of *The Great Terror,* a work on Soviet Russia that opened the eyes of many in the West to the atrocities of the Leninist and Stalinist regimes, John Braine, a phenomenally successful novelist in his day, Simon Raven, a better novelist and all round bad man, and George Gale, another ferocious scourge of Lefties. Most were heavy drinkers, highly literate, and company to Amis's taste.

A trip to Czechoslovakia in 1966 further convinced Amis that life under Communism was anything but fun. Not that he shared all of the Right's preoccupations; a spell teaching in Nashville, Tennessee, revolted him because of the casually expressed, callous anti-black bigotry of many of the university staff. The Amises finished off their second time in America with a tour going down to Mexico. For this, Amis provided himself with a cocktail-making kit, which Leader describes as being packed with 'bottles of tequila, gin, vodka and Campari, as well as fruit juices, lemons, tomato juice, cucumber juice, Tabasco, knives, a stirring spoon and glasses'. Cocktails could be made on the journey, with the car stopping for the first one at 11.30 in the morning. It was now important that alcohol was always present, that there was no danger of running short or, worse, completely out of the stuff. An earlier novelist had much the same practical approach and need for alcoholic security.

In *John Barleycorn: Alcoholic Memoirs* (1913), Jack London wrote:

> I achieved a condition in which my body was never free from alcohol. Nor did I permit myself to be away from alcohol. If I travelled to out-of-the-way places, I declined to run the risk of finding them dry. I took a quart, or several quarts, along in my grip.

Despite the subtitle of this book, London always denied that he was an alcoholic in any medically defined sense of the word. He was a drinker who drank socially and for the sake of like-minded company. Amis was also reaching a stage where his body was never entirely free from alcohol. For the last twenty or so years of his life – apart from a six-month gap, which did not seem to improve his health and temper – he drank heavily every day.

When not working on a novel, Amis liked a fairly early morning start to the day's drinking. Jeremy Lewis, in his hugely entertaining autobiography *Kindred Spirits*, remembered Amis in Peter Janson-Smith's office at the Oxford University Press in 1977, when Amis was compiling *The New Oxford Book of Light Verse*:

> Peter's office . . . was dominated by a gigantic, gleaming fridge . . .
>
> On the dot of eleven Kingsley would look at his watch, peer thoughtfully over his spectacles and say in a surprised voice, as though it had struck him for the first time, 'That's an interesting looking fridge you have there, Peter' . . . the fridge turned out to be choc-a-bloc with bedewed bottles . . . and so the meeting would progress, with much popping of corks.

Back in England, Amis occasionally met up with old friends from student days. It is odd and somehow disturbing that the two drinking stories he tells in his *Memoirs* of his oldest friends, Bruce Montgomery and Philip Larkin, both involve physical humiliation. Montgomery met Amis for lunch. He was obviously in a bad way alcoholically and he threw up at the lunch table. The other anecdote Amis produces is an account of Larkin at a poetry reading. Sitting on the platform and having drunk several pints of bitter, Larkin had an overwhelming need to urinate. He was wearing a very thick overcoat at the time and took the risk that the coat would absorb the discharge. It did not. Both these stories are told in preference to others that would, presumably, have put their subjects in a more engaging light. It is as if by publishing these particularly demeaning portraits of close friends Amis was venting some ancient spite. A deal too much energy is spent in the *Memoirs* in excoriating the characters of those who poured him drinks whose measures he judged to be on the mean side. Increasingly, as he grew older, he saw it as his due to be poured large and powerful drinks, a form of alcoholic tribute to his status as man and writer. Those who poured small measures were inadequate members of the human race to be scorned and vilified, as if this deficiency was a token of a wider and more shameful lack of character.

VII

As in life, so in the work – drink plays a crucial part in the novels:
It changes Jim's life for the better in *Lucky Jim* (1954); in *Take a
Girl Like You* (1960), Patrick Standish's rape of Jenny Bunn happens when they both get drunk at a party; Roger Micheldene, the
anti-hero of *One Fat Englishman* (1963), guzzles booze and food
like a vacuum cleaner. Drink in the earliest novels is used as a plot
device; by the time of *The Green Man*, the narrator is a fully paid-up
bottle-a-day man, but still able to function in running a pub and
conducting adulterous affairs. By 1986, drink flows like a river
through *The Old Devils*.

This mirrors the progress of drinking in Amis's life: drink as an
accompaniment to good times in his youth; a steady, heavy habit,
often spilling over into drunkenness in his early middle age; and a
drinking regime which became almost a full-time secondary
occupation in late middle and old age. D.J. Taylor, in a review of
Zachary Leader's biography of Amis, tells of a conversation with a
woman who knew Amis in his days as a young lecturer in Swansea
and said that what turned a charming and extremely funny man into
someone capable of gross and unforgivable behaviour was undoubtedly
his drinking.

A picture of how Amis appeared to someone outside his immediate
circle is provided by a book-dealer, John Baxter, in his book *A Pound
of Paper* (2002). Baxter wanted Amis to sign some first editions of his
novels and they met in the Coach and Horses in Heath Street,
Hampstead. Baxter was shocked at the fifty-seven-year-old Amis's
appearance: ' . . . he appeared twenty years older . . . Stooped, almost
shambling, he was myopic without his glasses, which he put on in the
doorway before peering around uncertainly.' Amis was perfectly
genial, despite still suffering from the previous night's session,
ordering first a pint of cider, and then going on to a double scotch.
Baxter's account leaves the impression of an amiable and modest, if
sharp-witted man.

The only rather odd thing about this is in the description of Amis as short-sighted. One of the irritating things about the film of *Lucky Jim* is not knowing what Jim's glasses are *for*. Ian Carmichael was not good casting as Jim Dixon anyway, being altogether too posh for the role, but he keeps taking off and putting on his glasses for no discernible reason. He is too young to need them for reading; if he is short-sighted why does he keep taking them off when he needs to see things? There are numerous photographs of Amis wearing glasses in later years, when many people have to, but even a slight shortness of sight in his earlier life could account for his dislike of the theatre, architecture and the visual arts. These things, and indeed much physical description of any sort, are largely absent from his early novels, apart from the close appearance of faces and bodies. The novels are largely constructed around the conversation of characters and the accompanying authorial running commentary on what they are thinking and feeling. Two other novelists, Evelyn Waugh and Anthony Burgess, whose books are composed mainly of what is *heard*, rather than what is *seen*, were both short-sighted, Burgess extremely so. The three, Waugh, Burgess and Amis, also shared a sort of defensive shyness, which could easily change to the offensive when they had drunk a sufficient amount.

VIII

A sufficient amount was very important to Amis.

Amis liked to be drunk. For a writer who debunked false emotions and high-flown language the nearest he came to any sort of elevated statement is in the words he puts into Maurice Allington's mouth in *The Green Man*. Allington is describing how he is drunk 'with that pristine freshness, that semi-mystical elevation of spirit which, every time, seems destined to last for ever'. To me, *The Green Man*, the novel of Amis's most closely concerned with drink, is also his most profound and compassionate book; a book about the protection of love from evil. There is an argument to be made that the novels of Amis's middle period, from *The Anti-Death League* (1966) to *The Alteration* (1976), are the most varied and interesting of his career, certainly more ambitious than the early social comedies, and not yet soured by the rancour of some of the later work. It is these books that seem to reveal the inner Kingsley Amis as a deeply troubled and far more emotionally complex person than the one met in the biographies and reminiscences of his friends. Amis was, like many other novelists, a good actor, able to assume many roles and disguises in his fiction and in life. The Amis of his last years is often pictured as an ogreish and extremely awkward character, but not everyone found him so. John McDermott, who wrote one of the first and best books on the author (*Kingsley Amis: An English Moralist*, 1989) and worked with him on putting together *The Amis Collection*, has told me what an amiable and charming man Amis was in all their meetings, a boozy lunch companion of course, but he was always that.

However, the alcoholic routine Eric Jacobs describes at the beginning of his biography of Amis would be punishing to a very much younger man, let alone one in his late sixties and early seventies. Whatever the ravages of the previous night, Amis would write for about three hours every morning and the drinking day would start at 12.30 with the first of two or three large malt whiskies in his local pub or at the Garrick. This would perhaps be followed by a bottle of wine with lunch, and a large Grand Marnier or perhaps two glasses of red wine after. A snooze in the afternoon, then he would resume work at five for an hour or two. More malt whisky; at supper, beer. The evening was rounded off with more whisky at about eleven. And so, presumably staggering, to bed.

It is said by some moralistic observers that drink destroyed Kingsley Amis. Well so it did; physically he was overweight and unable to walk far by his sixties, a tottering semi-invalid by his seventieth year. But mentally he remained remarkably acute. He worked every day, publishing ten books in the last decade of his life.

To Amis, drinking was a pleasure, providing a haven from the very real terrors that afflicted him, and enabling him to continue working at a high level. He had established a style of living that enabled him to survive; if this meant the ingestion of large amounts of alcohol that was just tough luck.

As a friend of mine once said, 'I drink so that I don't have to spend all my bloody time wondering if I should or shouldn't.' Or, as Wild Bill Davison, one of Amis's favourite jazz players, said, 'Christ, you have to drink to put up with the shit you have to put up with.'

CHAPTER 11

The Road to *Revolutionary Road*

Richard Yates (1926–1992)

I

ANTHONY BURGESS once wrote that the 'geniuses who are neglected are usually the geniuses who disturb, and we do not like to be disturbed'. As usual with any statement by Burgess this begs a lot of questions. Such as – what is genius? What is neglect? What is the nature of disturbance? He was writing about James Hanley, but his words could as well have been applied to Richard Yates, the novelist and short-story writer, neglected during his life and after his virtually unnoticed death in 1992 and in recent years undergoing a revival in interest. He was certainly a disturbing writer, both in his subject matter and in the lack of regard for any soft-heartedness in his readers. Great claims have been made for Yates. 'America's finest post-war novelist,' according to Scott Bradfield, who conducted a long interview with Yates shortly before his death. Perhaps. Time will sort that one out and may come up with a few other names that will surprise us. But Yates was a fine and original writer despite – or because of – his wretched life, dominated by ill-health and alcoholism. And if only one of his books survives it will surely be his first published novel, *Revolutionary Road*.

II

Richard Yates was born on the third of February 1926 in New York. His father, Vincent Yates, was distantly descended from the seventeenth-century Governor Bradford of Plymouth, and the nineteenth-century president Grover Cleveland, a lineage of which Yates was as proud as John Cheever was of his relation to another great New England family. But Yates's father was no New England grandee; for the most part of his life he worked as a salesman, rising no higher than assistant regional manager for the Mazda Lamp Division of the General Electric Corporation. Yates's mother had studied at Cincinnati Art Academy and wanted to be a sculptor. Both drank, sometimes heavily.

His parents represented two sides of Yates's personality that often appeared at odds in his work and life. There was his father, a businessman of a minor sort, prone to the occasional binge when the dullness of life got too much. Ruth, his mother, known as 'Dookie' by her children, was both artistically pretentious and conservative in her politics. These two conditions – artistic aspiration opposed to the need to earn a living in some mundane and depressing occupation – recur constantly in Yates's novels and stories. It was a problem he never fully solved for himself.

Like characters in a Yates novel, his parents did not have an easy – or long-lasting – marriage. Two children were born, Ruth and Richard, and the couple separated in 1929 when Dookie whisked the children away to Paris, where she intended to study sculpture. Paris was then inhabited by a small number of real and a much larger number of would-be writers and artists, most of whom returned home after a fling with bohemianism and settled back anonymously into their home towns. Dookie lasted for six months until her money ran out and she and the children returned to New York.

Yates remembered his childhood with bitterness. He was always, he said, 'the only new boy and the only poor boy' in a string of schools. The family lived an unsettled life. Dookie was sometimes hysterical, often drunk or only half-sober. Sometimes the breakfast table would be unexpectedly graced by the presence of some man she had brought home the night before. They moved frequently, flitting from one flat to another when Dookie was unable to pay the rent. The constant changing of schools and homes left Yates feeling insecure and friendless. His last and longest stay was at a progressive school, perhaps picked by his mother because it had its own psychologist on the staff. Yates was, as his biographer Blake Bailey says, 'the poorest, weakest boy . . . the smothered son of an unstable alcoholic sculptress'.

At sixteen, in 1942, tall and lanky, physically uncoordinated, an object of ridicule to school bullies, he found an outlet in editing the school magazine. He became determined early on that he was going to be a writer. Acting the part of the hard-bitten American journalist, he smoked almost continuous and had Dylan Thomas's habit of keeping a cigarette in his mouth and squinting through the smoke. When, at the end of 1942, his father died of pneumonia at the age of only fifty-six, there was no prospect of Yates going on to college. His father had been a heavy drinker and smoker who had been out of work for some time. He left no money and whatever allowance he had paid to his divorced wife ceased with his death. So Yates left school and got his first job, as a copy boy at the *New York Sun*. In 1944, at the age of eighteen, he was inducted into the US Army.

III

Yates failed the intelligence test that would have qualified him for training as an officer. Like many otherwise highly intelligent people, Yates could be surprisingly slow and obtuse in formal tests. As an infantryman, he saw active service in France and Belgium, and became a company runner delivering messages at the front line. He suffered permanent lung damage when he collapsed after continuing to carry out his duties despite suffering from pleurisy and pneumonia.

It was an early sign of the sheer doggedness that would carry him through the many subsequent years of neglect and poor health. When he returned from the war this six-foot-three tall man weighed just ten stone.

The war gave a second chance, in the form of the GI Bill, to all those who had missed out on their education while serving in the forces. Yates could have obtained a grant and put himself through college. That he did not do so may have been due to a lack of confidence in his intellectual capacity – the only subject he had done well in at school was English. The sense of inferiority he felt because of his lack of a college education lasted and later hampered him in finding teaching work in universities and colleges. He took a job as a junior writer on the *Food Field Reporter*, a trade journal for the food industry.

Life was not terribly satisfactory: he was living with his mother and now drank as much as or more than she did. He had the occasional girlfriend but nothing really to threaten life with mother. But, in 1947, he met Sheila Bryant. She was tall and pretty, the daughter of a failed British actor and his well-connected and near-fascist wife. She had as much reason to want to flee her home as Yates. His mother referred to her as 'that cheap little Irish slut'. Yates gave Dookie three hundred dollars as a goodbye gift and married Sheila. However, he was badly mistaken if he thought he was rid of his mother; she continued to touch him for loans and to come for dinner and pass out drunk.

Yates's next job was a slight improvement professionally. His story 'Builders' gives a pretty straight autobiographical account of his life at this time:

> ... in 1948, I was twenty-two and employed as rewrite man on the financial news desk of the United Press. The salary was fifty-four dollars a week and it wasn't much of a job, but it did give me two good things. One was that whenever anybody asked me what I did I could say, "Work for the U.P." which had a jaunty sound; the

other was that every morning I could turn up at the *Daily News* building wearing a jaded look, a cheap trench coat that had shrunk a size too small from me, and a much-handled brown fedora.

Indeed, at this time in his life, tall and stick thin, he might have had a role as a private eye in some late-1940s film noir. But the fine regular features of his face were undercut by the bags under his eyes, the look of lassitude and ill-health, partly due to his lung trouble, compounded by his four-pack-a-day cigarette habit and the amount of drink he was taking.

The autobiographical short story 'Builders' is mostly an account of the absurd job that its narrator Robert Prentice takes to supplement his job writing business copy. Prentice becomes a ghost-writer to a New York cabbie who keeps his amusing experiences on file cards in a huge bureau. For five dollars a time he commissions Prentice to write up the file cards as short stories, which they hope to sell to *Reader's Digest* or the movies.

There is all of Yates's life at the time in this story: the young married couple, not particularly happy; he tense and worried about his talent, if any, she pregnant and unsure of his talent; their tetchy conversations; the miserably low-paid jobs he gets; the ludicrous literary endeavours to attempt to raise more money (the cabbie and the stories written for him actually existed), and, more ominously and ubiquitously, drink. At a dinner with the cabbie and his wife, who are both teetotallers, a bottle of rye is produced and Prentice says 'that what I did next – and it took me a hell of a lot less time to do it in 1948 – was to get roaring drunk'.

There is a forecast of a whole lifetime of drinking in that sentence. The passage goes on: 'Soon I was not only the most vociferous, but the only talker in the room.' This is another attribute Yates carried into later life; the witty and pithy conversationalist giving way over an evening of drink to a garrulous, then hectoring, and finally manic monologist. It is a fault that sometimes bedevilled his work. 'Builders' is for the most part a funny and beautifully realised story, especially in the character and speech of the amazing cabbie, a man of few doubts and invincible ambition – but it is topped and tailed with sentimental and self-pitying asides from a supposedly older and wiser narrator.

IV

The stories written for the cabbie were short and sentimental, aimed for a specific market. Like any such work that is written calculatedly and cynically the stories failed, because to achieve a vast and indiscriminate audience the writer must have a genuine desire to please, and that was the last thing that Yates wished to cultivate.

Reading his own work and the accounts of his friends it seems that Yates had always had an ambivalent attitude to the worlds of work and art. The irony of a 'bohemian' writer secretly longing for a safe nine to five office job is quite novel in literary biography; but, after all, Wallace Stevens was vice-president of an insurance company, T.S. Eliot a perfectly efficient bank employee, and even Dylan Thomas scrupulously adhered to office conventions when he worked for a film company. What is odd about Yates is what might be called an anti-Gauguin tendency in him: the convention of a man throwing everything up and cutting free to 'find' himself is replaced by the figure, in his life and work, of a man who is egged on by his wife or lover to take up a free and bohemian life, but who remains reluctant and resistant. The character of Frank Wheeler in *Revolutionary Road* is a terrible and accurate portrait of a man who affects to despise his day job in business, who dreams of escape, but when offered the opportunity, turns away and realises, at first appalled but then comforted, that he actually likes the life of the office, the camaraderie, casual adulteries, and petty politics; he would rather endure these than be faced with his own inadequacy as a 'free spirit'. It is romantic nonsense to believe that somehow a life in Paris as a would-be painter or writer is in every way preferable to that of working in an office in New York, that such an escape is necessary to 'finding' one's true self. Of course it may be, on rare occasions – if you are any good as a writer. It depends what you are looking for. Unless a gift compels its holder to break away forever from a conventional working life – and that gift must give some evidence that it actually exists – then the artistic hopeful is probably better off in an office. And Yates, perhaps unsure of his gifts, insisted that a new job writing advertising copy for Remington Rand gave him more time to write what he 'wanted', although his stories were relentlessly rejected by magazines and publishers.

The test of which way he was to go came in 1951. Shortly after the birth of his first daughter, Yates was diagnosed with advanced tuberculosis and admitted to a Veterans' Hospital. He was there for almost a year; in that time he read enormously and when he came out it was his wife, Sheila, who suggested Paris. After all, if he was ever going to be a real writer . . . His mother, drunk, saw them off on the boat.

V

Paris did the trick for Yates. He was for the first time able to write when and how he liked in a city that had been the home of his greatest heroes, Ernest Hemingway and F. Scott Fitzgerald. He drank little; he was too tired after a day of writing to do anything much. After a few months the family moved south to Juan les Pins, where Fitzgerald had set much of *Tender is the Night*. Life there was far from glamorous; Yates had a small veteran's pension, but the lump sum of $2,000 he had brought with them was dwindling. But his literary luck turned in January 1952.

He sent his stories to Monica McCall, a literary agent in New York. From the beginning she believed in Yates as a writer. The editors of the magazines to which she sent stories were less impressed. Their rejection notes were full of words such as 'unpleasant', 'depressing', and 'cruelty'. McCall advised Yates to soften the ending of his superb story 'A Really Good Jazz Piano'. He refused, politely. McCall continued to send out his work.

Life on the Côte d'Azur was becoming financially impossible and when an aunt of Sheila's offered the family a basement flat in London they moved there in October 1952. In any case, the idyllic life of sun and sea in the South of France had been rather wasted on Yates. He didn't swim, and rarely ventured outdoors except to buy cigarettes. Despite his tuberculosis and weakened lungs, cigarettes were a necessity, a stimulus to his writing he could not do without.

He liked London; Sheila did not. But the move coincided with his first breakthrough as a writer. His agent sold his story 'Jody Rolled the Bones' to the *Atlantic*. This publication brought the inevitable letter from a publisher at William Morrow asking if Yates might have a novel 'that is free'. Seymour Lawrence of Atlantic also wrote enquiring if there was a novel in the offing. So, after a success in writing short stories, Yates became infected with the idea that writing a novel was the next and necessary step in any proper literary career.

He was now on his own in South Kensington. Sheila and their daughter had gone back to New York. He didn't move in literary circles; he was content with a few friends he had met at a pub, the Anglesea. He drank more when his stories were rejected by both English and American magazines, and was joyously buoyed up by the occasional sale. The superbly paced story 'Liars in Love' is a fictionalised portrait of Yates's life in London at this time.

In the story, Warren is in London on a Fulbright scholarship with his wife Carol and their two-year-old daughter. Carol is preparing to leave him and go back to New York. But this takes only the first couple of pages of the story. When his wife leaves him, Warren meets and begins an affair with a young prostitute, Christine. It is impossible to say how true to Yates's own life this was but in its brilliant portrayal of Christine and her rackety life, her self-deceiving lies and

heartbreaking lapses into truth this is one of the finest of Yates's stories and one that gives the lie back to all the accusations of heartlessness
in his characterisation.

VI

Yates returned to New York and to Sheila in 1953. He went back to
work at Remington Rand and remained there for the next seven
years. Working part-time, the strain of splitting his life in two began
to tell. He was a conscientious and good employee: as a writer he was
gaining mastery in the difficult art of the short story and working on
his first novel. Still not yet thirty, he suffered from feelings of rejection
and frustration that the honesty of his vision was constantly described
by editors as being too depressing to print. His marriage became a
succession of drunken rows and rants in which he excoriated his
successful contemporaries and bemoaned his own ill-fortune. A fifth
or more of bourbon a day was added to the four packs of cigarettes.
And in the midst of the ranting and hangovers and clouds of smoke
he began to write his first and greatest novel, *Revolutionary Road*.

He worked in the day, producing draft after draft. In the evening
he drank. Inevitably, he separated from Sheila and moved into a
small basement apartment on his own. It was, in the words of Blake
Bailey, 'cramped, dark, bare, roach-infested, nicotine-stained and
deeply depressing'. It was a precursor of the other dismal apartments
of much the same nature in which he would live all his life. He wrote,
and he drank and he smoked. After five years of work, *Revolutionary
Road* was at last finished and sent off to the publishers, Little, Brown.
Their acceptance was swift, and even before publication, Yates was
launched into literary New York. *Real* literary New York – he had
always been horribly in awe of 'real' writers, now he was meeting
them at parties and writers' conferences. Alcohol eased the way in
this world, in which he still felt little confidence in himself, and he
quickly became notorious as a falling-over drunk. Perhaps the very

completion of the novel and the opening of a doorway into a world he had always feared and envied and desired helped to unhinge him. There was a part of him that wanted literary success above all else; and another that wanted obscurity and the comfort of failure. A short time before publication, and after meeting a young woman, Barbara Singleton Beury, and inviting her to dinner in New York, he suffered a calamitous mental breakdown.

VII

Charles Jackson and Malcolm Lowry had both served their time in the alcoholic wards of Bellevue Hospital, and now, a generation later, it was Yates's turn. For Jackson, the experience was a source of shame; for Lowry an almost mystical exaltation. When Yates was admitted in 1961 to the Men's Violence Ward he was following in a long line of recorded experience that he must have known well. Much later he described the experience in his novel *Disturbing the Peace*. In a way this book was *The Lost Weekend* updated to the 1960s. Yates's book deals in great detail with the career and breakdown and eventual ruin of an alcoholic – or perhaps 'career' should be read as 'vocation'. In Yates's case, there was always a sense that he was somehow doing what was expected of a writer, and drinking was a big part of the job – it was how you proved yourself.

The account of John Wilder's committal in *Disturbing the Peace* follows almost exactly the chain of events as given in Blake Bailey's biography of Yates: what happens to his protagonist, John Wilder, happened to Yates.

At the beginning of the book, John Wilder is drunk. He rings his wife and boasts of some casual affair he has had in Chicago and then tells her that he can't come home because he is afraid that he will kill her. An old friend is dispatched to find him in the bar. Wilder is by now very drunk. His friend persuades him to let him take him to St Vincent's hospital (where Dylan Thomas had died in 1953). In the car he becomes agitated. At the hospital he becomes violent and has to be restrained. The doctor commits him to Bellevue and he is taken there, held down by medical attendants, shouting obscenities. At the hospital:

> . . . two big orderlies who dragged him still shouting toward a closed elevator, where a third orderly waited with a wheelchair, and they not only forced him into it but strapped him in. When the elevator door slid open they shoved him inside, and across the back of the chair was the stencilled word PSYCHO.

Wilder wakes to find himself in Hell. He is forced out of bed into the corridor and made to walk.

> Steel-mesh panels were being drawn across the folded bunks to prevent anyone from using them: this was indeed the corridor, the place for walking. It was yellow and green and brown and black: it was neither very long nor very wide, but it was immensely crowded with men of all ages from adolescence to senility, whites and Negroes and Puerto Ricans, half of them walking one way and half in the other, the dismaying variety of their faces moving into the glare of lights and then into shadows and then into the lights again . . . Then he saw that some weren't wearing pyjama tops but straitjackets, and he wanted to whimper like a child.

In this world that stinks of urine, rank sweat and stale cigarettes, where grown men piss themselves, masturbate in public, scream and shout nonsense, the black orderly, Charlie, is God. It is Charlie who distributes glasses of 'what looked like bourbon', actually paraldehyde, administered as a sedative. There are seven floors in the psychiatric wing in Bellevue, Wilder's doctor explains: 'Seven floors, each one worse than the one beneath, and this is the top. The worst. The Men's Violence Ward.' It is a week before he can see a psychiatrist and be released.

Wilder rests up in the country with his wife and small son. He drinks now secretly, a large shot of whisky every twenty minutes, 'like medicine'. The book is a succession of partial recoveries from booze and calamitous reversals into complete intoxication. He visits a psychotherapist and goes to an AA meeting; it is described sarcastically, his fellow drinkers portrayed as either simpletons or cynical backsliders. Immediately afterwards he goes to a bar and gets drunk. He falls in love with a young woman who introduces him to some amateurs who want to make a film about his time in Bellevue. They drive together up to Vermont to meet the young director. At the college he meets Nathan Epstein, a charismatic sixty-year-old philosophy professor. Wilder feels out of his depth intellectually and socially and proceeds to get wildly drunk. The result is another mental collapse. Another shrink afterwards. It would be tedious to go on and explore the full range of Wilder's obsessions, drunken rants and hospitalisations for manic and drunken behaviour, without the grace and brilliance of the novel itself. They are much the same thing as happened in Yates's own life, although those occurred within life, hour after hour, day after day, month after month, year after year and not in the mercifully brief compass of a book.

A very odd thing happens in the middle of the book, when Wilder, the drunken businessman, meets Chester Pratt, an alcoholic novelist, at a party:

> The important novelist was tall, all right, but thin to the point of frailty, and his drink-distorted face was that of a weak, sad boy more than a man.

The portrait is an unsparing one of Yates himself, but we already have Yates in the character of Wilder: the effect is that of Jekyll looking into a mirror and seeing Hyde staring back at him. Pratt even has a job writing speeches for Robert Kennedy, as Yates did for a time. The coming of Pratt is extremely bad news for Wilder; the novelist takes away his girl, Pamela, and the film director turns his attention away from Wilder's Bellevue story to adapting one of Pratt's novels. When Pamela returns it is because, ironically, she has left Pratt because of *his* drinking.

The characters of Wilder and Pratt are alter egos of Yates. The businessman, Wilder can stand for the office worker Yates was when writing his first novel in his spare time, dreaming of literary fame; Pratt is the 'real' writer Yates became. Both are alcoholics.

VIII

Yates's manic breakdown just before the publication of *Revolutionary Road* may have been a reaction to the change in his life that he knew literary recognition would make. He was dragged literally screaming from one existence to another, and lost his job at Remington Rand; from now on his income would depend on his writing.

His first novel was generally well received, but its placing of what is an almost unbearably tragic story in the suburbs of New York caused it to be misjudged by many reviewers as yet another rather sour satire about business types in the suburbs. *The New Yorker* dismissed the wonderfully drawn cast of the book as 'meaningless characters leading meaningless lives'. This review would have wounded Yates more particularly than any other. *The New Yorker* had already rejected his stories and would consistently reject every short story that Yates submitted over the whole of his thirty-year long writing life; at the end an editor asked Yates's agent to desist from sending the magazine any more stories. His failure to be printed in a magazine that regularly published Cheever, Updike and Malamud rankled deeply; it was as if he were never to be allowed to sit at the top table with the 'senior' writers. It is true that Yates's stories are consistently dark in mood and, read in bulk, can be depressing, but surely among all the often professionally glossy and less demanding work printed by the magazine, Yates could have been published.

After all, many of John Cheever's stories, dealing with the same suburban characters and published in *The New Yorker*, are very dark and disturbing. Perhaps the editors thought they already had their chronicler of the New England suburbs to hand.

The unfortunate truth is that, despite his considerable gifts, Yates did lack Cheever's poetic grace and sheer range of emotion and character: Yates's work was almost entirely based on his own life and he used family members and friends in his fiction, making little effort to disguise them, or his contempt for them. His ghastly mother Dookie becomes the poor insane Pookie in *The Easter Parade* and we have to ask why Yates didn't try just a bit harder to disguise or re-imagine her. The difficulty with fiction based so closely on personal experience is, as Kingsley Amis puts it in his essay 'Real and Made-up People':

> The writer whose direct experience gives him one satisfactory novel (as opposed to a short or very short story) in fifty years is very lucky. The rest of the time, thinness, repetitiousness, poverty of incident, scarcity of character supervene.

It was in *Revolutionary Road* that Yates succeeded, for the first and possibly last time, in achieving the necessary distance between his protagonist, Frank Wheeler, and himself: Frank and April Wheeler act out their tragedy and it is their tragedy, not the writer's. If we knew nothing at all about the life of Richard Yates we could still read and admire his novel as a work of art standing free of its creator.

And indeed the life that informed much of Yates's work was not one to be envied. At the age of thirty-five he was finally a published novelist; he was also an alcoholic. Photographs of that time show a tall and handsome but rather sickly looking man with enormous dark bags under his eyes and, inevitably, a drink in one hand and a cigarette in the other. His literary fame and good looks made him attractive to women, but he was virtually impotent. When drunk he was belligerent and insulting; like many physically weak men he could become violent when drunk. His hero was Scott Fitzgerald and he always felt keenly that his lack of education and good family had shut him out of the world of privilege. Indeed his clothes, the white linen suits and conventional jackets and ties that he always wore, assumed an almost parodic nature in the 1960s and 70s, when the creative writing students he taught and their more trendy lecturers wore jeans. As a veteran of the Second World War he felt uncomfortable with what he regarded as the facile and smug anti-Vietnam War opinions of his students. And more and more of them regarded him as hopelessly old-fashioned; his chivalric attitudes towards women were regarded as patronising and sexist, his realistic style, forged in the 1950s, was being overtaken by the first postmodernist models and was considered inadequate to describe what was seen as a new age.

The full and horrible story of his incessant drinking, mental collapses and committal to various institutions can be found in Blake Bailey's exhaustive biography. Richard Yates was an extraordinarily diligent writer who revised his work painstakingly and yet he could go for months and even years doing no creative work whatsoever, simply smoking and drinking himself into a stupor. His six later novels differ in quality, but all are better than most novels around at the time. None, except for *The Easter Parade*, was a commercial success. He worked, not very happily, teaching creative writing in various colleges, but he missed out on the prizes that went so regularly to those contemporaries he loathed. He could be sober when working, but seems to have developed a philosophy that to drink was not enough, it had to be done in as self-destructive a way as possible, as Fitzgerald and Hemingway and all his other heroes had done. There is something anachronistic about Yates and the career as a writer he hoped to have. If he had what Elizabeth Venant called a 'lifelong struggle with the whiskey bottle' it was a struggle in which Yates put up little resistance.

There has been a revival of interest in Yates, deservedly so, particularly after the release in 2009 of the film version of *Revolutionary Road*. But it is difficult to see him ever gaining a wide audience. It has to be admitted that his work is often grey and depressing, and Yates admitted that he was 'one of those writers who has the misfortune to write the best book first'.

That book, *Revolutionary Road*, is a very American book, one of those like *The Great Gatsby* that takes the American dream head-on and unflinchingly shows how it can become an unrelenting nightmare. There was no irony intended in the Founding Fathers' bequest of the rights to 'life, liberty and the pursuit of happiness' to the inhabitants of their new republic; it was Yates's special gift to show how cruel and illusory that pursuit can be and to what tragic depths it can bring us.

Acknowledgements

THIS BOOK is about the lives of writers, but also the works they produced – my thanks to their spirits and for the huge pleasure that reading and re-reading their work has given me.

More practical thanks are due to staff at the British Library, the London Library and the library of the University of Birmingham for their help in locating books and articles. I have enjoyed and benefited from discussing the subjects of the book, usually over a drink, with many friends, including Michael Barber, Alan Brownjohn, Philip and Sue Fisher, Nigel Hobbs, Jeremy and Petra Lewis, John and Anne McDermott, Nicholas Murray, and John Seaton. David Lodge read earlier versions of some chapters and gave me invaluable advice.

My agent, Charles Walker of United Agents, displayed his customary saintly patience faced with different drafts. My publisher, Duncan Proudfoot, has never been anything but enthusiastic. Amanda Keats, editorial manager of Robinson, and Una McGovern, the copy-editor, helped knock the manuscript into shape. In the remarkably complex world of photographic copyright, Linda Silverman located the sources of the photographs used.

Finally, as always, to Lynda and the whole Mamy clan, to my daughter, Lucy, and granddaughter, Bethan – at nine years old, still blessedly ignorant of the subject of this book.

Notes and Sources

A full bibliography of books and articles consulted and acknowledgements for general assistance can be found on page 239. The following notes are to indicate where I am particularly indebted to a work or the assistance of others. Where a printed source is clearly indicated in the text or in these notes, full details are listed under the author's name in the bibliography and I have cited them below only in short form.

Introduction

The vexed question as to whether alcoholism should be regarded as a disease is dealt with fully by Herbert Fingarette in *Heavy Drinking: The Myth of Alcoholism as a Disease*.

F. Scott Fitzgerald's list of physical complaints is from *The Crack-Up*. His story 'An Alcoholic Case' is reprinted in *The Bodley Head F. Scott Fitzgerald, Volume 6*.

Philip Larkin's poem 'The Life with a Hole in it' was first published in the Collected Poems in 2003.

An interesting psychiatric survey of writers and alcohol is by Dr Felix Post: Philip Hensher's remarks on this are from the *Guardian*. John Sutherland's comments are from his *Last Drink to L.A.*

The Le Fanu poem is printed in full in Graves's *The Irish Literary and Musical Studies*.

Chapter 1

Details of Hamilton's life are taken largely from the biographies by Sean French and Nigel Jones and the memoir by his brother Bruce Hamilton. Factual literature on ordinary pub life is surprisingly scanty, but the Mass Observation study of working-class pubs in the 1930s is valuable, as is the study by Steven Earnshaw.

Chapter 2

I am heavily indebted to the standard biography of Jean Rhys by Carole Angier and her research is so thorough and exhaustive that it is not likely to be superseded. A later biography by Lilian Pizzichini gives a different interpretation of the relation between Rhys's life and her fiction. Valuable sources for the early life and the later obscurity of middle age are in Rhys's autobiography *Smile Please* and the *Letters*. I am grateful for information from the late Sue Fisher who, as a child, lived next door to Mr and Mrs Hamer in Beckenham and more than once witnessed the homecoming of a drunken and boisterous Mrs Hamer.

Chapter 3

There is one full-length biography of Charles Jackson, by Blake Bailey. Other biographical information can be found in Mark Connelly's study of the novels, and in books, essays and articles by John W. Crowley, Max Wylie, Patrick A. McCarthy, and Dorothea Straus. Louis Paskoff is especially revealing about the relation between Jackson and his character Don Birnam. Details of the alcoholic wards of Bellevue Hospital in the 1920s and 30s are from studies and reports by Ernest F. Hoyer, Ruth E. Jones, and Vladimir G. Urse. The actor Ray Milland's experience of Bellevue is recounted in his autobiography. For details of the treatment of tuberculosis in the 1920s I am indebted to F.B. Smith's *The Retreat of Tuberculosis*.

Chapter 4

The pioneering biography of Lowry was by Douglas Day; however, the later one by Gordon Bowker benefited from a great deal more information about the novelist's life, particularly from interviews with Lowry's first wife, Jan Gabrial. Gabrial's own memoirs are the prime source for their years together in Europe and Mexico. Day also edited the first selection of Lowry's letters, a collection superseded by the two-volume collection edited by Sherrill E. Grace. The journal devoted entirely to Lowry, the *Malcolm Lowry Review*, is invaluable to the researcher. One article to be singled out is Patrick A. McCarthy's 'Lowry and The Lost Weekend', about the literary relationship between Lowry and Charles Jackson, a subject also dealt with by Victor Sage in the collection of essays *Malcolm Lowry Eighty Years On*, edited by Sue Vice.

Chapter 5

There seems to be a new biography of Thomas every five years or so. The most sympathetic to Thomas was the first by Constantine Fitzgibbon, but the fullest account is by Paul Ferris. Andrew Lycett adds yet more anecdotes of drunkenness and bad behaviour. Daniel Jones wrote as an intimate witness to Thomas's adolescence. Ralph Maud edited the early notebooks. The scholar David N. Thomas has published an enormous amount of new research concerning Thomas's life in Wales, most of it from sources ignored by other biographers; he has also produced what will probably be the closest we shall ever get now to a true account of Thomas's death. *Double Drink Story* by his widow, Caitlin Thomas, telling of their joint alcoholism, is possibly one of the most tasteless and spiteful reports of a marriage ever published. There are innumerable glimpses of Thomas drunk in books by his contemporaries and drinking buddies, chief among them Julian Maclaren-Ross, Dan Davin, and Rayner Heppenstall. On the other hand, Alan Brownjohn has told me of two encounters with Thomas at readings in London in the early 1950s; on both occasions Thomas was perfectly sober and professional. Robert Hewison's *Under Siege* is invaluable for its picture of London literary life in the war years. Randall Jarrell's quote is from his *Poetry and the Age*, Robert Lowell's from his collected letters.

Chapter 6

There are several biographies of Elizabeth Bishop: the fullest are Brett Millier's of 1993 and Megan Marshall's of 2017. Marshall is particularly valuable for the first printing of many revelatory private letters from Bishop to her psychoanalyst, her doctor, and friends and lovers. Millier's comments on Bishop's drinking come from an article in *Contemporary Literature*.

Remembering Elizabeth Bishop: An Oral Biography is a fascinating compendium of memories of Bishop's personal and public lives (two very different things); it includes the reminiscences of Howard Moss and Dan Gioia. Anthony Hecht's remarks are from *Melodies Unheard*. Reviews of Bishop by Tom Paulin and Michael Hofmann first appeared in the *TLS* and the *London Review of Books*.

Chapter 7

The first full biography was by Scott Donaldson. The recent *Cheever: A Life* by Blake Bailey presents more material from the 4,300 typed pages of Cheever's journals, a selection from which was first published in 1990.

The *Letters* were published by Jonathan Cape.

Chapter 8

The portrait of O'Nolan in McDaid's is a composite one, assembled from many accounts of his time in the Dublin pubs. The biographies to which I am indebted for details of O'Nolan's often confused life are by Anthony Cronin, and by Peter Costello with Peter van de Kamp. *Myles: Portraits of Brian O'Nolan*, edited by Timothy O'Keefe, is another invaluable source of memoirs by his friends and contemporaries. The best collection of the journalism is *The Best of Myles*, edited by Kevin O'Nolan. Evocative portraits of Ireland and particularly Dublin literary circles are given in John Ryan's book, in Clare Wills's *That Neutral Island*, and in Antoinette Quinn's biography of Patrick Kavanagh. The *Letters*, edited by Maebh Long, was published in 2018.

Chapter 9

Biographical details are drawn from Biswell's and Lewis's biographies, and Burgess's autobiographies. The discussion of pubs in the 1960s comes almost entirely from my own close and persistent observation as a young man.

Chapter 10

An example of the non-drinker's response to the literature of drunkenness is the review of *The Old Devils* that appeared in the *Spectator* (13 September 1986). The review was by Anita Brookner and her response was that of any well brought-up Hampstead intellectual asked to carve a human head for dinner. She wrote, 'It is impossible to overestimate the amount of drinking done in this novel . . . Drinking here is not undertaken to outwit the oppressions of the state or to celebrate natural good fortune: it is undertaken for the sole purpose of getting drunk.' Perhaps the editor of the *Spectator* could have pointed out: 'It is a novel, you see. Much of it is about people being drunk most of the time. Bit like murder in *Macbeth*.'

Getting drunk is the whole point of the exercise for Amis – see his exhortations to his friend Larkin to drink deeply (Amis, *Letters*, *passim*).

I am grateful to Jeremy Lewis, John and Anne McDermott, and Michael Barber for their memories of Kingsley Amis. The quote from Wild Bill Davison came up in conversation with the poet and jazz pianist Roy Fisher, who acted as Davison's driver on a British tour.

Chapter 11

The biography by Blake Bailey is the main source for details of Yates's life. The interview with Scott Bradfield adds much interesting detail. A long essay by Stewart O'Nan in *Boston Review* is a strongly positive revaluation of Yates' work.

Image credits

Dylan Thomas – © Hulton Archive/Getty Images

Malcolm Lowry – The University of British Columbia

Jean Rhys – Pictorial Press Ltd/Alamy Stock Photo

Anthony Burgess – © Mark Gerson/National Portrait Gallery, London

Flann O'Brien – © *The Irish Times*

Elizabeth Bishop – Mary Evans/Everett Collection

Patrick Hamilton © Bridgeman Images

Kingsley Amis – © estate of Daniel Farson/National Portrait Gallery, London

John Cheever – Paul Hoseros/Archive Photos/Getty Images

Charles Jackson – Margaret Bourke-White/The LIFE Picture Collection via Getty Images

Richard Yates – Illustration by Robert Risko

Bibliography

Amis, Kingsley, *Lucky Jim* (London: Gollancz, 1954)

Amis, Kingsley, *That Uncertain Feeling* (London: Gollancz, 1955)

Amis, Kingsley, *Take a Girl Like You* (London: Gollancz, 1960)

Amis, Kingsley, *One Fat Englishman* (London: Gollancz, 1963)

Amis, Kingsley, *The Anti-Death League* (London: Gollancz, 1966)

Amis, Kingsley, *The Green Man* (London: Jonathan Cape, 1969)

Amis, Kingsley, *What Became of Jane Austen? and Other Questions* (London: André Deutsch, 1984)

Amis, Kingsley, *The Old Devils* (London: Hutchinson, 1986)

Amis, Kingsley, *The Amis Collection* compiled by John McDermott (London: Hutchinson, 1990)

Amis, Kingsley, *Memoirs* (London: Hutchinson, 1991)

Angier, Carole, *Jean Rhys: Life and Work* (London: André Deutsch, 1990)

Bailey, Blake, *A Tragic Honesty: The Life and Work of Richard Yates* (London: Methuen, 2004)

Bailey, Blake, *Cheever: A Life* (New York: Knopf, 2009)

Bailey, Blake, *Farther and Wilder: The Lost Weekends and Literary Dreams of Charles Jackson* (New York: Knopf, 2013)

Baxter, John, *A Pound of Paper: Confessions of a Book Addict* (London: Doubleday, 2002)

Beaton, Cecil, *Portrait of New York* (London: Batsford, 1948)

Biele, Joelle (ed), *Bishop, Elizabeth and The New Yorker, The Complete Correspondence* (New York: Farrar, Straus and Giroux, 2011)

Bishop, Elizabeth, *The Complete Poems 1927–1979* (New York: Farrar, Straus and Giroux, 1983)

Bishop, Elizabeth, *One Art: Letters, Selected and Edited by Robert Giroux* (New York: Farrar, Straus and Giroux, 1994)

Bishop, Elizabeth, *Poems, Prose, and Letters* (New York: Library of America, 2008)

Bishop, Elizabeth and Lowell, Robert, *Words in Air: The Complete Correspondence between Elizabeth Bishop and Robert Lowell* (London: Faber, 2008)

Biswell, Andrew, *The Real Life of Anthony Burgess* (London: Picador, 2005)

Bowen, Stella, *Drawn from Life* (London: Collins, 1941)

Bowker, Gordon (ed), *Under the Volcano: A Casebook* (London: Macmillan, 1987)

Bowker, Gordon, *Pursued by Furies: A Life of Malcolm Lowry* (London: HarperCollins, 1993)

Brackett, Charles and Wilder, Billy, *The Lost Weekend: Screenplay* (Berkeley: University of California Press, 2000)

Bradfield, Scott, 'Follow the Long and Revolutionary Road' *The Independent*, 21 November 1992

Breit, Harvey, *The Writer Observed* (London: Alvin Redman, 1957)

Breit, Harvey and Lowry, Margerie Bonner (eds), *The Selected Letters of Malcolm Lowry* (London: Jonathan Cape, 1967)

Brinnin, John Malcolm, *Dylan Thomas in America* (London: J.M. Dent, 1956)

Brookner, Anita, 'Another Little Drink Wouldn't Do Us Any Good' *The Spectator*, Vol. 257, No. 8253, 13 September 1986, pp31–2

Burgess, Anthony, *Time for a Tiger* (London: Heinemann, 1957)

Burgess, Anthony, *The Right to an Answer* (London: Heinemann, 1960)

Burgess, Anthony, *Urgent Copy: Literary Studies* (London: Jonathan Cape, 1968)

Burgess, Anthony, *Homage to Qwert Yuiop: Essays* (London, Hutchinson, 1986)

Burgess, Anthony, *Little Wilson and Big God* (London: Heinemann, 1987)

Cheever, Benjamin (ed.), *The Letters of John Cheever* (London: Jonathan Cape, 1989)

Cheever, John, *Falconer* (London: Jonathan Cape, 1977)

Cheever, John, *The Stories of John Cheever* (London: Jonathan Cape, 1979)

Cheever, John, *The Journals* (London: Jonathan Cape, 1991)

Cheever, Susan, *Home Before Dark* (London: Weidenfeld and Nicolson 1985)

Connelly, Mark, *Deadly Closets: The Fiction of Charles Jackson* (University of America Press, 2001)

Cooper, Standford Lee, 'Eire's Columnist' *Time Magazine*, 23 August 1943

Costello, Peter and van de Kamp, Peter, *Flann O'Brien: An Illustrated Biography* (London: Bloomsbury, 1987)

Cronin, Anthony, *Dead as Doornails: A Chronicle of Life* (Dublin: The Dolmen Press, 1976)

Cronin, Anthony, *No Laughing Matter: The Life and Times of Flann O'Brien* (London: Grafton Books, 1989)

Crowley, John. W, 'Recovering the Author of *The Lost Weekend*: Notes on Charles Jackson' *Dionysos*, (5.2), 1993

Crowley, John W., *The White Logic: Alcoholism and Gender in American Modernist Fiction* (Amherst: University of Massachusetts Press, 1994)

Crowley, John W., 'A Charles Jackson Diptych' *Syracuse University Library Associates Courier*, (32), 1997

Dardis, Tom, *The Thirsty Muse: Alcohol and the American Writer* (London: Abacus, 1990)

Davies, John Booth, *The Myth of Addiction* (Amsterdam: Harwood, 1997)

Davin, Dan, *Closing Times* (London: Oxford University Press, 1975)

Day, Douglas, *Malcolm Lowry: A Biography* (London: Oxford University Press, 1974)

Donaldson, Scott, *John Cheever: A Biography* (New York: Random House, 1988)

Donoghue, Denis, 'Mylestones' *Times Literary Supplement*, 19 September 1968

Douglas, Donald B., 'Alcoholism as an Addiction: The Disease Concept Reconsidered' *Journal of Substance Abuse Treatment*, Vol.3, pp115–20, 1986

Earnshaw, Steven, *The Pub in Literature: England's Altered State* (Manchester: Manchester University Press, 2000)

Faulkner, William, *Collected Stories of William Faulkner* (London: Chatto and Windus, 1951)

Ferris, Paul (ed.), *The Collected Letters of Dylan Thomas* (London: J.M. Dent, 1985)

Ferris, Paul, *Caitlin: The Life of Caitlin Thomas* (London: Hutchinson, 1993)

Ferris, Paul, *Dylan Thomas: The Biography* (London: J.M. Dent, 1999)

Fingarette, H, *Heavy Drinking: The Myth of Alcoholism as a Disease* (Berkeley: University of California Press, 1988)

Fitzgerald, F. Scott, *The Crack-Up* (New York: New Directions, 1945)

Fitzgerald, F. Scott, 'An Alcoholic Case' from *The Bodley Head Scott Fitzgerald, Volume VI* (London: The Bodley Head, 1959)

Fitzgibbon, Constantine, *The Life of Dylan Thomas* (London: J.M. Dent, 1965)

Fountain, Garry and Brazeau, Peter, *Remembering Elizabeth Bishop: An Oral Biography* (Amherst: University of Massachusetts Press, 1994)

French, Sean, *Patrick Hamilton: A Life* (London: Faber, 1993)

Gabrial, Jan, *Inside the Volcano: My Life with Malcolm Lowry* (New York: St. Martin's Press, 2000)

Goldring, Douglas, *The Last Pre-Raphaelite: A Record of the Life and Writings of Ford Madox Ford* (London: Macdonald, 1948)

Grace, Sherrill E. (ed.), *Sursum Corda! Collected Letters of Malcolm Lowry, Volume I and II* (London: Jonathan Cape, 1995–1996)

Grant, Annette, 'John Cheever: the Art of Fiction No. 62' *Paris Review* (67), 1976

Graves, Alfred Perceval, *The Irish Literary and Musical Studies* (London, Elkin Matthews, 1913)

Hamilton, Bruce, *The Light Went Out: The Life of Patrick Hamilton* (London: Constable, 1972)

Hamilton, Patrick, *Hangover Square* (London: Constable, 1941)

Hamilton, Patrick, *The Slaves of Solitude* (London: Constable, 1947)

Hamilton. Patrick, *The West Pier* (London: Kaye and Ward, 1951)

Hamilton, Patrick, *Twenty Thousand Streets Under the Sky: A London Trilogy* (London: Vintage, 1998)

Hecht, Anthony, 'Awful but Cheerful' *Times Literary Supplement*, 26 August 1997, p.1024

Hecht, Anthony, *Melodies Unheard: Essays on the Mysteries of Poetry* (Baltimore: John Hopkins University Press, 2003)

Hensher, Philip, 'Black Dogs Behind the Typewriter' *Guardian*, 2 May 1996

Heppenstall, Rayner, *Four Absentees* (London: Barrie and Rockliff, 1960)

Hewison, Robert, *Under Siege: Literary Life in London, 1939–1945* (London: Weidenfeld and Nicolson, 1977)

Hofmann, Michael, 'Mostly Middle' *London Review of Books*, Vol 33 No.17, 8 September 2011

Holbrook, David, *Llarregub Revisited: Dylan Thomas and the State of Modern Poetry* (London: Bowes & Bowes, 1962)

Holiday, Billie and Dufty, William, *Lady Sings the Blues* (New York: Doubleday, 1956)

Hoyer, Ernest F., 'Exit: Alcoholic Wards' *The American Journal of Nursing* (20.6), 1920

Jackson, Charles, *The Lost Weekend* (London: John Lane, The Bodley Head, 1945)

Jacobs, Eric, *Kingsley Amis: A Biography* (London: Hodder and Stoughton, 1995)

James, William, *The Varieties of Religious Experience* (London: Longmans, 1902)

Jarrell, Randall, *Poetry and the Age* (London: Faber, 1955)

Joliffe, Norman, 'The Alcoholic Admissions to Bellevue Hospital' *Science* New Series, (Vol 83, No. 2152), 1936

Jones, Daniel, *My Friend Dylan Thomas* (London: J.M. Dent, 1977)

Jones, Nigel, *Through a Glass Darkly: The Life of Patrick Hamilton* (London: Scribners, 1991)

Jones, Ruth E., 'Alcoholic Episodes and their Nursing Care' *The American Journal of Nursing* (37.3), 1937

Kunitz, Stanley J. (ed.), *Twentieth Century Authors* (New York: H.W. Wilson, 1950)

Laing, Olivia, *The Trip to Echo Spring: Why Writers Drink* (Edinburgh: Canongate, 2013)

Larkin, Philip, *Collected Poems* edited by Anthony Thwaite (London: The Marvell Press – Faber, 2003)

Larkin, Philip, *Selected Letters of Philip Larkin: 1940–1985* edited by Anthony Thwaite (London: Faber, 1992)

Leader, Zachary (ed), *The Letters of Kingsley Amis* (London: HarperCollins, 2000)

Leader, Zachary, *The Life of Kingsley Amis* (London: Jonathan Cape, 2006)

Lewis, Jeremy, *Kindred Spirits: Adrift in Literary London* (London: HarperCollins, 1995)

Lewis, Roger, *Anthony Burgess* (London: Faber and Faber, 2002)

London, Jack, *John Barleycorn* edited by John Sutherland (Oxford: Oxford University Press, 1989)

Long, Maebh (ed.), *The Collected Letters of Flann O'Brien* (Victoria, TX: Dalkey Archive, 2018)

Lowell, Robert, *The Letters of Robert Lowell*, edited by Saskia Hamilton (New York: Farrar, Straus and Giroux, 2005)

Lowry, Malcolm, *Under the Volcano* (London: Jonathan Cape, 1947)

Lycett, Andrew, *Dylan Thomas: A New Life* (London: Weidenfeld and Nicolson, 2003)

Lykiard, Alexis, *Jean Rhys Revisited* (Exeter: Stride Publications, 2000)

Maclaren-Ross, Julian, *Memories of the Forties* (London: Alan Ross, 1965)

Mass-Observation, *The Pub and the People: a Worktown Study* (London, Gollancz, 1943)

Maud, Ralph (ed.), *Poet in the Making: The Notebooks of Dylan Thomas* (London: J.M. Dent, 1968)

McCarthy, Patrick. A., 'Lowry and The Lost Weekend' *Malcolm Lowry Review*, (33), 1993

McDermott, John, *Kingsley Amis: An English Moralist* (London: Macmillan, 1989)

Meyers, Jeffrey, *Edmund Wilson: A Biography* (New York: Houghton Mifflin, 1995)

Milland, Ray, *Wide-Eyed in Babylon* (London: The Bodley Head, 1974)

Millier, Brett C., *Elizabeth Bishop: Life and the Memory of It* (Berkeley: University of California Press, 1993)

Millier, Brett C., 'The Prodigal: Elizabeth Bishop and Alcohol' *Contemporary Literature* XXX1X, 1, 1998

Morris, Peter M., *A Survey of Dickens' Employments* (Birmingham: Peter Morris Books, 1996)

New York City Guide (New York: Random House, 1939)

O'Brien, Flann, *The Hard Life* (London: MacGibbon and Kee, 1961)

O'Brien, Flann, *The Dalkey Archive* (London: MacGibbon and Kee, 1964)

O'Brien, Flann, *The Third Policeman* (London: MacGibbon and Kee, 1967)

O'Keefe, Timothy (ed.), *Myles: Portraits of Brian O'Nolan* (London: MacGibbon and Kee, 1973)

O'Nan, Stewart, 'The Lost World of Richard Yates' *Boston Review*, 1 October 1999

Paskoff, Louis, 'Don Birnam's Dark Mirror' *Serif*, (10.3) 1973

Paulin, Tom, 'Newness and Nowness' *Times Literary Supplement*, 29 April 1994, p3

Pendery, Mary L., Maltzman, Irving M., West, L. Jolyon, 'Controlled Drinking by Alcoholics? New Findings and a Re-evaluation of a Major Affirmative Study' *Science*, New Series, Vol. 217, No. 4555, 9 July 1982

Pizzichini, Lilian, *The Blue Hour: A Portrait of Jean Rhys* (London: Bloomsbury, 2009)

Pope-Hennessy, Una, *Charles Dickens* (London: Chatto and Windus, 1945)

Post, Felix, 'Creativity and Psychopathology, a study of 291 famous men' *British Journal of Psychiatry* 165 (1994), 22–34

Quinn, Antoinette, *Patrick Kavanagh: a Biography* (Dublin: Gill and Macmillan 2003)

R., Marion May, 'Charles Jackson Speaks at Hartford A.A.' *The Grapevine* Vol 1, No 8, Jan 1945

Ratcliffe, Michael, 'Wilson, John Burgess [Anthony Burgess] (1917–1993)', *Oxford Dictionary of National Biography* (Oxford: Oxford University Press, 2004)

Rhys, Jean, *Wide Sargasso Sea* (London: André Deutsch, 1966)

Rhys, Jean, *Good Morning, Midnight* (London: André Deutsch, 1967)

Rhys, Jean, *Voyage in the Dark* (London: André Deutsch, 1967)

Rhys, Jean, *Tigers Are Better Looking* (London: André Deutsch, 1968)

Rhys, Jean, *After Leaving Mr Mackenzie* (London: André Deutsch, 1969)

Rhys, Jean, *Quartet* (London: André Deutsch, 1969)

Rhys, Jean, *Smile Please: An Unfinished Autobiography* (London: André Deutsch, 1979)

Ryan, John, *Remembering How We Stood: Bohemian Dublin at the Mid-Century* (Mullingar: Lilliput, 1987)

Schoeman, Ferdinand, Review of *Heavy Drinking: The Myth of Alcoholism as a Disease* by Herbert Fingarette, *The Philosophical Review*, Vol. 100, No. 3, July 1991, pp493–8

Smith, F.B., *The Retreat of Tuberculosis 1850–1950* (London: Croom Helm, 1988)

Steinman, Michael (ed.), *The Element of Lavishness: Letters of Sylvia Townsend and William Maxwell 1938–1978* (Washington D.C.: Counterpoint 2001)

Straus, Dorothea, *Showcases* (London: The Bodley Head, 1975)

Sutherland, John, *Last Drink to LA* (London: Short Books, 2001)

Thomas, Caitlin, *Leftover Life to Kill* (London: Putnam, 1963)

Thomas, Caitlin, *Double Drink Story: My Life with Dylan Thomas* (London: Virago Press, 1998)

Thomas, David N., *Dylan Thomas: A Farm, Two Mansions and a Bungalow* (Bridgend: Seren, 2000)

Thomas, David N., *Dylan Remembered, Volumes 1 and 2* (Bridgend: Seren, 2003–2004)

Thomas, Dylan, *Portrait of the Artist as a Young Dog* (London: J.M. Dent, 1940)

Thomas, Dylan, *Collected Poems 1934–1952* (London: J.M. Dent, 1952)

Thomas, Dylan, *Adventures in the Skin Trade* (London: J.M. Dent, 1969)

Tóibín, Colm, *On Elizabeth Bishop* (Princeton: Princeton University Press, 2015)

Turnbull, Andrew, *Scott Fitzgerald* (New York: Charles Scribners, 1962)

Urse, Vladimir G., 'Alcoholic Mental Disorders' *The American Journal of Nursing* (37.3), 1937

Vice, Sue (ed.), *Malcolm Lowry Eighty Years On* (London: Macmillan, 1989)

Wills, Clare, *That Neutral Island: a cultural history of Ireland during the Second World War* (London: Faber and Faber 2007)

Wylie, Max, 'Charles Reginald Jackson' *Serif,* (10.3), 1973

Wyndham, Francis and Melly, Diana (eds.), *Jean Rhys Letters, 1931–1966* (London: Deutsch, 1984)

Yates, Richard, *Revolutionary Road* (London: Methuen, 2001)

Yates, Richard, *The Collected Stories of Richard Yates* (London: Methuen, 2004)

Yates, Richard, *Disturbing the Peace* (London: Methuen, 2007)

Index